Sustainable Enterprise Architecture

Sustainable Enterprise Architecture

Kirk Hausman

CRC Press
Taylor & Francis Group
Boca Raton London New York

CRC Press is an imprint of the
Taylor & Francis Group, an **Informa** business

AN AUERBACH BOOK

CRC Press
Taylor & Francis Group
6000 Broken Sound Parkway NW, Suite 300
Boca Raton, FL 33487-2742

© 2011 by Taylor and Francis Group, LLC
CRC Press is an imprint of Taylor & Francis Group, an Informa business

No claim to original U.S. Government works

Printed in the United States of America on acid-free paper
10 9 8 7 6 5 4 3 2 1

International Standard Book Number: 978-1-4398-2154-1 (Hardback)

Visit the Taylor & Francis Web site at
http://www.taylorandfrancis.com

and the CRC Press Web site at
http://www.crcpress.com

To all the talented IT professionals who reach into the future with eager guiding hands to wrest order from chaos in the midst of constant change; and to Susan and our dear children, whose unflagging support has carried me through many challenges.

Contents

Preface   xv

Acknowledgments   xix

About the Author   xxi

Chapter 1   The Impact of Enterprise Architecture   1

    In This Chapter   1
    Simple Choice, Complex Impact   2
        A Strong Hand   2
        Opportunity Costs   3
        Ripples in the Pond   5
    Where the Only Constant Is Change   7
        Lilliput and Blefuscu   7
        Open Source and Open Standards   10
    The Best Solution   14

Chapter 2   Enterprise Planning   15

    In This Chapter   15
    Beyond Platform Selection   16
    Where Lies Success?   21
    The Architect   25
        The Chief Architect   27
        The Lead Architect   29
        The Business Architect   30
        The Technology Architect   30

Outsourced Architecture   30
Multiple Architects   31
Creating a Symphony   33
Governance   33
Architectural Models   36
Project and Program Management   38
Beyond Basics   40
Language Standard   40
Operational Environment   40
Virtualization   41
Mobile Technologies   41
Service-Oriented Architecture (SOA)   41
Whatever's Next   42
Summary   42
Resources   43

Chapter 3   Enterprise Architecture Challenges   45

In This Chapter   45
Complexity   46
Sources of Complexity   47
Opposition to Standardization   47
Enterprise Information Management   51
Sell the Value of Information   51
Avoid Drawing Fire   52
Look Beyond the Project   60
Align Technology and Business   61
Data Center Management   65
Consolidation   65
Automation   72
Virtualization   74
Plan for the Worst and Hope to Be Wrong   76
Summary   77

Chapter 4   Finding Value   79

In This Chapter   79
Impact and Return on Effort   80
Applying the 80/20 Rule   80
Expectations from Architectural Change   81
An Objective View   82

The Federated Enterprise   83
Legal Mandates   84
    Alphabet Soup   84
    Discovery and Retention   85
    Extended Legal Involvement   85
    Managing Risk   86
Beyond the End   88
    Planned Obsolescence   88
    Hidden Obsolescence   89
Good Enough Architecture   89
Summary   89

Chapter 5   Managing Identity   **91**

In This Chapter   91
The Many-Walled Garden   92
Identification   93
    What You Know   94
    What You Have   96
    What You Are   97
    Multifactor Identification   101
Authentication   102
    The Authentication Directory   102
    External Authentication   103
    Authentication Standards   103
    Single Sign-On   105
Authorization   107
    Access Controls   107
Identity Management   109
    Regulatory Mandates   109
    Business Drivers   110
    Identity Management Elements   110
    Identity Management Providers   112
Identity Management Strategies   113
    Implement Strong Identification   113
    Combine Authentication and Authorization   113
    Assign Rights to Groups   114
    Employ Identity Management Solutions   114
    Simplify the Garden   115
Summary   115

Chapter 6   Sharing Information   **117**

In This Chapter   117
The Value of Communication   118
    Communication Systems   118
    Network of Trust   120
    Collective Intelligence   120
Communication Technologies   121
    Asynchronous Communications   124
    Synchronous Communications   138
    Telepresence   142
Combined Collaboration   145
    Groupware   145
    Portals   146
Beyond the Boundary   150
Summary   150

Chapter 7   Storing Information   **151**

In This Chapter   151
Everything in Its Place   152
    File Storage   153
    Logging   153
    E-mail   154
    Repositories   154
    Virtual Computers   155
Storage Policies   155
    Scouting the Land   156
    Areas of Interest   156
Data Protection   166
    Backups   166
    Media Retirement   167
Summary   168

Chapter 8   Making Connections   **171**

In This Chapter   171
What Came Before   172
The World Wide Web   175
    Web 1.0   175
    Web 2.0   176
    Web 3.0   177
    Culture   179

The Needle in the Haystack   182
    Ranking   182
    Caching   183
    Bogus Information   183
    Name Squatting   184
    Typos and One-Offs   185
    Name Service Poisoning   186
Inter, Intra, and Extra   187
    Internet   188
    Intranet   189
    Extranet   189
Summary   189

Chapter 9   Anytime/Anywhere Computing   **191**

In This Chapter   191
Mobile Technologies   192
    New Technologies   192
    Network Connectivity   194
    Extending the Enterprise   195
Accessibility   195
Mobile and Remote Access   195
    Mobile Limitations   197
    Remote Desktops   198
    Transport Security   198
    Kill Pills   199
    Device Interaction   199
    Signal Boosters   200
Policy Requirements   201
Summary   201

Chapter 10   Virtualization   **203**

In This Chapter   203
Virtualized Services   204
Virtualized Applications   204
Virtualized Desktops   205
    Remote Desktop Clients   205
    Virtual Appliances   206
Virtualized Servers   207
Virtualized Networks   208
Cloud Computing   209

Comparing Cloud and Traditional Application
    Life Cycles   209
Types of Clouds   210
Cloud Flexibility   212
Best Practices   212
Summary   216

Chapter 11   Enterprise Sustenance   **217**

In This Chapter   217
Project Management   218
Hardware   219
    Firmware   220
    Drivers   221
    Components   222
    Tech Refresh   222
Software   226
    Testing   227
    Deployment   227
    Update   229
    Directory Entries   233
    Passwords   233
Summary   234

Chapter 12   Enterprise Security   **235**

In This Chapter   235
The Process of Security   236
    Security Is like an Onion   236
    Program Rather than Project   236
    Explain Why   237
    Standardize and Simplify   238
Common Enterprise Threats   238
    Load Only in the Nursery   238
    Secure the Network   239
    Secure the Data   239
    Secure the Applications   240
    Defend the Enterprise   241
    Malware Defense   243
    Network Protection   243

Defense Against the Unexpected   243
    Emergency Response Planning   245
    Don't Forget the Little Things   245
Summary   245

Chapter 13   Recovering from Disaster   247

In This Chapter   247
Continuity of Operations Versus Disaster Recovery   248
    Continuity of Operations (COO)   248
    Disaster Recovery (DR)   249
Planning for Recovery   249
    Business Impact Analysis (BIA)   250
    Risk Assessment (RA)   251
    Construct a Plan   251
Technology in Recovery Planning   252
    Alternate Data Center   252
    Alternate Equipment   253
    Alternate Communications   253

Summary   255

Chapter 14   Future Computing   257

In This Chapter   257
Bigger Is Better   258
Supercomputing   260
Distributed Computing   261
Grid and Cluster Computing   261
    Volunteer Computing   262
    Grid Computing   262
    Cluster Computing   263
Distributed Computing and the Cloud   264
The Sustainable Enterprise   264
    Equipment Replacement and Disposal   264
    Energy Options   265
    Reducing Consumption   265
    The Right Location   266
Summary   266

Index   267

Preface

The term "architecture" comes from the Greek words for "chief builder." When we discuss architecture, it is usually in terms of the style of design and arrangement of elements in a physical structure. This book addresses architecture as well, but in terms of the design and arrangement of elements in an extended network enterprise. This book does not address specific technologies or vendor products, which would rapidly become out of date. Instead, the book is intended for anyone charged with coordinating enterprise architectural design in a small, medium, or large organization. As you progress through this book, you are encouraged to consider the various elements of your own particular network environment and to develop strategies for mid- to long-term management and sustainable growth.

Throughout the book, you will be introduced to ideas and considerations that may fall outside of your past experience and current job requirements. You should try to set aside any existing bias for a particular style of licensing, vendor's products, or favorite framework for governance and consider their potential in application within your own enterprise. Enterprise architecture requires an understanding of all technologies, strategies, and data consumption throughout the enterprise, and so you should always strive to continue to broaden your knowledge of existing as well as emerging trends and solutions. It is not enough to say, "There, now I have created perfection," because ours is a trade faced with constant change—there are no once-and-forever solutions, only strategies that will weather the changes bought by the future.

The concepts presented in this book are useful whether your role is that of a CIO or Chief Architect in a very large network enterprise or simply as "the person" faced with management of a small organizational network. *Sustainable Enterprise Architecture* was written with the following people in mind:

- Designated enterprise architects
- Technology managers
- Technology implementers
- Chief information officers
- Students of technology trades
- Project managers
- Instructors and trainers for IT architectural practices
- Anyone charged with or inheriting technology management duties

How This Book Is Organized

This book is organized much like a book on structural architecture, starting with a solid foundation of frameworks and general guidelines for enterprise governance and design. The book covers common considerations for all enterprises, and then drills down to specific types of technology that may be found in your enterprise—or that may be useful if added. Finally, the book covers strategies of protecting enterprise resources and briefly examines technologies and strategies that are only just beginning to take a place in the modern enterprise network.

- Chapter 1 provides an introduction to the concept of enterprise architecture, with considerations for decision making early in the process of constructing a new enterprise network or in planning for a realignment of existing technologies.
- Chapter 2 examines the various architectural roles that may be needed, and identifies common pitfalls in enterprise architectural planning. This chapter also addresses the use of formal governance methodologies.
- Chapter 3 reviews challenges that may be encountered in implementing enterprise change and considerations for establishing the organizational value created by architectural realignment.
- Chapter 4 examines common expectations for various types of enterprise architectural projects, risk management considerations,

and the extension of technology life-cycle planning from purchase through disposal.

- Chapter 5 examines authorization, access control, and directory service integration.
- Chapter 6 reviews various mechanisms for communication and collaboration.
- Chapter 7 addresses considerations for information storage and data management policies.
- Chapter 8 reviews the impact and use of Web-based technologies, spanning the solutions developed in Web 1.0, 2.0, and beyond.
- Chapter 9 provides an examination of mobile computing and security in the anywhere/anytime enterprise.
- Chapter 10 examines types of virtualization that may be implemented within an enterprise network, along with best practices for implementation and management of virtualized technologies.
- Chapter 11 reviews strategies for hardware and software technology refresh and the application of project management practices in protecting the long-term viability of an enterprise network.
- Chapter 12 addresses security and risk management strategies for protection of the enterprise against accidental or intentional threats.
- Chapter 13 reviews considerations for disaster recovery and continuity-of-operations planning.
- Chapter 14 closes the book by providing a glimpse into newly emerging technologies and strategies for "green" computing.

Each chapter is intended to build on the knowledge and understanding of the topics presented earlier in the book, to develop a thorough understanding of the challenges and opportunities presented by management of enterprise resources within a well-designed architectural strategy. Although I have coordinated enterprise architectural projects in many different venues and across all scales of network enterprise, I am always told why every enterprise is unique. I have generally found that the technologies used by these organizations are unique in the same way.

I challenge you to consider your own unique environment and find alignment with the concepts presented in this book, to build a style and arrangement of solutions and policies to protect your enterprise and allow it to continue providing the greatest organizational value into the future.

Kalani Kirk Hausman

Acknowledgments

I would like to acknowledge the tremendous help in developing this book provided by the remarkable staff at CRC Press and Taylor & Francis, in particular John Wyzalek, and with all of the editorial and production staff members operating behind the scenes to make our work possible. Special thanks are also due to Theron Shreve of DerryField Publishing Services, without whom this book would never have come to be, to his colleagues Lynne Lackenbach and Marje Pollack, and to my agent and constant guide, Carole Jelen of Waterside Productions.

About the Author

Kirk Hausman is employed as an Assistant Commandant at Texas A&M University and specializes in project management, enterprise architecture, IT governance, security and business continuity, information assurance and regulatory compliance. He has a background that includes digital forensics, WMD/wide-area disaster response planning, pandemic response planning, and technology audit practices in higher education, corporate, and health care venues. His experience includes application design, data resource management, network architecture, server and storage virtualization, strategic technology modernization, network and backup centralization, research computing, and large-network business continuity/disaster recovery planning. With a Master's degree in Information Technology, Kirk has served as a senior research scientist in the fields of cyber terrorism, cybercrime, and cyber security, and he lectures regularly on uses of technology in education, solutions for persons with disabling conditions, and strategic architectural planning to improve enterprise efficiencies. Kirk has served as a subject-matter expert before both Houses of the Texas State Legislature and has more than 20 books currently in print, together with numerous articles and white papers addressing enterprise architecture, cyber terrorism, and IT governance. Kirk's professional certifications include the CISSP, CGEIT, CRISC, CISA, CISM, and CCP, together with a wide assortment of technology- and regulatory-specific designations.

Chapter 1

The Impact of Enterprise Architecture

In This Chapter

- An introduction to the concept of enterprise architecture
- An examination of the opportunity costs and ripple effects of decisions made in an enterprise setting
- Considerations for the inclusion of open sources, open standards, and commercial elements in an enterprise network

A house built on unsteady footing will be forever under repair, and the same is true for technology implementations. Information technology has extended into almost every area of business and operational coordination, becoming the glue that holds the modern world together. When an information technology choice is made, the effect of that choice ripples out like the ring of water around a stone dropped into a pond. Poor planning can lead to many problems immediately and for years to come. Decisions made alone, without consideration of the impact each decision may have on other aspects of the overall enterprise, can create turmoil.

Note: The strategies presented herein are not targeted at a particular product or technology. Where examples include such details, they simply reflect actual architecture projects in which the identified solution was implemented.

This text provides an understanding of the mechanisms available for enterprise architecture that will allow planning to be extended from the immediate into a three- to five-year range. These strategies have been used successfully within many different types of organizations, from small office settings through large educational and global commercial enterprises. This text is intended for business and technology professionals, particularly those serving in the capacity of chief information officer (CIO), information technology (IT) director/manager, or some other form of lead architect, but will be understandable to any reader interested in the practice of technology enterprise architecture.

Simple Choice, Complex Impact

It is simple to claim that technology is complex, difficult to understand, and requires an extensive background in many aspects to fully grasp the intricacies of its planning. This claim lies behind the omnipresent need for technologists in almost every business—from small one-office sites to large, globally deployed endeavors—and is brought up regularly to justify salary improvements and yearly technology modernization expenditures.

Counterarguments can be made that each technology choice can be made by a committee or group of information technology professionals and managers, noting the extreme lack of business process integration and project management in many information technology implementations. Although it is true that any choice should be reviewed by a group of skilled individuals, to attempt piecemeal technology decisions is to court failure and heartache. It is imperative that a single office own the business process responsible for overall technology strategy, in order to ensure that all selections fit into a cohesive, interwoven mesh of connectivity.

A Strong Hand

Information technology managers have recently begun to implement formal project management practices in order to avoid the never-ending, constantly changing spectrum of offerings that must be addressed in today's marketplace. Before project management became a formal part of the enterprise, a single application could take many years in successive attempts, only to be discarded ultimately because the need no longer existed or some other alternative was found in the meantime. The ugly term "feature creep" is a constant enemy to progress in any technology endeavor. When user expectations meet regulatory requirements and operational mandates, clear objectives and scoped guidelines must be in place to allow the steering committee to hold onto the project's original purpose. It is far too easy to attempt to take a simple calculator application and try to shoehorn in e-mail, calendaring, human resource training, NASA image galleries, and the kitchen sink when programmers and users are set free to do as they please.

A technology architect must possess both business acumen and technological savvy in order to filter through user requirements and sift out "need" from "want," while also seeing past the technobabble jargon that technologists are wont to use even when dealing with normal mortals who struggle with their VCRs. The architect must identify future technology trends, emerging opportunities, and evolving security requirements. Between the thousands of new viruses created each year and the increasing complexity of regulatory requirements, architects are kept very busy just honing the skills of their trade before they can begin its practice.

Opportunity Costs

Economists know that when a purchase is made, it is made at the expense of other selections that might have been purchased instead. The opportunity cost of a technology selection can be very significant when money is spent to obtain needed skills, implement new solutions, and train users in their operation. Selection of an application platform or code base may later affect the ability of the business to react in an agile manner to changing requirements. A decision on the standard programming style that will be used, such as J2EE or .NET, can affect the options available for authentication platform or provider selections.

Figure 1.1 presents an example of one such common technology project—the selection of a new e-mail platform. This need might arise in response to a consolidation of business units or merger, as a result of new purchasing mandates, or as a part of a technology modernization effort.

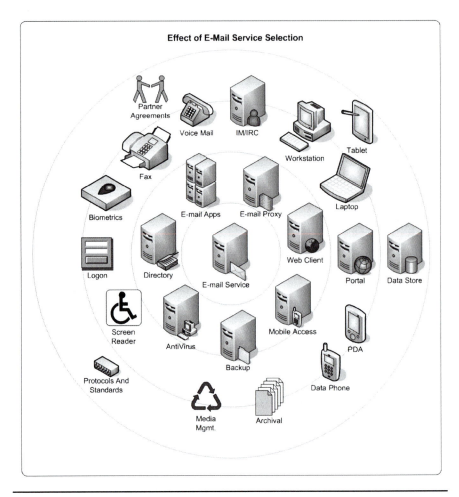

Figure 1.1   Effect of e-mail service selection on other related technologies.

The unwary might perceive selecting a new e-mail platform as a simple process, since all platforms use a standard known as the Simple Mail Transport Protocol (SMTP) to transfer messages from sender to recipient. Certainly, however, cost and features are important in the selection, so accountants and users may offer input as well. A committee typically collects user requirements and preferences, identifies purchasing options, and makes a recommendation to upper management, where a simple "go/ no-go" response drives the selection forward.

Ripples in the Pond

Moving beyond the simple issues of cost and features within the e-mail service itself, selecting an e-mail platform will also affect the type of directory service that can be used for log-on authentication, which in turn will affect the choices available for user log-on and identification as well as options for accessible interfaces, encryption, and other extended requirements for connectivity within the enterprise.

Services

The selected platform may need to be interoperable with other e-mail–enabled applications, in which case the code base and authentication systems must be able to integrate with the new selection or applications may need to be rewritten or abandoned. Network fax and voice mail systems may be integrated with the e-mail service to deliver other content into users' inboxes, while instant messaging and chat functions may provide online awareness and synchronous communication integration with the asynchronous e-mail that is the heart of this selection.

Some e-mail services may provide options for proxy relay systems in remote offices that are not always connected to the business network; others may provide a feature-rich Web-based client that allows users to access e-mail through the Internet. Push-type mobile e-mail technologies such as Research In Motion's Blackberry and Microsoft's Smart Phone allow users to avoid the need to log-on to access e-mail—each item is sent directly to the user's device when received. Selection of a particular platform may affect how users access e-mail on local and remote workstations, mobile computing devices, and newer technologies such as data-enabled telephones.

Business

As e-mail becomes one of many types of communication that users require, organizations are beginning to blend together asynchronous and synchronous means into a common one-stop location—often referred to as a portal. Here, users may receive targeted news, engage in threaded discussions, share documents, manage schedules, read e-mail, chat with other team members through instant messaging, and review operational readiness using business intelligence solutions such as dashboards and automated scorecards.

Whether or not an e-mail selection needs to fit within such an enterprise communication suite, it will also affect data storage, backup solutions, records retention practices, and media management controls based on all applicable regulatory and operational mandates. Defenses must also be integrated to protect against e-mail–borne threats, particularly as more users access their mail through small portable devices whose limited resources cannot support fully featured antivirus defenses. Selection of an e-mail platform affects options available for defenses to filter out spam (unwanted electronic "junk mail"), viruses, and other undesirable content.

Business continuity and disaster recovery planning must also be integrated with the selection. Large-scale disasters such as the terrorist attacks of September 11, 2001, hurricanes such as Rita and Katrina, and fears of contagious pandemics have shown the value of the business continuity of operations that can be provided by adequate planning and effective electronic communications, where the selected platform may be the only means of coordinating a geographically dispersed staff.

Beyond

Thus a simple e-mail service selection will have far-reaching effects by determining all protocols and standards that may be used to access, protect, and consume its functionality. It will affect internal users, operational planning, and external issues such as partner agreements or contract-worker access. Because the e-mail service is only one component of many, each of these other choices will, in turn, affect many other elements of the extended technology enterprise.

Unless the architect is fully cognizant of all such issues, including both business requirements as well as the technologies involved, a misstep may limit options later or even require a total overhaul of the system down the road. A manager or information technology professional who is not skilled in enterprise architecture can easily cost a business significant opportunities, even if the selection at first seems best based solely on user requirements and cost analysis.

Where the Only Constant Is Change

In this text, we will examine the strategies that allow an enterprise to be agile enough to take advantage of new opportunities, while at the same time being stable enough to allow recovery and continuity in the face of disaster, regulatory mandate, or significant shift of business focus. Before walking that path, it is important to be forewarned: Change is often opposed. This opposition pervades the entire spectrum of information technology solutions—which may seem odd in an environment where the only constant is change.

Lilliput and Blefuscu

In Jonathan Swift's *Gulliver's Travels*, the primary character encounters the tiny inhabitants of an island called Lilliput. Lemuel Gulliver discovers that the people of Lilliput are embroiled in a bitter war with their neighbors on the island of Blefuscu. The war is being fought over a difference in the way that eggs must be eaten (Lilliput legislates that eggs must be eaten only from the smaller, pointed end, while Blefuscu claims that eggs must be eaten only from the larger, rounded end). The big-end/little-end difference separates these people so strongly that a long and bitter war has been fought over the issue.

Because both solutions allow an egg to be eaten, the choice of starting at one end or the other seems a poor cause for conflict. This is nothing compared to the passionate manner in which technologists are divided, with arguments over who "gets root" (has an administrative level of system access) or which method of log-on authentication to use escalating to heated brawls or thousands of pages of research "proving" the One True Way.

It is said of the popular dish *pad Thai* (Thai noodles) that there are as many recipes as there are chefs who prepare it. This is also true for technology, as every technologist will have his or her own One True Way and every enterprise will have its own set of needs and preferences. Before we begin our study of the strategies that may be used, it is important to understand that entrenched information technology professionals will have their own best option.

An architect must have the strength of vision necessary to stand firm and persuade these individuals that some choices must be made from a larger perspective in order to reap the greatest benefits for the organization overall. A few of the arguments that may be encountered include the following.

Root. In information technology circles, position and status are often conveyed to the administrator who has ultimate access rights. By having a root administrative account, these individuals proudly proclaim that they are trusted enough or responsible enough to have this access—and they often fight fervently to get or keep this type of account and to avoid anyone else having a higher level of administrative access.

Silos. Consolidation of information is a driving force in many efforts to reduce administrative requirements, hardware costs, licensing fees, and data exposure. This is counter to the traditional structure, in which individual business units maintained their own technologies, data, backups, and administrative controls in independent silos with total autonomy. Regulatory mandates and cost controls are driving consolidation efforts, posing a threat to the legacy of autonomy and control.

Big iron. Traditionally, large enterprises relied on large, dedicated systems. These "big iron" mainframes still have a place in the enterprise, but they are being challenged by technologies that rely on decentralized nodes or grids of interconnected lower-capacity systems to generate the same level of operational capability. Although Beowulf-style superclusters made from off-the-shelf personal computing hardware have provided greater computing power than all but the largest dedicated supercomputers, those who are used to the "big iron" style of computer hardware and software often find it difficult to trust applications and platforms that are based on small-computer models.

Platform. Perhaps the most hotly debated topic in any information technology environment—the choice of a particular operating system or programming language as the standard—can turn even the most mild-mannered geeks into a hostile angry mob. Even the manner in which programs are written can set off a blizzard of protest and justification for an alternative. Attempts to include service-oriented methodologies or new programming styles such as rapid-prototyping "scrum" techniques can cause projects to halt while technologists argue the relative merits of one technique over another or one standard over another.

SOA and Scrum: Service-oriented architecture (SOA) programming techniques rely on standards for connectivity, rather than requiring all code elements to combine into a single massive application. Implemented as modular stand-alone sub-applications that communicate with one another, this method allows multiple development teams to work on pieces of a project in isolation—provided the interfaces are designed according to a set of agreed-on standards. This programming style often relies on Internet connectivity among the application segments, which rely on Web services and other standards for common communication interfaces.

The "scrum" method of programming extends this paradigm by seeking to create a prototype before requirements are completed. The prototype can be evaluated and then a new version produced based on feedback to include more user requirements, following on the old military adage, "Doing anything is better than doing nothing, even if it is wrong." Because the developers are always running ahead of feedback, the parts that are kept afterwards are already completed rather than just being started. This results in a lot of discarded code, but as Thomas Edison noted regarding his thousands of failed attempts, "I have not failed, I have found three thousand ways not to make a light bulb. All I need is one way that works." Scrum programmers may have already created a code element that can be reused later, as they look for the one right way to fulfill user requirements.

Technologists will passionately defend their One True Way to such an extent that this conflict may add months or even years to a simple technology selection process. It is here that the architect's vision and understanding must be used to move things along, because behind everything else, it doesn't matter which end you eat from. It is only important that you meet all requirements.

Open Source and Open Standards

The most fundamental level of conflict underlies any selection of standards or platforms, and in consolidating business units and technologies. This argument divides technologists with a level of passion that borders on religious hysteria, with proponents on both sides of the argument creating huge bodies of data and propaganda machines spewing out reams of arguments about the Only Way that is always best. At its simplest, this argument is over whether free open-source software (FOSS) is inherently better than commercial software whose source code is not provided to end users.

Note: The source code is the actual computer-language instructions used to write a program in a language such as C, FORTRAN, Java, or Visual Basic. With this code, developers can examine how the program works in detail and can change parts to create their own unique version of the software.

Open Source

Open-source software proponents often identify the success of the LAMP stack as a platform for architecture. A stack is simply a collection of applications or standards designed to work together, and LAMP stands for Linux (an operating system), Apache (a Web server), MySql (a database application), and a programming language such as Perl or PHP. This arena of technology is generally able to move faster to embrace new types of technology than commercial suites can, and proponents note that thousands of programmers are constantly adding new functionalities of all types.

Tip: Even in fully integrated commercial enterprises, FOSS rapid development can be leveraged to test emerging technologies before buying into a commercial product. As an example, the DotNetNuke open-source portal is often used to evaluate the viability of a portal within commercial Microsoft enterprises before implementing a full SharePoint Portal server. Many useful tools and utilities exist within the open-source space, though they are intended for use in commercial enterprises.

Not all open-source software is free; many commercial products operate within this space, including commercial versions of many elements of the LAMP stack. Conversely, not all free open-source software is written for the LAMP environment—many such applications are created to operate within commercial software environments such as Apple's OS-X or Microsoft's popular Windows platform.

Openly shared source code has spawned hundreds of versions of popular technologies, such as the more than 700 versions of Linux that are currently identified. Unlike commercial application vendors such as IBM's WebSphere and z/OS or Microsoft's Windows environments, many businesses operating within the open-source space generate a revenue stream by providing support and updates to free products. Because an open-source enterprise may make use of products produced by hundreds of different developers, the greatest cost to operating this type of enterprise is often the effort needed to get all the pieces to work together.

Businesses that must identify all intellectual property used in their enterprise due to regulatory mandates such as the Sarbanes-Oxley Act of 2002 may need to dedicate effort toward identifying the source of application code elements used within the open-source community, and will want to identify alternatives in the event that a developer decides to sell a popular product to a commercial vendor or ceases to work on the application.

Because each piece is created by a different developer or group, the interface may seem complex to users who are more accustomed to a standard look and feel as present in commercial application suites; however, user training and the selection of standard solutions can minimize the impact of this variation. Implementing an architecture based on FOSS technologies may also encounter resistance from users who rely on alternative devices such as screen readers, Braille displays, and eye-tracking control devices, which are not always compatible with some programming styles. Alternate character sets may also pose issues for some FOSS applications moved into a global space, depending on the skill of the individual programmer.

Warning: Not all open-source efforts meet approval based solely on the lack of licensing fees. When the Commonwealth of Massachusetts decided on the OpenOffice FOSS application suite, lobbying groups representing residents with disabling conditions brought up many barriers to using the open-source solutions.

Commercial Off-the-Shelf (COTS)

With free alternatives available, why do commercial application suites dominate current enterprises? These suites are popular because they work together seamlessly, can be set up or recovered rapidly because there are fewer configurable options, and are familiar to most users. Fully integrated suites such as Microsoft's Office and IBM's WebSphere allow users to pick and choose from a range of applications designed to work together. This integration extends from application-level interoperability through standardization of the user interface, so that standard control functions can be found in the same location across platform elements. The ability to find a File -> Save or Print option in the same location every time makes these platforms and packages much more attractive to many users and can translate to a shorter learning curve and enhanced productivity when new applications are introduced into the enterprise network.

Although open-source equivalents exist for almost all commercial packages, they are seen as lower-quality or less featured products by commercial software proponents. One of Novell's OpenOffice developers noted at the 2006 LinuxWorld conference that a spreadsheet that opened in Microsoft's Office Excel program in roughly 30 seconds took almost 3 hours to open in Calc, the FOSS OpenOffice equivalent. This issue is only a problem for businesses with complex spreadsheets, but the one-for-one compatibility issue is valid.

Commercial vendors generate a revenue stream through licensing fees, which may be one-time or recurring. Open-source advocates note that user comfort with the standard interface and licensing investments may create a "vendor lock-in" that can be exploited by the technology vendor. Proponents of commercial enterprises note that a clear upgrade path will exist in moving from current technologies to emerging future versions, because vendors will want to make it easy to move to their newer versions.

Commercial technologies may be easier for some users, because they are built following accessibility and global character set requirements. The standard interface for administrative tools and user applications may also make it easier to replace key personnel during turnover, because those who are experienced in a commercial technology such as SAP or Oracle/PeopleSoft will find another implementation of the same technology very similar. Disaster recovery may also be easier for large enterprises when they can simply order replacements for damaged or lost equipment, which will arrive preinstalled with the desired commercial technologies.

Note: Open-source advocates have long noted that Linux might have a stronger market share if the larger computer manufacturers offered pre-installed open-source options rather than the dominant Microsoft Windows platform. However, the flexibility of the platform itself makes this a difficult task, because there are more than 700 recognized distributions of the Linux platform alone—before considering the numerous forks of packages that might be arrayed atop the Linux operating system. A few manufacturers, such as Dell, offer a limited Linux option. These are typically based on one of the commercially supported Linux distributions, in order to ensure that clients can find support at need.

Open Standards

A tangent to the open-source vs. commercial technology argument is the often-used term "open standards." Legislation has even been proposed in several state legislatures to mandate that all purchased technologies must support open standards. Open standards are those that can be used by any technology designer to create a solution that will work with all others of the same type. The SMTP e-mail transport protocol is one such, as a part of the TCP/IP communications protocol suite.

Open standards are fundamental to the global Internet, and they must be present for both information sharing and future-proofing an enterprise. Whether an open-source or commercial off-the-shelf architecture is ultimately determined to be correct, connectivity and accessibility must be based on open standards. Without these standards, critical functionality might be lost in future updates or records retention compromised if new software cannot read older files. Numerous standards have been recognized for document interchange, such as the Microsoft Office Open XML (OOXML) or the Open Document Format (ODF) developed by the OASIS group. One of the most-often-used open standards for document interchange is the Portable Document Format (PDF) created by Adobe Systems and used for many corporate and governmental sites to ensure that critical documents can be examined and reproduced across a wide range of software platforms and printer devices.

The requirement for using open standards may sound daunting, but it is not; for example, almost all word processing applications can store and access documents in text format, whether in ASCII, EBCDIC, or Unicode (formats used by different computer types to store character data). Plain text, while perhaps not as visually appealing as other formats, is an open standard by which these applications can share information—even between commercial (Lotus, Microsoft Office) and open-source (OpenOffice, Star Office) word processors.

The Best Solution

Beyond all else, which is the best solution? Ultimately, as long as the technology does the job efficiently, can be supported and maintained, and provides an acceptable return on investment, then it is a good solution. While academics and die-hard geeks can argue over the Platonic ideal of the "ultimate best" technology, the only best solution is one that can be accomplished so that the next can be addressed.

Technology is not a goal—it is a support function that allows business to be conducted, and sometimes a tool that may provide new opportunities for client and user services. Most organizations have neither the technical skills nor need to access source code and build their own versions of common applications, while all organizations need the greatest value for their dollar. Whether an enterprise pays commercial licensing fees or pays for integration support of free open-source software alternatives, technology will remain a costly proposal. The strategies described in coming chapters will help minimize this cost, allow long-term operational planning, and produce a robust and agile enterprise.

Chapter 2

Enterprise Planning

In This Chapter

- An examination of elements to consider in enterprise architecture
- Identifying measures of success and common pitfalls
- A review of the architectural roles and requirements for each
- Considerations for formal governance and framework adoption

Before a building can be constructed, a detailed layout of all the structural, environmental, decorative, and functional elements must first be compiled. This detailed layout, called a blueprint, ensures that adequate resources and room to expand are present and that all elements will work together in the final product. The blueprint is reviewed many times before construction begins to ensure that elements from many different disciplines will work together well—that electrical and plumbing fixtures are properly placed, that the windows and doors produce the desired effect, and that the materials specified are suitable to the environment.

Before an enterprise network can be constructed, or further developed from its existing state, a design similar to a physical construction blueprint must be created. Instead of building codes and construction methodologies, this design must identify the guidelines and strategies that will form the basis for the network architecture, along with standards and frameworks that will be used to guide its creation.

The next few chapters will examine these overarching details, before we dig more deeply into individual technological elements in the remainder of the book. This chapter focuses on the function and traits of an enterprise architect, information technology governance principles, and several architectural frameworks that can be used as templates for developing an enterprise network architectural plan.

Beyond Platform Selection

Many attempts at enterprise architectural planning revolve around selection of a particular technology as the standard that will be applied to future purchasing choices. Such a "platform architecture" might include listings of approved hardware platforms, operating systems, desktop configurations, office productivity suites, content management and database management systems, programming languages and development tool suites, collaboration platforms, directory and identity management solutions, and even mobile technology solutions approved for staff use or purchase reimbursement.

Architects of commercial platforms may select a particular vendor stack, such as Microsoft or IBM, for enterprise-wide standardization in order to ease integration and planning. Open-systems architects may select only a set of standards around which all purchases must be made, with minor platform or application variation allowed at the user or facility level if deemed worth the added complexity. Regardless of the particular approach chosen, selecting standardized platform architectures can provide direct benefits that are easily conveyed to stakeholders:

- Economies of scale can be gained through aggregated purchasing mechanisms spanning multiple business units that formerly purchased technologies in an ad-hoc manner using locally directed funding. Enterprise-wide licensing and per-processor licensing models can often save tremendous amounts of money compared to individual per-user licensing throughout a medium-to-large organization.
- Applications are more easily integrated and tested, depending on the level of commonality provided through platform specification. The more elements of the platform architecture are shared, the greater is

the ease in initial implementation and later additions of functionality. Selecting a standard or vendor with a large body of third-party offerings allows an organization to readily adopt newly emergent technology offerings as they reach viability.

- Users and technical support staff can be more efficient throughout the enterprise, as they can gain a greater working knowledge of a smaller number of disparate solutions. This can reduce both staffing and training requirements, and allow greater mobility within an extended organization to meet marketplace agility needs. When all applications are standardized, a user trained in the standard suite of productivity applications will require very little training if he or she is transferred to another department.

- Selecting widely used platform architectures provides a greater body of community support when issues arise or when new technologies are being implemented. When problems or questions arise, it is easier to find effective solutions if the platform architecture is in common use and enjoys strong community involvement in implementation and development.

- Future control is simplified because only the initial selection process must include all possible competing alternatives. After the platform architecture has been identified and detailed, future selection needs only to evaluate alternatives within the identified platform's offerings.

Enterprise architecture would be greatly simplified if platform selection was its only feature. Within small, well-funded organizations, many of these "low-hanging fruit" may be plucked readily as value-for-effort. However, selection of a single platform specification to be implemented across a medium-to-large organization will rapidly encounter many stumbling blocks, often including the following:

- Many packaged applications rely on a particular set of technologies for operation. Legacy equipment such as automation and equipment control systems may rely on an embedded control technology, while other applications may only operate against a particular type of relational database management system (DBMS) such as an Oracle or MySQL instance. Changing these solutions to meet newly-identified platform architectural guidelines can be problematic, requiring time, effort, and expense in acquiring alternatives that fit within the identified platform—assuming that such an alternative exists. Application virtualization systems are often tied to the fundamental architecture of the network itself, relying on the authentication and access control system to control application package assignment, deployment, and updating. The architect can address this issue by carefully identifying all such dependencies before beginning enterprise reconfiguration actions, so as to avoid mid-upgrade loss or instability of key services that can stall or terminate enterprise-wide projects.

- Replacement of existing, working systems may be beyond the budgeting ability of many organizations and business units. While there are times when a functional but expensive enterprise solution may be tossed out in favor of an alternative (a scenario we will examine later in this book), the majority of businesses must enact incremental evolutionary change rather than outright revolutionary change simply because the cost of replacing everything outweighs the benefits of immediate standardization. An architect's knowledge and understanding of existing revenue streams and any constraints on stream allocations are critical to understanding and successfully planning the scope and pace of enterprise-transforming projects.

- Changes in technology standards, development of new offerings, and the constant evolution of network threats can often outrun an established platform specification. By the time an organization can transition its technologies to meet the new standard; several new versions of an identified platform option might have been developed to add new features or close vulnerabilities not identified at the time of the original assessment. This is particularly true when dealing with governmental agencies, educational systems, and organizations with complex bureaucracies, because of the lag between specification and purchase. An identified best-in-breed at the time of original product evaluation might be woefully inadequate compared to later entries into the same application space by the time the new fiscal year rolls around and funds are available for acquisition. The architect must constantly review emerging technologies and keep abreast of changes in common technology devices, configurations, and uses.

- The scale of need and expertise may vary widely within an organization, creating a requirement for different levels of operational capability that may not be reflected by a one-size-fits-all platform specification. A commonly encountered version of this involves the dominant enterprise Microsoft platform, which includes both desktop (Access) and server (SQL Server) relational database solutions. Both solutions use a similar interface for query/view design and share many elements in common; however, the workgroup-scale Access application is not suited to the same level of concurrent use as its more robust SQL Server counterpart. Conversely, training to support each relational database (RDBS) application differs greatly in the level of expertise required, because the workgroup product lacks many of the index, trigger, stored procedures, and other features necessary in its enterprise counterpart. Proper project management practices during the planning phase will aid in achieving an effective transformation by identifying existing solutions that are in place and compiling skills and responsibility matrices to identify available resources, both human and technological, as well as any shortcomings that must be met by acquisitions or training.

- Partner organizations may not follow the same standards, creating difficulties when the platform architecture must interoperate with that of another organization whose decisions are made along a differing standard or cycle of upgrade. This problem becomes more apparent as organizations are increasingly coupled with partners for service provision, regulatory mandate, or business opportunity. Poorly selected platform architecture or the choice of little-used technology standards can create barriers to business integration and lose opportunities for the organization well beyond simple issues of whether the solution meets an originally identified specification. This problem arises often during mergers and acquisitions when platform architecture decisions have followed different courses in the originally separate organizations. As an example, elements of the U.S. Department of Homeland Security experienced difficulties with e-mail between organizational elements when the department was created from previously separate functional organizations. Platform differences caused communications difficulties between some divisions of the new organization, even though all were using the same underlying standard (SMTP) for e-mail. Use of common platforms and applications in architectural redesign will reduce the likelihood of poor interoperability with partner organizations or external services, such as hosting or cloud computing providers.

Customization of operating system, application, and service configurations beyond accepted industry standards should be kept to a bare minimum to protect both interoperability and upgrade potential.

- Individual business units or key stakeholders may be unwilling to accept the platform architectural specification. As we discussed in Chapter 1, a wide range of technology preferences may factor into the local mandates provided by business-unit IT decision makers. In addition to preference, individual business units may lack the expertise and skills necessary to implement a newly specified platform standard—particularly one that differs considerably from the platform architecture currently in use. Matrices and surveys of existing resources compiled during the planning phase will help identify requirements for training to upgrade support capabilities. The platform architect should also ensure that support leadership is included in the technology council that provides change management controls, to ensure that issues are presented, considered, and addressed before initiating a change.

- Implementation of alternative standards or platform specifications without a review of service impact or analysis can compromise service availability and user capabilities, and may create push-back from user and management-level consumers in addition to technical support teams. This type of issue is common when movement to an older standard platform is necessary due to a merger between organizations when the main organization is using older software versions than the newly acquired organizational element. Users who have become accustomed to features and functionalities provided by the newer software may experience significantly reduced efficiency due to a lack of certain features. Users may also feel "cheated" by being forced to roll back to the "outdated" application platform or software standard.

Certainly, these are not the only barriers to adopting a platform specification, but they illustrate clearly why the practice of enterprise architecture must take into account elements that extend beyond the range of platform specification alone. Beyond specification of a set of standards or vendor products through which the enterprise will operate, the enterprise architect must also consider integration and communications requirements, application-specific requirements, available and emergent communications protocols, business integration mandates, legislative and regulatory compliance constraints, scale and scope requirements, event management and alerting, reporting mandates, storage and architectural requirements, identity management mandates, and a wealth of other aspects that we will examine later in the book.

Without guidance and consideration of these elements both in their current form and following emergent trends, the enterprise architect may make short-term decisions that fail to provide longer-term efficiencies—in fact, some decisions can even create greater cost burdens if improperly applied. Architecture is more about plotting a course through a variety of choices than about making a particular application selection. Technical frameworks and standards must be balanced against the strategic goals of the business while minimizing the negative impact of any changes on the end user. Rather than being a goal, technology must always remain a means to facilitate user requirements.

In the end, a project that produces the desired change in technology but negatively impacts user and client service remains a failure. According to the Project Management Institute (PMI), roughly two-thirds of all projects fail. To avoid expending unnecessary effort on failure, the enterprise architect must know when to initiate a project, when to decide the time or resources are not right for a particular change, and when to call a halt to avoid spending resources on a failed effort. Always remember that sunk costs (money already spent) should not be used to determine whether to continue a failing or troubled project.

Where Lies Success?

Successful enterprise architecture must convey some form of advantage to the organization or it serves no purpose. While it might once have been possible for an organization to gain a competitive edge by using e-mail for internal communication or a website for user contact, these solutions are now used by such a broad range of organizations that they create no operational advantage. Although doing without them might have a negative effect, their presence alone no longer constitutes a particular competitive advantage. Enterprise architecture must provide additional value to the organization, as we will examine in detail in Chapter 4.

A few qualities that may indicate successful enterprise architecture include:

- Providing a clear upgrade path to future technologies
- Defining standards for interoperability with current and emergent technologies
- Minimizing undesirable redundancy and optimizing fault tolerance
- Reducing risk and enhancing continuity of operations
- Reducing support and operational costs
- Improving operational opportunities for interaction and mobility
- Recognizing architecture as a valuable contribution to the enterprise

It may at first seem strange that one indicator of a successful enterprise architecture is that the architecture is recognized as valuable. However, architectural choices can have a profound effect on an organization's capabilities and opportunities for future growth. An architecture that is completely in the background, which is never noticed by the users and stakeholders, may be too readily discarded as an unnecessary effort or expense during organizational changes or economic cutbacks. It is important for long-term viability that not only should good decisions be made, but that they must also be communicated to implementers and users. Successes, failures, and even near-misses should also be conveyed to primary stakeholders so that the value of the architecture remains known, identifiable, and justifiable within the overall business plan.

An enterprise architect may be aided by other architects, a change management council, or an integration competency center to ensure that all decisions that are made fit within all necessary technologies and operational mandates. However, it is the architect's vision of the enterprise that guides all policies, standards, guidelines, and specifications that will be enacted within this scope. The enterprise architect must be able to convey the value of this vision to both stakeholders and implementers, and must be able to see far enough ahead that decisions made today allow opportunities in the future.

As with any project, the project manager (enterprise architect) must be selected as early in the process as possible and must be given the authority to negotiate for necessary resources and designate standards for architectural changes. There can be only one person in the role of chief architect: Effective responsibility cannot be assigned to a group.

In smaller organizations, the enterprise architect may also be the chief technologist or lead developer. This can be acceptable in a small venue, as the architect may be able to learn and consider all possible aspects of the organizational technology needs. In larger organizations, it is important to distinguish enterprise architecture from development and information technology implementation. While nontechnical managerial staff members cannot be effective enterprise architects because they lack the necessary understanding of service interrelations, even effective IT professionals may be a poor enterprise architects if:

- **Their personal preferences for technology specification do not provide the best opportunities for their organization as a whole.** Many organizations attempt to bypass the tendencies discussed in Chapter 1 by placing a nontechnical individual into the CIO/chief architect's position. While this may avoid the problem of information technology preference, it creates a situation in which the primary decision maker responsible for architectural vision must rely primarily on the advice of others—a situation akin to sheep asking wolves to advise them. This also leads to project selection in isolation, where a change in collaboration platform might be decided on without considering the impact on related services such as an organizational intranet portal or a customer management system that leverages the collaboration platform for critical functionality.
- **Their vision lacks clarity and understanding of the needs of the organization, or changes too often to provide a useful direction.** Nothing can doom an enterprise architectural effort more effectively than a leader who does not know where the organization is going. Fuzzy goals tend to lead to unremarkable results that lack metrics for assessing success. Like a boat without a tiller, an architect without direction tends to lead nowhere. Worse, in some ways, is the architect whose vision changes with each new month's trade journals or based on which stakeholders have most recently argued their needs. An inconstant leader can cause implementers to waste valuable time jumping from project to project, at times working only to undo what has just been partially completed because the architect has just heard about the newest process-of-the-month. Nothing illustrates more how lost a leader is than such wandering in the wilderness of alternatives.

- **They are unable to convey their vision to stakeholders, implementers, or business consumers.** The most knowledgeable technologists, skilled at every aspect of their craft and instilled with the most incredibly clear vision of successful enterprise architecture, are useless if they cannot effectively convey their vision and its value to others. Many technologists eschew the "soft skills" necessary to project management, negotiation, and selling the idea of their vision and its worth to the organization. For those to whom technology itself becomes the goal, conveying its value beyond existence appears unnecessary. This form of tunnel vision can doom an enterprise architectural effort to failure. The most beautiful painting in the world has no value if it is kept in the dark—so too with an architectural vision.
- **They fail to remain knowledgeable about technologies in use and in development.** While the CIO/chief architect should focus on aspects of technology that extend beyond the day-to-day implementation details, it is impossible to command the respect of information technologists charged with implementing the vision without maintaining a thorough knowledge of current and emerging technology trends. Not only may architects miss potential opportunities, they may lose the support and input from individuals whose expertise may carry the key to greater success. Buy-in from implementers within the technology service arena is often developed only in the presence of expertise on the part of the architect. While this role need not have deep expertise in all areas, the architect should be an expert in at least one area and conversant in the functions of all others in order to best gain the trust and support of other technologists. Knowledgeable architects can also bridge disparate skills as a force multiplier, producing an outcome greater than that possible by team members acting apart.
- **They fail to lead.** Worst of all possible architects are those who are so busy gathering requirements, evaluating options, negotiating with their peers, reporting to their superiors, and getting feedback from stakeholders that they never do anything. It is easy to slip into a routine so filled with the process of developing architectural guidelines that nothing is ever produced as a result. The pursuit of perfection is seductive and pointless—what must be accomplished is a solution that is good enough for the current business needs and good enough to allow the next generation of technologies to be managed in turn.

Table 2.1 IT Maturity Models

Level	Maturity	Management	Architecture
4	Value	Information improves business process and cost recovery	Processes exist to resolve strategic/tactical conflicts
3	Service	Capacity and service levels managed	Standard architecture, applied inconsistently
2	Proactive	Performance, configuration, and change management are automated	Architecture managed in some business units
1	Reactive	Basic event response, backup/recovery, and help desk	Departmental-level architectural management
0	Chaotic	No consolidation, operations are left to deployment staff	All decisions made in isolation

Source: Gartner Research.

Many different means can be used to measure the current state of architectural guidance and management within an organization. Table 2.1 provides a simplified maturity model based on those offered by Gartner Research. Far too many organizations operate at the lowest levels of maturity, where decisions on architecture and implementation are missing altogether or function in chaos merely as reactions to the latest problem or need. Proactive effort and cost is generally far lower than reactive, because reactive actions include resources necessary to undo what has been done in addition to resources necessary to implement the new course of action. Without a higher level of planning, coordination, and vision, these organizations cannot take advantage of the true potential of their IT resources.

The Architect

If a successful architecture can produce advantages, then what makes a good architect? This question is tied closely to the job the CIO/chief architect must perform in order to effectively identify, strategize, and resolve organizational needs and technology drivers that affect the enterprise. The architect is responsible for many tasks, such as:

- **Identifying data and its movement.** The enterprise architect must identify data that is being managed and maintained throughout the enterprise, along with the paths through which it is transferred, archived, or eliminated in order to properly plan for its continuity under a formal architectural style. Many times, the identification and elimination of undesirable redundancy in data stores can produce strong benefits from direct cost savings in hardware, software, and support to indirect cost savings through security of sensitive or protected data.

- **Defining technical architectural guidelines.** Standards, technology selections, protocol selections, guidelines for identity management, update management, security and recoverability statutes, computer use policy specifications, and all other aspects of the technology architecture must be coordinated by the enterprise architect in the overall vision.

- **Integrating existing resources.** The enterprise architect cannot, in almost all cases, simply throw away everything that exists and replace it with new solutions. Embedded systems, legacy equipment, merged business units, and partner relationships may all bring different technology solutions into the enterprise. The enterprise architect must plan for the inclusion of these elements into the strategy.

- **Communicating the vision.** The enterprise architect must convey the benefits of the vision to stakeholders, the details to the implementers, and the benefits and purpose to the users. At the same time, this communication cannot be one-way. The enterprise architect must constantly be accepting useful input to be included in the evolution of the vision to encompass emerging needs and solutions.

- **Improve quality.** The results of the enterprise architect's efforts must provide value to the organization, improving the quality of information technology operations. Architects whose solutions simply replace existing systems with a different version of the same thing may find it difficult to justify the continued expense without some measure of value or quality improvement. Careful metrics identified before and after each phase can aid in the identification of the value provided, requiring the architect to practice more than simple technology selection in order to be a success.

- **Program management.** Strong project and program management skills are vital to ensure that all phases of architectural reconstruction are handled in an efficient manner using well-defined strategies. In addition to maintaining technology operations, which many former IT managers are more than capable of continuing, the enterprise architect must manage numerous projects simultaneously to control costs and ensure that activities on the critical path are addressed ahead of activities with flex remaining. It is far too easy to seek "easy" projects to illustrate ongoing success to sponsors, but this can lead to missed deadlines and cost overruns when those easy projects are not ones that must be completed first to maintain overall project and program timelines.

The Chief Architect

A CIO/chief architect must be able to perform equally well in the business and technology arenas. It is here that the ability to identify business needs and shareholder expectations of value is essential in order to later convey the purpose and benefits resulting from enterprise architectural deliverables. Identifying opportunities to improve the organization through productivity, efficiency, or asset gains is as important as identifying inefficient architectures, poor buying models, and outdated solutions currently in place.

Providing a Plan

The chief architect must be able to identify the purpose of information technology solutions, align them with business requirements, and communicate their value to both technical implementers as well as nontechnical stakeholders. Subordinate IT professionals at times may want to try out new solutions that have no applicability to the current business environment—distinguishing new business opportunities from expensive toys is a valuable skill for the chief architect. The chief architect must be willing to simply say "no" to nonproductive projects and inefficient ways of doing business. The chief enterprise architect is rarely a popular person, as entrenched professionals with established professional and personal standing can be very influential when complaining about changes that are made counter to local preferences.

The chief architect must always be looking to the future, identifying crises that may emerge as a result of new network threats or emerging technologies. Disaster recovery and business continuity may hinge on effective IT planning, in which good decisions and an eye to potential large-scale disruption may keep the business on track while competitors fail. Concerns about global pandemics, terrorist activities, and natural disasters all add to the scope of an enterprise architect's planning, because decisions now may determine whether an organization survives or simply ceases to exist in the worst case.

Communicating the Vision

Chief architects must be able to see the big picture but paint it on small canvases. Translating the vision into simple, concise pieces is vital both to educating stakeholders and conveying directives to those responsible for executing planned changes. A solid business case for each primary element, along with strong project management skills that can bridge multiple projects into a cohesive program within a common framework can aid in rapidly identifying a process gone awry or one that is being ineffectively implemented. Unhappy implementers can often be identified here, where their lack of enthusiasm may be adversely affecting project success and timeliness.

Chief architects must be equally at home talking to primary stakeholders as to individual users, as they are comfortable communicating in the language of business as technology. They must be able to effectively convey elements of the vision at all levels of the business, but also be able to dig down to the individual details of the application of the vision so that communication can flow both ways. Ultimately, they need to be able to sell the idea to stakeholders, convey it to implementers, and document everything so that metrics can be measured against the process of change. Like all project managers, enterprise architects may spend up to 90% of their time communicating among implementers, change management functionaries, stakeholders, project sponsors, peers, and individual users.

Balancing Value and Risk

The chief architect must be able to identify value in the present architecture, as well as identify missing elements that need to be filled. Many times, some elements of efficiency can be acquired rapidly. These "low-hanging fruit" are easily obtained, and it is important to identify these for initial implementation in order to show value—but care must be taken to ensure that jumping too quickly does not incur undesirable opportunity costs, excluding opportunities for greater improvements later. Establishing clear business goals and balancing them against selected technology solutions is not a simple task, as each choice may close off other alternatives later.

Chief architects must identify metrics and goals for success and failure, while also planning and identifying risks that will arise from each step toward these goals. Cost and risk factors and various constraints must be considered during each planning phase, both at the immediate per-project level and across the entire enterprise planning process. Adding vulnerability or exposing protected data during a transitional phase may not be legally allowable under regulatory and operational mandates, while relying on a technology that is still in the incubator stage may produce an unacceptable level of risk to future-proofing guidelines and purchasing requirements. Security and regulatory compliance must always be considered in strategic planning to ensure that assets are not exposed to risk during transition.

The Lead Architect

In support of a chief architect, a lead architect may participate in senior management forums, serve on the change management council, or lead implementation groups in applying the strategies developed from the chief architect's vision. In small to medium enterprises, these roles are typically combined. A lead architect will often lead forums, integration competency center reviews, requirements-gathering initiatives, and other similar tasks necessary to identifying business and technology elements for integration into the overall architectural plan. This role is particularly valuable when attempting to integrate multiple cross-enterprise initiatives during mergers.

The Business Architect

Organizations that employ complex application solutions or ones with public-facing business applications such as Web shopping carts or business intelligence portals may find it necessary to assign a business architectural role. Whether combined with the chief architect's position or implemented separately, the person holding this operational role must understand and translate all business strategies and processes into requirements that can be addressed through technology selection or development.

The business architect's role may include technology planning for business-to-business, business-to-consumer, partner integration, service-oriented-architecture selection, and management of heterogeneous or legacy application suites that require data gateway translation or information transfer for operation.

The Technology Architect

The technology architect role becomes necessary in organizations that employ a wide range of technological solutions, or in which application development or customization is used extensively. This role requires deep technical experience, often in one or more programming disciplines, and the technology architect acts to ensure that application development and modification are performed within the strategies detailed from the chief architect's vision.

The technology architect is responsible for guiding application design style selection, such as service-oriented, scrum, or waterfall-type development, as well as testing new techniques and technologies for potential use within the extended enterprise. Though often considered the most fun job, this role of the technology architect is not just to try out all of the new technology toys, but to be able to draw a hard line when a solution reaches end of life or is determined to fall outside the organization's needs.

Outsourced Architecture

Some aspects of enterprise architecture can be outsourced to external expertise. In general, this is done in order to gain access to skills that are not present or not present in sufficient depth within the existing human resources of the organization. When making a strategic change in storage architecture or federated identity management, outsourcing the planning roles can be effective while internal personnel are being provided the necessary training to understand a new solution's implications. During mergers and acquisitions, for instance, an outside expert may be able to begin the migration process while local IT resources are retrained into the parent organization's architecture.

Outsourcing the developing of a strategic guide or blueprint may provide a means to save time within limited internal enterprise architect resources, or when internal political issues provide the need for an outside viewpoint to settle on one solution as the common thread for development of a strategic vision. Documentation of existing resources can also be outsourced in order to save time and to reduce the impact of internal business-unit politics on discovery and resource identification. Critical functions such as enterprise architectural change or security may be outsourced in some cases, but responsibility for services, regulatory compliance, and data protection ultimately remains with the organization.

One additional area that lends itself well to outsourcing is that of testing and compliance review. Testing new technologies for a fit within the enterprise architectural vision may be best performed by a third party in order to ensure that findings reflect technology interactions and not simply local preferences. Similarly, compliance audit and review should be performed by a dedicated or external agency in order to ensure that internal bias or simple familiarity do not cause the review to overlook areas of concern. Audit functions must not be conducted solely from within the IT organization, as it is impossible to obtain a fair and thorough report of variance when the individual reporting an issue is subordinate to the functions or personnel being assessed.

Multiple Architects

Small to medium-size enterprise architecture can easily be coordinated by a single chief architect, with additional supporting focused architects added to cover capacity shortfalls as the enterprise scope expands. This can produce an optimized architecture, capable of the most complete synthesis of homogeneous network coordination with the greatest possible reduction in data and network complexity and cost. As enterprise networks increase in size or span multiple business units with independent purchasing capabilities, the load may be distributed across multiple architects' purview, provided the organization has matured to some form of matrixed structure. A single chief architect or chief technology officer must still be identified in all cases, because someone must ultimately make choices between alternatives and be responsible for success or failure of the effort.

Distributed federated architecture for very large enterprises can be configured serially or in parallel, depending on the nature of the enterprise and its goals, as noted in Figure 2.1. Serial architecture divides individual aspects of the overall architectural vision so that each element is guided by its own chief architect. Communication among the chief architectural roles creates a community environment within the coordinated guidelines dictated by each architect's contributions. This is similar to a university or corporate environment in which each business unit operates within a negotiated general vision but maintains some aspects of localized control.

Parallel architecture is more like a city, in which no common vision is implemented and each silo makes decisions for access within its own

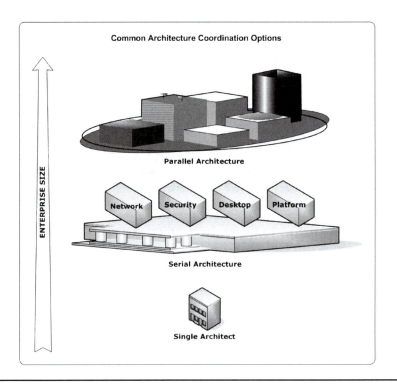

Figure 2.1   Architecture coordination as enterprise size increases.

boundaries. Multiple autonomous heterogeneous silos of parallel operation yield localized responsiveness at the cost of opportunities for efficiency, much like physical city planning efforts. Parallel architectural
control scenarios tend to experience large undesirable redundancies in
data, hardware, and staffing requirements and do not adapt to wide-scale
upgrade as well as more closely coordinated architectural forms. This is
the least efficient format for large enterprise networks, as differing architectural decisions may generate standards conflict, compromise security,
and create large areas of overlapping expense and operational effort.

Creating a Symphony

Federated architectural solutions, whether distributed serially or in parallel, must have a central chief architect to set basic policy and provide the
highest-level vision—all other forms of federated architecture will produce conflicting internal elements and impair long-term efficiency and
viability. This need is seen in many other operational arenas: Cooking,
music, education, corporate control, and military strategy all rely on coordination under a designated leader in order to avoid chaos.

Without a master chef, the sous-chefs and all others working in a commercial kitchen might produce a variety of very nice dishes but would be
very unlikely to create an integrated masterpiece of culinary art. A general
officer in the military may rely heavily on the support of senior staff officers, but in the end must make decisions alone so that an army can move
toward a single purpose. The federal Sarbanes-Oxley legislation formal-
ized responsibilities built into the framework of corporate governance,
mandating specific attention and control in the corporate sector. A master
conductor must work to bring together the disparate instruments present
so that an orchestra can produce a symphony—one that will differ from
the same music played by the same orchestra under a different conductor's
baton. Each of these scenarios represents the same need found in enterprise architecture—someone, ultimately, must hold the baton.

Governance

The art of enterprise architecture relies on similar high-level coordination
to gain advantages in agility, cost reduction, and operational efficiency.

The symphony that can result from effective coordinated enterprise governance depends on a clear vision, strong leadership coupled with executive buy-in and support, and an effective means of communication with those responsible for their own areas of expertise. Some assessments detail the process of enterprise architecture as follows:

1. **Creation**—Identification of the business drivers and requirements that create a need for enterprise coordination. This may be a simple need for cost-effective technology utilization, or made more complex by regulatory mandates and partner intercommunication requirements.
2. **Discovery**—Identification of the individual protocols and technologies that come together to form the executive-level vision that will guide technological development, purchase, and organization.
3. **Implementation**—Enacting changes, developing policies, communicating requirements necessary to implement the vision in actual terms.
4. **Governance**—Overseeing and managing the process that guides technology decisions, implementation actions, and all other decisions that fall within the guidelines of the technology enterprise.

However, governance is more fundamental than first appears in this process. Enterprise architecture translates business requirements into technology planning that must include strategic and operational decisions. These decisions must in turn contain decision making for capacity, cost, recovery, survivability, and future-proofing that must be more than theoretical abstracts. Governance is more about communicating between strategic roles (CEO, CFO, CIO, business-unit leaders), operational roles (managers, partner representatives, regulatory agents), and infrastructural roles (integration competency centers, information technology implementers, training staff).

Without some mechanism for governance, lines of communication and authority can become hopelessly tangled and doom the architectural effort before it has even begun. Many formal systems for information technology governance exist, including:

- **Information Technology Infrastructure Library (ITIL).** Perhaps the most widely adopted standard for enterprise governance, the

ITIL is a best-practice set of guidelines for operational control. Because of the level of detail in the ITIL, it can produce revolutionary change—with all of the benefits and costs that entails. Without strong management commitment, care in training and specifying each ITIL process, and planning for a three- to five-year implementation effort, this methodology can be a bit hard to handle. As a living document, the ITIL continues to evolve to meet new challenges that follow emergent technology standards and options and is widely used in large enterprises such as governmental and multinational corporations.

- **Control Objectives for Information Technology (CobIT).** This detailed governance model produced by the Information Systems Audit and Control Association (ISACA) grew from an audit and control methodology and is also widely recognized, with a strong community supporting its continued evolution. Its sponsoring agency, together with the IT Governance Institute, produce a large number of focused-compliance guides to help CobIT apply more specifically to individual guidelines that may apply to specific industries and business sectors (Sarbanes-Oxley, COSO) and to specific technologies (zOS, Linux, SAP).
- **ISO/IEC 27002.** The British governmental 7799 standard was adopted by the International Standards Organization as ISO 17799, which enjoys wide use throughout many business sectors—although it is often found combined with other governance methodologies due to the large number of translation guides that exist to bind this standard's elements with those of the other methodologies. The ISO/IEC 27002 standard has since replaced the older ISO 17799 standard, reflecting changes and more recently emergent requirements.

Many other formal systems exist for information technology governance, and any sufficiently detailed system with a strong community of support and regular updates to its standards could benefit the architectural process. Control objects from the ITIL, CobIT, ISO 17799, and other similar standards are aligned in many different studies, allowing organizations to use elements of those that fit best. It is vital that enterprise architects include an understanding of information technology governance in their planning and vision. Few organizations of significant size will find that a single governance or control standard meets all possible needs, so methodologies are often layered at different operational levels (as shown in Figure 2.2).

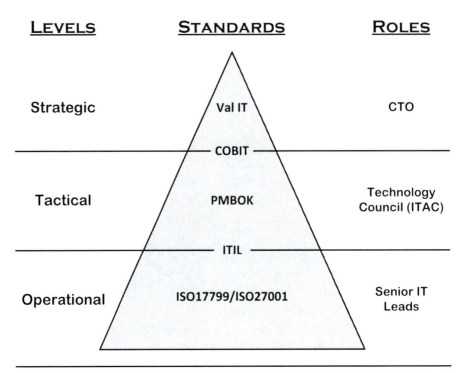

Figure 2.2   An example of governance layering to address needs at different organizational levels.

Architectural Models

In addition to an understanding of governance methodologies, the chief architect should also have an understanding of formal architectural frameworks that can be used as fundamental models during the architectural process. These frameworks can provide extraordinary resource, although many carry an inherent bias toward specific technological viewpoints and should be considered in that light. Formal enterprise architectural frameworks include options such as the following.

- **POSIX 1003.23.** One of the earliest formal frameworks for enterprise architecture, this standard was developed by the Institute of

Electrical and Electronics Engineers (IEEE) as one of several standards related to software compatibility for Unix operating system variants. Because of its origins, this standard is coupled closely with Unix and Unix-like platform environments.

- **The Zachman Framework.** A widely-accepted benchmark model, this framework was developed by the Zachman Institute in order to model enterprise architecture in terms of scope, business model, system model, technology model, and other detail when measured against the standard questions asked: what, how, where, who, when, and why. As a high-level model, the Zachman Framework provides an excellent starting point for architectural theory.

- **The Open Group Architecture Format (TOGAF).** TOGAF has been developed by the Open Group, a consortium of information system vendors, software suppliers, and user organizations. It is a very detailed, extensive living document that can be used as a starting point for developing commercial platform enterprise models, though its origins couple the document itself more closely to the open systems methodology.

- **The Federal Enterprise Architecture Framework (FEAF).** This framework emerged from a series of policies and guidance efforts within the U.S. federal government, aimed at providing a standard framework for planning interoperable and sustainable computing. It derives details from earlier governmental standards, including the Office of Management and Budget's (OMB's) EA Assessment Framework, the General Accounting Office's (GAO's) Information Technology Framework, the Treasury Enterprise Architecture Framework, the Generalized Enterprise Reference Architecture Model, the Performance Reference Model, the Data and Information Reference Model, the Application-Capability Reference Model, the Technical Reference Model, and other similar frameworks. It is detailed, extensive, and continues to be updated to reflect the changing needs of governmental IT enterprises.

- **The Gartner Enterprise Architecture Framework.** Developed by Gartner Research, this framework attempts to provide a comprehensive model for the development of both commercial and open-source enterprise environments. It is divided into parts, with half of the model addressing technology, while the other half addresses business strategy and process. Although it remains less developed in terms of a body of reference guides and compliance checklists, this framework enjoys steady growth in the body of documentation and research provided by its parent organization.

- **The North American State CIO Enterprise Architecture (NASCIO).** An emerging leader in enterprise architectural planning, this model is developed by the National Association of State Chief Information Officers (NASCIO), which is composed of representatives of the 50 state CIOs. Coupling well with other models, this model has broad applicability throughout both commercial off-the-shelf and open-source enterprise environments. Because it is derived from ongoing state-level CIO efforts, this framework remains a living body of data.

Tip: As with governance methodologies, elements from the formal frameworks can be combined in order to better meet the needs of each enterprise's unique setting. As an example, the State of Michigan makes use of elements from both the Gartner and NASCIO frameworks in the continuing development of its Strategic Plan, with very positive results to show from this effort.

Many mappings exist between the various enterprise framework models to better allow translation and combination of their useful elements. With attention to potential source bias, they can serve as an invaluable resource when attempting to identify boundaries within an unplanned ad-hoc enterprise seeking focus.

Project and Program Management

A common fallacy encountered in many organizations is the idea that technology must drive business and operational mandates. Business goals must always drive the logical decision making that produces a technological outcome, or the technology will become an end unto itself rather than a means to facilitate business operations. Aligning these requirements is the most important task to be managed by chief architects as they develop their vision and then implement it into real-world elements. Beyond documenting requirements and technology solutions, architects must also engineer metrics and measurement criteria into each element to be able to identify and illustrate the benefits or costs incurred during implementation.

This is not the end of the requirements for an enterprise architect, by any means. The chief architect must also plan each element with clear goals, milestones, and completion criteria before seeking or providing approval for each stage. The architect must be the final arbiter when negotiating solutions to conflicts that arise during planning, acquisition, implementation, and adoption of each change—which relies far more heavily on the project management skills of the architect than on detailed knowledge of the technologies involved. Ultimately, the architect must plan, design, guide, and monitor the ongoing fluid process of development throughout the enterprise and all of its associated business elements and technologies.

While the process of enterprise architecture never ends, individual elements must be clearly identified with a scope, planning guidelines, completion criteria, and other elements common to discrete project management. Leadership, communication, negotiation, problem solving, resolving cultural impact, meeting regulatory mandates and standards, quality control, and other aspects of formal project management play a critical role in the success or failure of a chief architect's contributions. Operational elements within small and medium-sized enterprises may not always need a formal scoping document, formal change control committees, and a detailed risk analysis for each tiny change that may be enacted. However, knowledge of these techniques is vital to knowing when they have become necessary—particularly as the enterprise scale increases.

In addition to operational technology management, the chief architect must be comfortable in some type of formal project and program management methodology. It is important that any other lead architectural roles also involve these principles, but they are imperative for the central architectural role. Note, however, that there are many different formal project management styles. General project management techniques often bring benefits beyond focused-methodology management techniques, such as those that focus closely on quality control or documentation mechanisms specific to particular technologies. More general techniques often address business drivers that may factor into long-range planning without being obvious in short- and mid-term architectural assessments.

Beyond Basics

The chief architect must always be looking toward the future, identifying trends and emerging strategies that will play a part in the next cycle of enterprise evolution and the ones beyond. The architect must have an understanding of the impact of decisions made in creating and implementing the central vision, to avoid closing doors not yet even glimpsed ahead. This can at times be a journey fraught with peril, as many unanticipated consequences can arise from small differences in technology.

Language Standard

The adoption of a programming standard, such as the Java J2EE language, works very well in the resource-plentiful PC environment but may not always scale well into mainframe OS architectures, where thousands of processes may be sharing a vast but not unlimited resource pool. Even though the language can perform within both environments, the manner in which applications must operate can vary widely in such circumstances. Similarly, the selection of an object-oriented programming language (Java, .NET) can create disruption if developers have previously used a traditional language (ANSI C, COBOL), because of the fundamental differences in how these types of programming languages transfer information.

Operational Environment

Environments that must support real-time operations rely on different solutions than those required for high-volume transactional processing, distributed computing, or detailed business intelligence analytical processing. The data structures necessary to support each type of operation differ in terms of resource consumption, scalability, data throughput, metadata organization, 24/7 availability, security, recoverability, and many other factors. Beyond the data structures, user interface design, reporting, and other tools will vary widely among tasks, and decisions can have a strong impact on many of these tasks. Selection of an operating system platform, user office suite, application suite, data management solution, programming language, development suite, and all of the other elements of the technology implementation plan can amplify or negate business drivers present in each scenario.

Virtualization

The potential for technology virtualization seems almost limitless as enterprises take advantage of huge resource and storage pools, enhanced network bandwidth, and improved management utilities. Users can now remotely access their desktop workstations from anywhere in the world, while server farms and their attendant power requirements are collapsing by half or better as hardware server sprawl is being channeled into a smaller number of powerful servers supporting software system emulations.

Virtual storage solutions can make use of every scrap of space throughout an entire enterprise, while others may ensure that necessary data is available on the best connected server by replicating a virtual volume throughout the enterprise. Combinations of high-performance computing strategies and service virtualization have led to the virtualization of entire network infrastructural elements into "the Cloud." These solutions promise incredible advantages in utilization, efficiency, and cost management—and the decisions made today will affect their availability down the road.

Mobile Technologies

As network bandwidth and portable computing power increase, the office is leaving a physical building and becoming more a matter of availability anywhere, anytime. Weather, sports, navigation and other personal interest data is readily at hand, while network management and server console access no longer requires anything more than a WiFi hotspot at the local coffee house or a cellular data link from the back nine at the local country club. The ability to remotely access and manipulate information that remains safe on its host system can help to alleviate business issues for corporations working across national boundaries that may restrict where information may be exported. The ability to virtually access supercomputing power from a mobile handheld device is one of the most powerful causes for change in the modern enterprise.

Service-Oriented Architecture (SOA)

As remote access and network connectivity improve, many enterprises are adopting the service-oriented approach to application development. By making use of Web service standards such as SOAP and UDDI to pass information between applications, programmers can work simultaneously on different parts of a larger application without having to worry about using the same language or parameter-passing mechanisms. All that is required is that a set of standards is used for the information exchange itself—often a variant of the XML specification. This has the short-term benefits of both rapid development and platform independence that allows a heterogeneous enterprise to take advantage of solutions developed using this methodology. However, the varied nature of development and the distributed processing potential of SOA solutions can complicate technology modernization and disaster recovery planning.

Whatever's Next

Emerging developments in optical and quantum computing offer glimpses into new mechanisms for cryptography and data mining that are simply not possible using today's technologies. The synthesis of asynchronous e-mail and threaded discussion boards with synchronous chat and instant messaging systems is extending into data-based communications for voice-over-IP (VoIP) and teleconferencing, where a shared whiteboard can be used to share doodles across a dozen participants in a dozen different countries. These issues and more must be considered today by the chief architect, so that strategies will already be planned if they later reach commercial viability. Built atop yesterday's decisions, the enterprise architect must make choices for today that will offer options for tomorrow.

Summary

In order to succeed, an enterprise needs a coordinated architectural vision. Ultimately, this requires that someone be responsible for creating the vision, presenting the implementation, and resolving the inevitable conflicts that follow change. The architect must be knowledgeable in a wide range of technologies, information technology governance, existing architectural models, project management methods, and a wide range of both "hard" and "soft" skills needed to gain support and engagement in the process of turning the vision into a functional enterprise.

The architect must always be learning, looking to the future, and communicating with all involved parties. Enterprise architecture is not a goal; it is a process for implementing long-term business requirements within an environment of constant change.

Resources

The IT Infrastructure Library (ITIL)
   http://www.itil.co.uk

Control Objectives for IT (CobIT)
   http://www.isaca.org

Gartner Research
   http://www.gartner.com

North American State CIOs
   http://www.nascio.org

The Open Group Architecture Framework (TOGAF)
   http://www.opengroup.org

The Zachman Insitute
   http://www.zifa.com

Federal Enterprise Architecture
   http://www.whitehouse.com/omb/egov/a-1-fea.html

Chapter 3

Enterprise Architecture Challenges

In This Chapter

- An examination of challenges faced in applying architectural designs to an enterprise network environment
- Considerations for risk management in enterprise architecture planning
- Examination of the need to establish value and achieve business alignment in enterprise architecture strategies

During the months prior to the turn of the millennium, millions of dollars and tens of thousands of hours of time were spent addressing the "Y2K" issue. Until that time, programmers had designed databases and applications to handle date-years as two-digit numbers, assuming the preceding "19" to reflect the century. This was a simple oversight in planning, but one that had a tremendous potential to disrupt electronic data management. After a great deal of effort and expense, the problem was resolved in time to greet the year 2000 without significant impact, making this the largest and most widespread IT problem ever to be corrected in time to avoid catastrophic results.

As the world has become more integrated through Internet connectivity, issues of high-level planning and strategy have an increased impact on business viability. Strategic drivers for information technology expense are not as clearly obvious now as in the days before the Y2K bug, but a few guiding principles can make an equally valuable contribution to an organization's long-term operational capacity.

This chapter focuses on high-level guidelines, providing a framework for detailed strategic planning that will be examined in later chapters of this book. Before we delve into guidelines addressing enterprise information management, data center practices, and protective planning concerns, however, complexity issues warrant special attention,. These guidelines are applicable to any organization that uses more than a handful of stand-alone computers, storing no data of interest or worth.

Complexity

In the fourteenth century, a Franciscan friar called William of Ockham expressed a maxim that is widely applied today to economic, medical, and scientific endeavors. This maxim is generally known as "Ockham's razor." Commonly used as a practice for simplifying assumptions being made when observable evidence has been taken into account, the original form of Ockham's maxim is very applicable to the information technology enterprise:

"Entities should not be multiplied beyond necessity."

The renowned physicist, Albert Einstein, noted much the same in his famous statement:

"Everything should be made as simple as possible, but not simpler."

Essentially, both statements suggest that we should always simplify whenever possible, but not oversimplify. These thoughts should be kept firmly in mind whenever an enterprise architect considers any question of implementation or strategic planning.

Sources of Complexity

A common rule-of-thumb employed by CIOs, IT directors, and other technology architects in making strategic technology decisions is that the support requirements and costs associated with technologies increase by the square of the number of similar solutions used. Thus, having two workstation operating systems will require approximately four times as many resources as having only a single platform; while having three standard user application suites might require as much as nine times the effort to coordinate, integrate, and update all three in comparison to an enterprise employing a single standard suite. Table 3.1 details a few of the potential sources of enterprise complexity that may be encountered.

The business value of information technology can be affected by the complexity of its implementation. Enterprise architects must consider complexity issues not only in technology selection, but also in terms of the number of resource silos and the level of undesirable redundancy present in any enterprise that has not recently been reengineered from whole cloth. The issues surrounding desirable and undesirable redundancy will be discussed later in this book. Here, it is enough to recognize the need for simplification and standardization in order to provide a level foundation atop which other strategies can be constructed.

Opposition to Standardization

Whenever standardization is considered in an organization, opposition is almost guaranteed. Beyond simple issues of budgetary constraint, commonly raised issues include:

- **User familiarity**—Opponents to standardization often note existing user familiarity with the disparate technologies under consideration for replacement, and the potential disruption that may occur during transition. This is a short-term problem that may be addressed by user training and awareness as a part of the update project's requirements. The architect should, if possible, identify the platform in use by the majority of existing users, as selection of that as the new standard will reduce public outcry because proponents already exist among the current user base.

Table 3.1 Common Sources of Complexity

Source	Impact
Identity management	Directory services and identity management determine almost all other aspects of an enterprise network. Commercial solutions include technologies such as SunONE, Novell's eDirectory, and Microsoft's dominant Active Directory, while open-source shops commonly employ Lightweight Directory Access Protocol (LDAP) solutions such as the common OpenLDAP service. Federated identity management solutions aid in transferring credentials across authentication boundaries, allowing disparate technologies to integrate more transparently, but they risk compromising multiple authentication systems if the IM server is compromised. Federated systems also create risk because administrative access can temporarily associate account credentials, providing an easy mechanism for unauthorized access to protected resources.
Application stack	The application stack includes technologies such as the operating system, user suite, Web server, and many other technologies that together make up the operational environment for servers and workstations within the enterprise. Deeply integrated enterprises may make use of a single vendor's stack, such as IBM's popular WebSphere environment or the familiar Microsoft server/service/client suite of products, while the open-source LAMP stack is comprised of applications from dozens if not hundreds of sources. The basic L-A-M-P stack itself is not wedded to a particular source, as Linux has hundreds of possible sources and variations, while the Apache Web server and MySQL database platform are developed by separate vendors. Even the "P" in LAMP can reflect several options for application development—Pearl, PHP, Python, and Primate are all used interchangeably here. Without standardization, users can encounter difficulty when moving from one area of an organization to another, while update projects and upgrades become complex to plan and implement across a varied spectrum of products.
Application development (*continued*)	At the most fundamental level of development, the selection of programmatic style and language affects development and customization of applications used in anything other than default configurations.

Table 3.1 (*Continued*)

Source	Impact
Application development (*continued*)	Selection of object-oriented programming languages, such as Java and Microsoft's .Net languages, will affect the manner in which applications access and manipulate data, compared to traditional languages such as ANSI C, FORTRAN, and COBOL. Implementation of a service-oriented architecture (SOA) development practice can add to the complexity of an enterprise as well, gaining rapid application development and deployment capability at the cost of internal consistency across all application elements. Retention of legacy applications within SOA wrappers can further increase complexity by avoiding the process of legacy software retirement. Application design and testing for multiple platforms can add tremendously to the cost of development.
Interconnectivity	Modern enterprise networks may require connectivity for external operators, partner organizations, Internet users, mobile access devices, and a wide range of implementations that fall outside the technical envelope that can be mandated within the enterprise itself. Requirements for encryption, credentials management, and even the protocols implemented for access must all take into account the potentially widely varying solutions presented here. Selection of an industry-standard platform can help mitigate this risk somewhat.
Protection	Legislative mandates may include specific requirements that must be addressed in enterprise planning, such as the Health Insurance Portability and Accountability Act (HIPAA) requirements for segregation of Protected Health Information (PHI). Complexity may also be added where access and storage mechanisms must include encryption or where access controls mandate specific protocols. Many governmental and research organizations may need to impose classification systems for Mandatory Access Controls (MAC), as opposed to the more common Discretionary and Role-Based Access Control (DAC, RBAC) mechanisms used in other enterprises. Careful planning is required to ensure that resource access is granted appropriately, denied to unauthorized access attempts, and reviewed regularly.

- **Functionality**—Potentially the most valid complaint that may be raised is the question of functionality present in the current solution that may be missing in a newly named standard. Mature technologies such as word processors and spreadsheet applications are beginning to converge on common features and expected functionalities, while specific advanced media manipulation software may still be required in special cases. The enterprise architect should not expect to achieve a 100% standard suite that will fulfill all users' needs. In achieving a standard platform and user suite, it may be necessary to implement limited variations based on cost or need factors. Managing the exceptions and controlling variation are challenges that must be continuously addressed. Enterprise architects who strive too hard toward total compliance may find strong opposition together with documented need opposing new standards, while those who are too flexible may find that exceptions become the de facto standard regardless of the planned end state.

- **Compatibility**—When selecting a standard platform or application suite, it is important to consider compatibility with existing file stores and application protocols. Legacy technologies may require additional interface solutions to allow operation within a standardized environment, while years or even decades of past documents and files should not be rendered unavailable due to the change. It is important to consider format-translation and accessibility requirements when selecting a new standard. Use of more common file format standards can aid in future technology transitions and architectural changes.

- **Monocultures and biodiversity**—Opponents of integrated commercial off-the-shelf solutions often note the potential for a technology monoculture, where vulnerabilities in one vendor's products may comprise the entire stack. This is commonly reflected against the need for biodiversity in crops and herds to ensure that a single contagion is not able to affect the entire stock. This analogy fails under close scrutiny, however, because enterprise networks are not automatically protected by diversity as in biological farming. Viral programs capable of spreading through multiple vectors (blended threats) can pass across many different technology variations, while recent viruses have been written to allow cross-platform transmission as well. Unlike biological contagions, new viral programs can be created at will using simple GUI-based tools to target as many different platforms and vulnerabilities as the author desires. The advantage of desirable diversity within layers of security will be addressed later in this book, but diversity alone will not automatically improve platform and application security—it simply complicates patch management efforts and slows large-scale disaster recovery efforts.

Enterprise Information Management

It is important to understand the purpose of enterprise information management and enterprise information architecture so that its value becomes apparent during budgetary planning. Without executive buy-in and support, enterprise architects will find themselves in the unenviable position of being asked to work miracles while being held accountable for even the most minor glitches, all without a budget to meet an ever-growing swell of requirements that information technologies present. In Chapter 4 we will address the value gained from architectural planning in greater detail. Here, it is enough to know that even the best plan will fail if it cannot be conveyed to stakeholders and sponsors. The architect must be not only the designer of a cohesive vision but also the herald of its virtues, to avoid being simply swept under the rug.

Sell the Value of Information

Without a comprehensive effort to plan and organize available data, an organization risks far more than simply losing data on a client, patient, or other person of interest. Poorly constructed information architectures can create barriers that oppose efforts to identify data already present, while siloed architectures that segregate resources in an undesirable manner can prevent data mining, data sharing, and other value-added capabilities of well-considered plans. Information has value as a strategic resource, because operations can come to an abrupt halt without this information. The loss of e-mail for a few hours can shut down a business for the day, while the loss of Web services can cost many thousands of dollars every minute for organizations that depend on Web access for product sales.

Companies such as Amazon, eBay, and Google are all good examples of organizations that depend on network availability simply to conduct business, while many other companies have corporate websites offering goods, services, and customer contact capabilities. Without adequate planning, valuable data and key services can be impaired if inadequately protected. An enterprise architect must identify which elements of the information architecture act as currency within the organization's operational envelope, in order to plan and negotiate for sufficient resources to identify, acquire, manage, and use information and needed information technologies. The value of IT programs must be made clearly evident to stakeholders and users alike, particularly when an architectural change creates disruption or change to the users' day-to-day experience. The architect should look for the "low-hanging fruit" that easily generate return on the initial investment, while looking down the road for longer-term benefits that might require greater planning, effort, and expense to achieve.

Avoid Drawing Fire

A popular cartoon by Bill Mauldin printed during World War II showed an illustration of an officer, standing proudly and boldly in the face of oncoming fire from the enemy while two GIs huddled in the foxhole at his feet. One of the GIs says to the officer, "Would you mind not drawing their fire while inspiring us, Sir?" This humorous aside should be kept in mind whenever a decision is made to include controversial or newly emergent technologies into enterprise planning. A network enterprise is not the place to test beta versions of new software, nor to implement wholesale change to meet the latest fad in computing practices, software, or information delivery.

An excellent example of drawing fire while trying to do the right thing comes from the attempt to establish the OpenDocument Format (ODF) as a mandatory requirement within the Commonwealth of Massachusetts' information technology strategies. In addition to user groups voicing opposition to the change from the more familiar Microsoft Office user suite, the state found itself addressing a wide range of concerns. The strongest objections came from organizations representing persons with disabling conditions who might be barred from working with the state or accessing its offered services because of the relative scarcity of accessibility-related development applied within the open software environment, specifically the OpenOffice suite of products that was being considered for ODF document creation and management. What had seemed a simple, easy decision intended to inspire the integration of open-source solutions into governmental networks instead brought the state firmly into the crosshairs of some very concerned groups.

Outsource Carefully

Outsourcing is an obvious movement within the IT arena that regularly draws fire, particularly after the economic downturn that left millions out of work. The outsourcing of jobs is a hotbed of concern during difficult economic times, while the outsourcing of data processing can present very difficult challenges as more and more legislation is enacted to impose liability and rules governing information exposure and data protection. The European Union has already enacted specific legislation that addresses the types of information that may be transmitted outside its borders and has defined a specific listing of partner countries that may share this data. Some countries, such as China and France, have enacted legislation that restricts what information may be provided to network users accessing data from within the respective countries. Partner agreements and outsourcing efforts can become enmeshed in the politics of an organization's host country, as well as all other countries where the data is stored or processed—or even countries through which the information is transmitted.

Outsourcing should be undertaken only when necessary, with careful consideration of the laws and rules governing information and its release in all applicable countries. It is far easier to control data and address legal issues by selecting outsourcing agencies with operations within the same geopolitical region as the host organization, compared to requirements for filing suit or recovering exposed data under a separate set of laws and rules governing information protection, privacy, and other similar hot topics. Developing legislative actions may even prevent some types of outsourcing arrangements, as in the case of the U.S. State Department's decision to eliminate ThinkPad laptops from their approved purchasing list after IBM sold the popular platform to the Chinese Lenovo Corporation. It is far easier to streamline operations locally than to outsource (particularly when considering offshore outsourcing services) and later be forced to return operations in-house, and enterprise architects should use this tool only when it is truly appropriate or necessary to avoid adding undesirable complexity to the host organization's operational environment.

Protect the Data

Being suddenly naked in public is a common nightmare, but one that is not nearly as disturbing as having the sensitive or protected data of millions of clients revealed inadvertently. A number of laws pertaining to the liability of information exposure came under consideration following the spectacular data exposure of information about more than 26 million veterans and active-duty military personnel when a laptop containing this information was stolen from the home of a Veteran's Administration employee. This is not an isolated event, by any means—sensitive data from millions of clients has been exposed through loss of backup media, security compromise, and inadvertent disclosure. Credit card agencies, universities, medical facilities, and information clearing houses are common targets for identity thieves seeking useful information on large numbers of people at once.

It is not enough to plan how to handle the public reaction following data loss, because many articles of legislation include very strong penalties that follow automatically. The Health Insurance Portability and Accountability Act (HIPAA) is an excellent example of the type of legislation that may affect an organization as a result of data exposure. This act includes specific penalties, including very stiff per-item fines, whenever Protected Health Information (PHI) has been disclosed. Beyond direct legal and cost factors that may affect an organization, loss of customer trust can be even more devastating to an organization. Few acts will draw public outcry as rapidly as an accidental disclosure of data that could be used for identity theft, credit fraud, or other person-affecting actions. Because of a simple household burglary, now 26 million veterans and service personnel must forever monitor their credit and watch carefully lest someone misuse the stolen information.

Include Security at All Levels

An enterprise architect must include security when planning every level of the enterprise architecture. Because most computers can be booted directly from a Live CD or USB flash drive (Knoppix is a good example of a media-bootable operating system), physical access to any computer presents an attacker with almost immediate results. Security cannot be "bolted on" later; it must form the basis for enterprise defense, data encryption during storage and transport, and be deeply integrated into application development standards.

Attackers Have Tools Too

An organization's most sensitive data is readily accessible without an encrypted file system strong enough to resist tools that are available on the Internet. Many tools originally intended for law enforcement and security purposes can also be used by attackers to access sensitive information. Figure 3.1 shows an example of the type of data recovery that can be conducted using the Forensic Toolkit package.

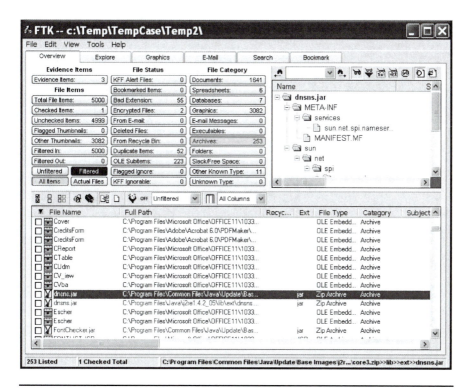

Figure 3.1   The Forensic Toolkit being used on an unencrypted drive.

Figure 3.2 shows the use of this same tool to rapidly example files of interest to an attacker after only a brief window of access to an unprotected system.

Commercial forensic suites include products such as the Forensic Toolkit, as well as offerings from Encase, Paraben, and many other vendors. FOSS-developed tools also exist, such as those preinstalled on the popular Helix bootable forensic CD based on the Knoppix Linux distribution. Using tools already installed on this insert-and-run package, an attacker can examine running processes, extract stored passwords and form data, search for specific types of files, or even replicate an entire hard drive for later deep analysis. These functions are invaluable to the professional forensic investigator, but they are equally available to potential attackers seeking to bypass access control mechanisms to gain unauthorized access to protected resources.

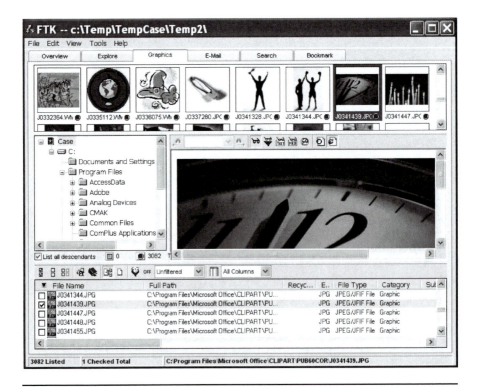

Figure 3.2 The Forensic Toolkit being used to examine image files.

Encrypt in Storage and Transmission

An enterprise architect must keep abreast of current and emerging security threats and mechanisms for system exploitation and malware operation, while also remaining cognizant of physical security and user training requirements. All enterprise planning should first identify all resources and the requirements for protecting each resource before beginning implementation plans. Encryption and data protection should be included whenever data is stored, transmitted, or processed—particularly in service-oriented architecture (SOA) implementations, where legacy integrated systems may not include the capability for more modern types of data transmission security or endpoint validation.

Security Must Be Layered

Security is not encryption, authentication, firewalls, filtering policies, run-time authorization, antivirus/antispam applications, or intrusion-detection systems—it is all of these and more. Security should be included at the most basic level and then layered in order to strengthen a network's defenses. Figure 3.3 illustrates a simplified model of network defense including host-based and network-based defensive applications, along with firewall barriers shielding an externally exposed data management zone (or, sometimes, demilitarized zone, DMZ) as well as an internally protected shielded subnet.

An illustration of enterprise defensive concepts has much in common with early physical defenses employed to protect against invading armies. It is often said that a castle is only as secure as its least protected gate, and this same thinking must be applied when the enterprise architect is evaluating architectural plans. Most large networks are placed behind a boundary defense, as is often the case when individual business elements are allowed to maintain and update their own systems within the overall organizational network. A single unpatched or insufficiently defended system can be compromised and used to bypass boundary defenses for attacks against other systems within the protected network.

Note: One desirable complexity may be to implement devices from different vendors for defensive layering. By including products based on different technologies at the external and internal boundaries of the

DMZ, for example, the same hacking toolkit cannot be used to bypass both barriers. Complexity can add to security when layering protections, although this only increases security—a skilled attacker can eventually bypass multiple defensive layers, whether they are constructed from a single vendor's offerings or developed using a wide assortment of products.

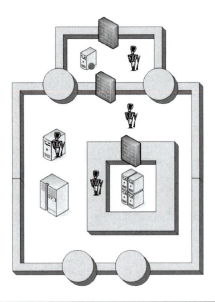

Figure 3.3 A simplified network defensive strategy employing defensive applications on guard against intrusion, malware, or misuse, and firewall barriers creating a DMZ and shielded subnet.

Conceal the Inner Workings

Like a castle, a protected network relies on standardized rules for passing through its gates. Defensive applications act as guards and turn away undesirable traffic, while ensuring that legitimate requests are passed only to the appropriate destination. Some systems may require defenses against internal threats, requiring additional layering to create shielded subnets and protected safe harbors for legacy systems or sensitive data. By exposing only encrypted Web service interfaces, external applications can interact with protected data stores and application services within these defended areas using a black-box approach. This type of defensive strategy secures even the manner in which information is arranged from easy outside observation.

Proactively Implement Standards

Many standards exist for securing information and networks, including architectural models such as CObIT and ITIL (see Chapter 2). In addition to these guidelines, many industries are evolving mandated security practices that can be used to plan proactively for future state defensive requirements. As one example, the Payment Card Industry (PCI) Data Security Standards provide a basic framework for protecting data related to credit card transactions (see Table 3.2).

Table 3.2 PCI Data Security Standards

Standard	Implementation
Build and maintain a secure network	Install and maintain a firewall. Do not use default settings for passwords and other security parameters.
Protect cardholder data	Protect stored data, including backup media. Encrypt data during transmission across public networks.
Maintain a vulnerability management program	Employ regularly updated antivirus software. Develop and maintain secure systems and applications.
Implement strong access-control measures	Restrict data access to least necessary. Assign a unique ID to each user. Restrict physical access to cardholder data.
Monitor and test networks	Monitor and log all network access to cardholder data. Regularly test security systems and practices.
Maintain an information security policy	Maintain clear security policies. Ensure adequate training and awareness.

Source: MasterCard International.

Even if an organization does not currently employ credit card handling practices, the same standards can be applied in a proactive manner when planning for future-state architectural defense. If the organization later falls under the PCI requirements, the protections will already be in place; if not, these standards remain good practices for data defense. If a public data exposure occurs, it is far better to be able to prove due diligence in attempting to defending sensitive or protected information than to be found negligent in this area. Doing nothing to prevent an exposure is certainly going to draw fire.

Look Beyond the Project

As we discussed previously, strong project management skills are vital for the CIO and any other lead architectural roles. This dictum can be misleading, however, if it is applied too thoroughly without an eye toward the big picture. Projects are discrete, with a clear beginning, identified term, and identifiable closure. Enterprise architecture may include many projects in the architectural management program, but while projects have a defined end, operational practices are ongoing and often cyclical in nature. Security, for example, is never a goal that will someday be attained once-and-for-all-time. Security is a relative state, subject to continued changes as new attack techniques are developed or personnel are moved between assignments. Tens of thousands of new viruses are released each year, along with hundreds of other potential sources of malware and network exploitation. Adding in social engineering and ever-increasing computing power, the potential threats to an organization's network become almost infinite.

Enterprise architects must plan for reactive immediate-term solutions, address current trends and evolving requirements, while moving always toward the supportable future-state enterprise that is yet to exist. Selling IT projects as quick-return "low-hanging fruit" projects can create impossible expectations or unrealizable goals. The enterprise architect must also maintain awareness of the ongoing value provided to an enterprise through incremental changes and cyclic technology modernization efforts. Formal project management skills should be employed, but with an understanding that the big picture is always evolving, always moving to reveal more of the road ahead. Strategy and vision must be the ultimate drivers for all of the more finely focused implementation projects.

Align Technology and Business

The most fundamental but sometimes difficult concept to convey is the idea that technology must follow the business, and not the other way around. Many failed IT projects try to shift an organization's operations to fit a newly purchased or newly developed application. Certainly there are many very fine application suites for human resource management, accounting, inventory management, and the many other tasks necessary for a modern organization to operate. Solutions such as SAP, PeopleSoft, and Great Plains include a wide range of modules to suit the needs of different business environments, but it is not enough to select a product and then expect an organization to shift its operational processes to suit. Information technology is a logistical element that supports other operational functions within an organization, and it should not be considered as more. At the same time, it must not be discounted as an afterthought or add-on to be maintained by convenience. The addition of new technologies may make new service offerings possible, if the enterprise architect can convey details of the new offering to executive staff members throughout the organization in terms that can be understood by technical lay persons.

Apply Clear Governance Principles

An enterprise architect must be sensitive to business drivers during the full technology life-cycle process, from specification through tombstoning. Planning and procurement affect successful projects just as thoroughly as skills planning and user training. This is where a formal IT governance framework can function to improve coordination with other business elements by aligning enterprise operations with the overall organizational governance model. Governance and planning should be kept separate from functional management, as the skills and focus needed for these roles vary widely. Clear ownership and responsibility must be tied to the management of each project, while an overall vision provides guidance and coordination with the rest of the organization.

As a related matter, personnel promotion should not provide the only mechanism for incentivization, ensuring that skilled and effective technologists are not moved into management roles purely to provide recognition of their success. According to the "Peter principle," it is easy to promote individuals out of positions as a result of their excellent performance, only to find that they are unsuited to their new roles. Individuals may thus be promoted only until they reach one place beyond their peak skill level, leading to dissatisfaction and reduced operational efficiency enterprise-wide.

Plan Ahead and Stick to the Plan

A common maxim states that "Form follows function." While this is certainly true for sharks and submarines, it is amazing how complicated and internally inconsistent an IT enterprise can become over time. The key to a successful initiative is to have a plan and to build toward the goal, with regular checks to ensure that the goal remains valid and that efforts are achieving desired movement toward the goal's end state. Starting with modest testing will help to ensure that the new technology meets an actual need before building unwarranted expectations or creating concerns about change. With a clear plan and identified requirements, it is far easier to reach the necessary solution than when the end goal is indistinct or incompletely conveyed to the implementation staff. Above all, start at the top and build interest and support downward, to ensure that funding and reasonable expectations are in place before user requirements and preferences turn "feature creep" into a nightmare of complexity and unending revision.

Collaborative Technologies Are Vital

Collaborative technologies form the communications core, whether planning for a simple technology modernization project or a rip-and-replace total enterprise overhaul. Such technologies include e-mail, task assignment, ticket management, calendaring, virtual meeting spaces, threaded discussion boards, wikis, shared document storage, voice and video teleconferencing, voice mail, instant messaging, and a host of emerging methods for communicating and organizing groups of participants. Before a project is undertaken, it is absolutely imperative to ensure that all appropriate collaboration technologies and a formal communications plan are in place to promote communication among users, implementers, and governance roles.

Remain Agile and Flexible

Modifying architecture in production is much like trying to change tires on a moving car or performing brain surgery on oneself. Elements of the operating network environment, from data stores to authentication and Web services, may already be operating at or above optimal capacity or may be tied to divergent technologies that do not integrate well. The lead architect must be wary of pitfalls such as planning the reallocation of a database server that also happens to have an active Web-facing reporting utility, or a Web server that hosts small yet vital resources not identified in the initial review. Flexibility is necessary when making plans, to ensure that service disruption is minimized. This must be tempered by formal project management procedures and a firm change management process in order to avoid employing too much flexibility.

Maintaining flexibility becomes more complex during long-term planning operations, as the driving factors change from year to year as technology and regulatory mandates evolve. While wireless connectivity and mobile communication might remain a hot topic from one year to the next, issues of security or application development might swap places in terms of organizational priority as a result of a newly emergent threat or programming style. Because data and voice-over-IP (VoIP) telephony compete for the same bandwidth, network infrastructure upgrades might move ahead of technology modernization projects to ensure that adequate bandwidth is available before the new and shiny gear is connected.

Avoid Too Much Good

Enterprise architects perform a constant juggling act to balance expenditures, resources, and requirements. Surprisingly, too much of a good thing can be as bad as lack of interest. A new SOA-based Web service coupled to an existing tried-and-true application can rapidly overrun available capacity and connectivity, if the demand exceeds the throughput of any element in the chain. New portal deployments often suffer from overly enthusiastic user interest, because users find sudden need for expanded access to their whole team or operation as soon as the potential is demonstrated. Jumping too far, too fast can lead to problems in storage overrun, load balancing, and service availability. New technology projects should always be monitored carefully to identify overly successful solutions and apply controls or add resources to suit. The use of cloud computing hosting can help reduce the impact of suddenly vital new offerings by allowing an expansion of network and system resources at need by simply purchasing additional capacity. We will examine cloud computing and other virtualization practices later in this book.

Too much of a good thing can also be a problem when implementing security measures. It is easy to make layered defenses so unwieldy that users find ways to bypass controls just to perform common tasks. If the password policy calls for highly complex 14-digit passwords that change every 40 days, users may start writing down the latest version in a convenient place. Business intelligence applications often generate the same type of threat, as it is very easy to get lost in reports and dashboards showing how well operations are performing when measured against how they were doing this morning or ten years ago—regardless of whether this information is useful to the organization.

The same can be true of security practitioners, where the ability to log and monitor every action within the entire network can become a goal unto itself. Too much logging and data mining can sometimes get in the way of simpler updates and less flashy tasks that are fundamental to network health. Focus in the wrong area or misplaced trust in defensive technologies alone leads to vulnerable systems and a false sense of security. It is easy to miss an ongoing brute-force attack against a server hosting the company's SSL-encrypted website if the fancy monitoring tools are happily logging that hits are up and encryption is in place.

Plan on Partners

Organizations are increasingly integrating external connectivity for business-to-business (B2B) partner relationships, business-to-consumer (B2C) automated shipping management, and mobile workspace management. Industries may use specialized processing services or clearing houses for data management and mandatory reporting, such as in the case of caregiver integration with health insurance provider systems for billing and client account management. Services are increasingly moving to an online format, particularly with the explosion of SOA-based Web services exposing applications that could previously function only within an isolated internal network.

The savvy planner must constantly watch for opportunities and pitfalls presented by partnering solutions, and avoid being taken unawares by emerging regulatory mandates or upcoming potential mergers requiring connectivity with partner organizations. It is here that standards must be applied throughout the data center and the organization's networked resources at every stage, so that it is not a sudden scramble to implement connectivity on a truncated timetable because of a new partnership.

By planning proactively for partnerships, the lead architect can act to improve business agility as well as the potential for success in future-state strategic planning efforts. Although the creation of a standard Data Center Markup Language (DCML) remains in a nascent state, following accepted standards such as the PCI Data Security Standards can help prepare to meet the virtual neighbors.

Data Center Management

Internal users are most aware of changes to their desktop, but an organization is most affected by changes in the data center. Solutions implemented within the data center affect internal users, external users, partner interconnectivity, and even the way in which the organization communicates with itself. Many of the "low-hanging fruit" projects in an enterprise are focused within the data center, where divergent authentication systems and server sprawl increase complexity and cost.

Tip: Changes to the user's desktop operating system or user productivity suite are most likely to concern users, while changes within the data center are most likely to concern information technology implementers. The lead architect must work to control this reaction before, during, and after planned changes to the data center. Training is critical for both technologists as well as users in order to ensure that the proper skills are in place prior to need.

Consolidation

Consolidation into a centralized or limited number of shared data centers provides the most obvious step for dealing with disparate silos of information technology and expertise. By standardizing architecture and reducing administrative and procurement costs, architects can show a quick return on investment while freeing up resources for future projects. Consolidation will require not only a restructuring of technology resources, but also a realignment of planning, budgeting, and procurement compared to planning and acquisition at the individual departmental level. Cost savings are generally identifiable within the first year of operation following consolidation projects.

Opposition Will Arise

As we discussed earlier, opposition to standardization and centralization can be varied and impassioned. Fears abound at the loss of authority and direct access by local implementers, while issues of strategic budgeting and personnel costs must be moved up the organizational hierarchy. A key factor to successful consolidation and shared service projects is to ensure that funding is managed as a budgeted expense, rather than impressed upon individual departments as a per-system or per-person cost. It is too easy to build antagonism toward a consolidation project by identifying individual business units whose per-system or per-person costs appear to be lower in direct comparison with other units, obscuring the overall reduction in cost or expansion in capability for the organization as a whole. Opt-in cost-recovery programs tend to multiply this problem, because business units with adequate resources may work to avoid sharing, while the "have nots" find themselves pooled together without sufficient funding or resources to fulfill basic requirements. Critical services should be considered cost-of-business or commoditized operational costs and budgeted accordingly, rather than operated under outdated cost-recovery models that often create competition and conflict between organizational units within the same overall enterprise.

Benefits Will Be Near- and Long-Term

Consolidation within the data center can aid in organizational decision making through integration of cross-departmental information and increased information availability to key decision makers. Resource savings are also obvious targets for consolidation and shared service efforts, because economies of scale can be applied to common requirements such as file storage, patch control, database management, and collaboration technologies. Because these factors can be more easily tracked and maintained, overruns and shortfalls in capacity or cost can also be identified much more easily in a consolidated environment. Resource utilization is generally improved by consolidation, combining services onto more robust systems able to handle greater capacity with a similar administrative requirement.

Consolidation may not always produce direct cost savings, as the resources freed up by consolidating redundant systems and services may be used to add value and functionality elsewhere within the enterprise. Architectural leads must ensure that executives understand the value to be gained through reinvestment and reallocation following a consolidation effort. These cost savings and reallocated technologies can play a large part in moving the organization toward a more regular cycle of technology update and modernization or in adding new service options to facilitate emerging needs.

Modernization Becomes a Process

Cyclic technology refresh, update and system modernization is a key goal when planning long-term enterprise network strategies. Consolidated resources make long-term budgetary planning possible, with a clear life cycle and maintenance strategy for both software and hardware solutions within the enterprise framework. This minimizes the impact of technology evolution, because a portion of the network can be updated each year rather than all at once or on a random basis driven by product release or technology emergence.

Consolidation and shared services can also improve service delivery by increasing the transparency between services and through a more seamless method of access for users and consumers. The "one-stop shop" becomes more efficient when service resources are well connected and built around common technologies. This ensures that clients are not greeted with a public-facing resource site in which some elements are unavailable due to network lag or synchronization issues that may arise when integrating widely varying services into a single interface.

Boundaries Can Be Better Protected

Consolidation allows improved security by minimizing the transmission of data between services and reducing the surface area of exposure. When each information silo must possess copies of sensitive data for its own operations, the potential for accidental exposure is much greater than when data is secured within a central store that is transmitted only through tightly controlled access. Not only is it easier to maintain and update a smaller number of systems within a consolidated network, it is also easier to justify capital expenses for defensive technologies to harden the data center network and to provide adequate bandwidth for remote sites that will no longer have all resources sited locally.

Consolidation Extends Beyond Centralization

While backups, updates, and maintenance can be performed more rapidly within a centralized site, care must be taken to avoid isolating remote sites from access to necessary services. Authentication and user provisioning for remote sites require planning and may include additional technologies to offset slow or intermittent network access. Higher-bandwidth always-on solutions such as cable modem and DSL service are reducing the dependency on demand-dial modem networks and dedicated telephony-based lines, but mobile users and remote sites may still be isolated from full-time, dependable connectivity. The lead architect must have a clear understanding of the network before moving resources to a consolidated model.

Facilities Must Be Adequate

Beyond network connectivity, consolidation projects rely heavily on adequate facilities for the consolidated hardware. Data center and server targets for consolidated services are often more robust than their departmental counterparts, requiring greater capacity for power and thermal dissipation. Soaring energy costs can create cost overruns for consolidated architectures, because ambient air movement is typically not sufficient to cool most data centers even though individual departmental servers may be able to sit in a refitted closet without a need for dedicated air conditioning. Not only do servers consume a great deal of power, they generate heat like small toaster ovens—but they do so continuously, not just during breakfast.

It is not always possible to simply scale up power feeds and air conditioning within an existing structure, which can lead to a very unpleasant surprise halfway through an extended consolidation effort. Capacity planning includes long-term research to ensure that the hottest months of the year are considered when evaluating capacity requirements. Layout and organization within the data center can also affect cooling and power distribution, creating hot spots or requiring renovation to strengthen floors beneath large uninterruptible power supplies.

Larger data centers may separate power and processing facilities in order to implement more efficient DC-based power distribution. Water-based cooling systems, popular with technology geeks trying to overclock their systems for maximum performance (that is, alter the settings to exceed the manufacturer-recommended maximum speed), are now evolving into effective solutions for cooling large data centers, where water or oil can be used to circulate heat away from servers more efficiently and more quietly than forced-air cooling allows. Such extensive changes, however, require a wholesale shift in facilities planning as well as in server acquisition procedures.

As recent events have shown, facilities planning must also include factors such as potential terrorist activities and natural disasters. Data centers in the World Trade Center were completely lost as a result of the terrorist attack of September 11, 2001, while some located in the vicinity of New Orleans were literally buried in mud and sewage when levees failed following Hurricanes Katrina and Rita. Even backup sites along the Gulf Coast became unsupportable when evacuation efforts drained available fuel supplies needed to run backup power generators long-term. Organizations whose centralized consolidated resources are located in high-visibility or geographically risky locations constantly gamble on the continued performance and long-term viability of their data centers and the services they support.

Consolidation Includes the Help Desk

Another key issue to address when considering consolidation or shared services is to ensure that the help desk function is maintained. Users may not care which server holds their e-mail or how their file storage is being backed up, but they will most certainly care about how their problems can be communicated to the responsible IT professionals. Whenever human resources are consolidated, users may feel that they are losing access to their local IT support that was both responsive and directly available at need.

An effective help desk can aid tremendously in the acceptance of consolidated services by reducing the time between user contact and effective problem resolution. While this may not be as friendly as having an IT professional in the office next door, it can go a long way toward providing user satisfaction. Failure here can close the door to future projects, because users become wary of losing control or level of service. Another useful option is to retain existing support personnel in office space proximate to the consumer base, but to structure help desk functions to allow online support from any help desk operative. Users can retain the feeling of being well supported while gaining access to support skills across the enterprise by employing virtual teaming, instant messaging between support professionals, and centralized telephone and Web-based contact mechanisms for users to request help.

Tip: When building interest in consolidation projects, concerns about the loss of local control can often be addressed by examining existing interdependencies. Stakeholders may not be aware that they already depend on networking, authentication, name resolution, or other services provided centrally or externally. The perceived loss of control is often merely that—a perception that control exists currently, without considering the interwoven nature of an enterprise network.

Consolidation Is Not Limited to Technology

Operational capability often relies on information technology to such an extent that even a short time without access creates a tremendous cost or service disruption. Organizations are faced with the need to address a global marketplace, which may include requirements for maintaining data stores within specific geographic locales. Web-based services and applications are extending the full benefits of being "in the office" to a wide range of highly mobile users, which again may rely on services hosted at multiple locations. Rather than attempting to provide a full set of deep skills to all site locations, large enterprises can take advantage of remote management solutions to create a consolidated group of highly skilled professionals able to address issues arising in disparate locations. Local staff members remain necessary, as many powered-down systems still require someone to turn a key or press a button. However, businesses can reduce the number of wide-but-shallow skill sets found in remote sites and individual business units, where a single isolated support individual may be called on to perform many different tasks.

Tremendous advantages can result from standardizing technologies and implementing remote management solutions for console access, patch control, application deployment, and user support. A core group of highly skilled technical responders can address problems across a large enterprise as emerging issues are identified by help desk personnel, without requiring every site to have its own expert in security, networking, authentication, or any of the many other technologies that can be found in a modern organizational network. Although these "jacks of all trades" may enjoy jumping from one task to another, the deeper skills available with dedicated staff and trained expertise can reduce downtime and improve operational recovery windows following an incident.

Desirable Redundancy Can Be Acquired

Consolidation focuses on minimizing undesirable redundancy in service, system, or operational capability. There are times when redundancy can be desirable, and consolidation can facilitate this as well. An organization can improve its resistance to challenges by reinvesting cost savings from eliminated redundant servers, services, and personnel in desirable redundancy of key functions.

Redundancy can be desirable at many levels, including:

- **Personnel**—Load-balancing expertise within a consolidated support team reduces the impact of the loss of a key individual and allows members of the team to take vacations without risk to the organization's ability to operate in the event of an unforeseen crisis.
- **Service**—Rather than having a dozen dedicated departmental e-mail servers, an organization might instead have a centralized system able to fail-over automatically to clustered backup hardware in the event of a server crash.

- **Storage**—Where local resources may be maintained on limited hardware, centralized storage can make use of more efficient and fault-tolerant RAID (redundant array of independent disks) storage solutions capable of automatic de-duplication, single-instance storage, and a wide range of other storage management options that can allow existing storage to enjoy an extended lifetime before needing replacement or expansion.
- **Load**—High-demand user interfaces and SOA module connectivity can create high levels of demand on user-facing systems. By mirroring information and service available across multiple systems, user experience can be maintained even during periods of peak use.
- **Network**—Backup network connectivity and caching servers can reduce the load on centralized services when accessed from remote locations. Authentication services, name resolution, and even file and Web caching can all improve user access while reducing the load on the central network and data center systems.
- **Site**—A backup data center may be considered mission-critical for some organizations. When widespread disaster or extended power outages isolate an organization's data center, a backup site outside the affected area can take over operations and provide a means for communication and organization during recovery efforts.

Automation

Automated solutions for deployment, backup, update, and patch control should be implemented whenever possible. These solutions act as a force multiplier for the available IT support staff, alleviating repetitive and cumbersome chores and allowing attention to be directed to less easily addressed issues. Standardization is absolutely vital here, to reduce complexity in system configuration across the enterprise and make automated management possible. When consolidating services into a single environment, automation strategies can reduce human administrative requirements significantly and free up resources for additional projects.

Automating Updates

Thousands of new viruses are released each year, requiring almost hourly updates to defensive applications protecting key data stores, e-mail gateways, and user desktops. These updates are so time-critical that they cannot be left to manual efforts at update and management, and require an automated centralized solution to provide continuously updated protection against the constant onslaught of viruses, worms, and other malicious code (malware).

Only slightly less numerous are updates and patches to operating system and application files, which may be released on a set schedule or ad-hoc as providers add functionality or correct emergent security issues. Patch control can become tremendously unwieldy across a large distributed enterprise unless an automated patch management solution is employed. Microsoft's Windows Software Update Service is a common patch management solution used in Microsoft enterprise networks, while Linux users have similar solutions in the Up2date and Yum services that leverage native RPM package management through a comfortable user interface. Many other solutions afford patch control capabilities as well, such as Novell's popular Zenworks product, used in Netware and SUSE Linux enterprise environments.

Automating Protections

Automation can extend beyond simple updates to include backup and restoration, such as image-based deployment systems able to wipe and reload an entire computer in a matter of minutes. In these solutions a source computer is first configured and updated with all applications installed; then the source "image" is captured. This image can then be copied to target systems, which can then be deployed in a fully ready state, without requiring extensive human action to set up and configure common settings and applications. Standardization is critical here, to reduce the number of images and the complexity of the deployment solution.

Backup solutions exist to copy files and data stores to a safe location each night, each hour, or according to whatever criterion is desired. Some of these systems provide near real-time recovery from a bare-metal hardware failure and replacement, though the network and storage requirements for constant-backup solutions can consume significant resources within the data center. By automating backup and recovery solutions, valuable information can be protected from loss or corruption. Care is required in media management and encryption of stored data to avoid accidental data exposure due to lost or stolen backups.

Supporting Automation

Although automated systems can perform arduous repetitive tasks, human operational staff remains necessary even in the most heavily-automated enterprise. Logs must be reviewed regularly to ensure completion of updates and backups. Backup media should be regularly tested for recoverability, and retired on a regular schedule to protect against loss of critical data at an inopportune time. Human operators are needed in order to configure initial system images, and to ensure that patches and updates do not create problems within the test network before they are deployed to the production environment.

Enterprise architects may hear concerns from IT professionals afraid they may be automated out of a job, but the architect should emphasize that automation is a tool that can multiply the effectiveness of the IT professionals—not one that can remove the need for them outright. Even self-service password reset solutions, file-recovery utilities, and ad-hoc database reporting tools require configuration and management in order to provide automated results to end users.

Virtualization

Virtualization allows a single server computer to host multiple virtual servers, which function as if each were on a separate system. Each server can have its own dedicated processing power, memory allocation, and storage. Virtualization allows enterprises to bring together multiple services and standalone applications and run them all one a small number of physical servers. This can decrease energy costs and increase resource utilization, particularly when consolidating multiple systems that spend most of their CPU power idling. Xen, VMWare, and Microsoft are some of the vendors producing virtualization host software, many versions of which are free or provided with the server operating system at no additional charge. More robust versions of some virtualization software solutions can be used to automatically load-balance virtual systems and perform other management tasks, though these are typically commercially licensed.

Many in One

Because each virtual system functions as if installed on its own hardware, a single computer can host virtual servers of many different types (illustrated in Figure 3.4). Windows, Linux, and other operating systems can be installed as virtual machines with independent operational characteristics and resources. Even the priority of resource access can be assigned, restricting less critical services to allow key services access to the lion's share of available host resources when necessary.

Virtualization is an excellent way to test consolidation procedures and to begin the data center consolidation process, because each host can remain linked to the authentication services of an organizational unit without affecting other systems on the same host. Virtualization provides an easy mechanism for creating test networks and technology demonstrations, because multiple systems can be run side by side with provably equal resource allocations. Before diving into procurement procedures, demonstration versions of many software products can be installed on virtual servers running on existing hardware. Even a single laptop can be used to host an entire network, provided it has sufficient resources available for all operating hosts, while alternative hosts can be turned on or off at will where resource constraints apply.

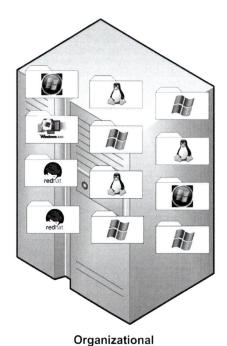

**Organizational
Virtualization Host**

Figure 3.4 A simplified example of virtualization with a single host supporting multiple heterogeneous virtual servers.

Virtual Operations

Because each virtual server is stored as a set of files on the host system, a backup made from a virtual server can be transported to a new host as rapidly as the media can be mounted. This can speed disaster recovery immensely, because it eliminates the need for matching hardware and lengthy configuration. Continuity of operations can also be enhanced through the use of virtualization, because a large number of virtualized hosts can be run on less expensive hardware at a backup site, with minor changes to allocated resources. Although these virtual hosts may operate at reduced efficiency, the ability to continue normal operations can be a tremendous benefit to the organization while replacement primary hardware is acquired.

Not all services can be virtualized well, particularly where the full system resources of a host computer are required for complex resource-intensive tasks. However, the ability to relocate virtual servers between hosts by simple file-transfer operations can add greatly to the effective load balancing of operational resources. Rather than trying to find more memory to fit into a physical server, a virtualized server can just as easily be moved to a different system that already has the necessary resources—taking with it all the configuration settings and even network identities of the original virtualized host. Many services developed in cloud computing environments can be automatically updated to provide additional storage, network, and processor power as needed, based on cloud hosting contractual resource allocation limits.

Plan for the Worst and Hope to Be Wrong

Consolidation, standardization, automation, and virtualization are all important considerations when planning data center operations. However, the lead architect must remain aware of internal and external threats that go far beyond whether the door is locked or the power feeds are adequate. Contingencies, fallback plans, disaster recovery, and continuity of operational planning must be included at every step, both during consolidation activities and during ongoing normal operations.

When sunspot activity knocked out the power grid across many of the northeastern states and parts of Canada in August 2003, disaster recovery sites hours away were still within the same area of effect. During the Gulf Coast evacuation before Hurricane Rita, even sites many hours away were found to be inadequate, because fuel supplies and housing needed for relocating staff could not be found. Tsunamis, hurricanes, volcanoes, earthquakes, sunspots, and many other uncontrollable events can have a tremendous impact on an organization and the technologies needed for its continued operation.

Other problems are man-made but equally threatening, such as viruses and other malicious code. Even defensive technologies can sometimes prove dangerous to operations, as when the popular McAfee antivirus suite incorrectly identified many business applications as a threat and quarantined or deleted application files needed for database management, business awareness, and many other functions. Recoverability must be a factor in network planning, and effective systems virtualization can speed recovery thresholds immensely.

Even concerns over the potential of threats, as in the case of severe acute respiratory syndrome (SARS) or a swine flu pandemic, could lead to isolation of operational staff or facilities. By conducting proper disaster recovery and continuity of operations planning within the data center, an organization can remain viable in times of crisis. If the business is forced to operate by running virtualized hosts on laptops from an out-of-the-way data center, at least it may still be able to maintain minimal support for key customers while its competitors are blacked out.

Summary

Technology is not the solution to business requirements, but it can provide the means for an organization to remain viable and even to gain an advantage if properly directed. Standardization and a reduction in complexity are vital if an enterprise is to gain access to true economies of scale, automation, and efficient control. Although some complexity and redundancy can be desirable in order to defend a network adequately, these are areas where rapid proof of value can be found by the lead architect charged with enterprise renovation. Effective information management and data center controls can provide tremendous return on enterprise restructuring projects. Problems like the Y2K bug do not fix themselves—they are fixed by carefully guided management strategies. The reins must be firmly in hand before the next crisis arises, as it is inevitable that something will eventually go wrong. Recovery from disaster or attack is not a matter of "if" but of "when."

Chapter 4

Finding Value

In This Chapter

- Applying the Pareto principle
- Identifying common expectations of enterprise architecture projects
- Planning for risk management
- Considerations for planned technology retirement

An old Jamaican saying goes: "New broom sweeps clean, but old broom knows the corners." An enterprise architect charged with re-conceptualizing an existing infrastructure might do well to remember this adage. It is very easy to imagine sweeping aside all that exists in favor of a nice, clean, uncomplicated solution that perfectly embodies the architect's vision. However, hidden value might be lurking within the existing state, and an overly zealous effort to get rid of everything old could easily discard this value as well. It is important to ensure that sunk costs do not become a deciding factor for future purchases and strategies, but whenever cost recovery is an option, care should be taken to conserve as much value as possible.

Technology modernization and network rationalization efforts frequently require rip-and-replace changes, but it is important to identify reusable components and technologies for salvage and transfer to the new architectural format. Existing skill sets and detailed knowledge of localized network and system issues should not be overlooked when planning for major change. Whenever possible, existing resources should be reallocated, updated and reused—whether these resources are human or technological.

In this chapter, we will examine examples of value that may be conserved or sought during architectural realignment projects. The rest of the book will then examine specific enterprise elements and network management options in greater depth.

Impact and Return on Effort

The Pareto principle, also known as the 80/20 rule, is a management principle that evolved from the observations of the Italian economist, Vilfredo Pareto. Presented by Dr. Joseph Juran and named for Pareto's original observations, the 80/20 rule states that in many settings, 80% of consequences are derived from 20% of causes. This means that roughly 80% of all trouble tickets will be opened by roughly 20% of the client base, or that approximately 80% of available security options can be implemented through 20% of the overall security effort. Applied to technology management, this is a useful tool for understanding the impact of application development, resource allocation, user productivity suite selection, and a variety of other broadly applied strategies.

Applying the 80/20 Rule

When developing a new application, the 80/20 rule suggests that 80% of the final product will be achieved during the first 20% of time spent in development and testing. When user interface preferences and feature creep are added into such a project, this can easily be the case—it is if not 90/10 or worse. Conversely, users may only consume 20% of the features of a productivity suite to complete 80% of their work, rendering further development effort beyond these core features effectively "gold plating" (functionality beyond the specified scope of the project).

The 80/20 rule can also be applied when selecting standard technologies for use across the enterprise, by first identifying the key functionalities and

existing user familiarities that comprise the bulk of the current environment and then working to incorporate the remaining 20%. This is not
to say that majority should rule, but it does reflect the value that exists
within an established solution. If a technology were wholly without value,
it would not likely be fulfilling a role in the existing architecture.

Expectations from Architectural Change

Before delving into specific metrics that can be used to assess the
impact of enterprise architectural realignment, it is useful first to
understand some of the common expectations that may be held by stakeholders. Table 4.1 details some of these expectations.

**Table 4.1 Common Stakeholder Expectations
of Architectural Realignment**

Operation	Expectations
Standardization and consolidation	Reduced complexity will require less training, management, and support. Reduced product count will streamline purchasing and acquisitions. Less effort will be required for installation and patch management. Integration will be simplified among elements of the enterprise.
Modernization and reorganization	Capacity will be increased for information storage, processing, and delivery. Improved or updated feature sets will be present. Simplified organization will improve agility with regard to new technology initiatives.
Integration and federated identity management	Data sharing and availability will be increased. Barriers between authentication pools will be reduced or eliminated (the "single sign-on" wish). Interface consistency will improve access and availability for partners and external consumers. Collaboration will be improved, either internally or externally.

Stakeholder expectations will strongly affect the subjective assessment of an enterprise architectural project's success. It is important to convey successful gains to stakeholders throughout the realignment process. Subjective perception of success can be strongly affected by small gains such as reduced product count easing evaluation and contract negotiations, or a reduced deployment envelope achieved through reduced variety in the types of deployed technologies.

An Objective View

Objective metrics are also needed in order to assess the impact of architectural change in a manner that is not subject to subjective assessment and argument. Many different systems have been evolved to create lists of possible metrics. Individual metrics typically fall into one of several general categories:

Quality: A measure of the performance metrics for personnel, users, or partner consumers of provided services

Efficiency: A measure of the cost per unit of storage, processing, or support for each client supported

Uptime: A measure of the raw time during which services are available to consumers

Alignment: A measure of the alignment of services and competencies with an organization's business strategies and goals

Extensibility: A measure of the ability to integrate services with other solutions, both within the enterprise and with external partners

Individual metrics can be identified and assigned relative values to best fit specific business goals and may include such measures as the number of full-time employees dedicated to patch management each year or the number of lines of code generated by each programming staff member in a month within a specified limit of errors-per-line. A vast number of other metrics can be identified, and the lead architect should identify as many as possible before initiating changes. If challenged on subjective grounds, these objective measures can be used to prove the value gained through change.

Note: The measure of uptime should not be limited to the time a particular server is in operation, but should also include periods of network instability, service unavailability, and any other times during which the target service is not reliable from the perspective of its consumers. To measure service uptime accurately, it is not enough to count the number of seconds between system reboots, because overload and instability can remove a running server from a functional state just as easily as turning off the power.

The Federated Enterprise

Enterprise planning and execution will take time to implement correctly and with a minimum of disruption to users and business units. Because the process can be somewhat protracted, it is important to identify useful tools to provide integration and federation of resources during the mid-migration period. Two common types of federated technology solutions involve identity management and data.

1. **Federated identity management.** These solutions sit above the various authentication pools and provide translation or synchronization between security principals. Sometimes referred to as a meta-directory, a federated identity management solution can improve transparency between legacy solutions and a modernized or consolidated architecture. As legislative mandates for accountability and privacy increase in number, such meta-directories fulfill compliance reporting and control functions beyond simple authentication translation.

2. **Federated data.** The concept of federated data management evolved to meet the growing need to track information as it passes through an organization's various applications and data stores. Such meta-data may be aggregated information or it may be "data about the data," and it is often used in data warehouse and business intelligence applications. The service-oriented architectural approach to application design also makes use of data federation in order to decouple storage of data from transfer and processing between disparate modules. Standards such as XML and UDDI expand information to natively include meta-data that may be useful in data federation.

Legal Mandates

Value may be present or gained through technology renovation in many forms, though few issues are potentially as threatening to an organization as compliance with legal mandates and regulatory requirements. Many acts of legislation and industry standards require detailed documentation and certification of compliance in order to avoid fines, fees, or other negative results. Any efforts made to develop or realign an enterprise must take into account existing and emerging legal requirements from the very start. It is difficult—sometimes impossible—to go back and implement controls to review past actions or data access. For example, logging must be in place before a service is exposed for production use, because without this logging from the initial entry into service, it may be impossible to comply with privacy or regulatory mandates that may be imposed.

Alphabet Soup

Legislative responses to issues such as data loss, privacy violations, and fiscal accountability have generated an ever-growing number of "alphabet soup" legal requirements that the lead architect must include in enterprise planning. These include items such as the Sarbanes-Oxley Act (SoX), the Gramm-Leach-Bliley Act (GLBA), the Health Insurance Portability and Accountability Act (HIPAA), the Federal Educational Rights Protection Act (FERPA), the Children's Online Privacy Protection Act (COPPA), and a host of other similar articles and regulations.

Each item carries its own potential pitfalls when applied to the enterprise. HIPAA mandates for segregation of health care clearinghouse data from other organizational access may complicate data storage, backup, and archival planning. Mandates for truthful disclosure of intellectual property ownership under SoX may complicate the use of free open-source software, where individual package intellectual property (IP) ownership may be difficult to document.

Many of these articles have common themes, however, making it easier to integrate specific requirements for compliance into more general planning steps. Privacy laws such as COPPA, HIPAA, and GLBA all include provisions for the privacy and protection of personally identifying information, as do industry regulations such as the Payment Card Industry Data Security Standards (PCI DSS). Following recent large-scale accidental data exposure events, it is likely that additional legislation will follow to address backup media and other responsibilities in the management of such information.

Knowledge of all the constraints and regulatory mandates affecting an enterprise is critical to the chief architect's ability to implement mandatory controls while avoiding wasted effort on regulations that may be mistakenly applied to an organization. HIPAA provides a ready example of an often-misapplied set of rules and requirements, because many organizations do not fall under its scope of application even if some health-related information is maintained in the organization's data systems.

Discovery and Retention

Because so many legal investigations and compliance reviews require access to electronic records, long-term planning should include provisions for information archival and reporting, as well as establishing standards for data retention policies. Subpoena management practices should be firmly in place before requests for data are received, in order to ensure continuity of operations and minimize operational impact due to motions for legal discovery.

Multiple articles of legislation under review may impose mandatory data retention for Internet service providers and other agencies responsible for the storage, processing, and transmission of information that could be useful to law enforcement investigations. A chief architect can provide great value to the organization by including data archival, storage, and handling options in long-term enterprise strategy.

Extended Legal Involvement

Beyond information technology–specific mandates, legal requirements can also include more generalized mandates that must be considered. Issues such as the control and proper disposal of toxic chemicals such as lead and cadmium found in many circuit boards can affect media disposal and end-of-life-cycle technology management constraints.

Accessibility requirements under Section 508 of the Rehabilitation Act must also be considered during authentication and data access planning. Complex multifactor or biometric authentication systems may prove too difficult for individuals with physically disabling conditions to operate, while public-facing applications may be unusable by some consumers if they do not support assistive screen-reading technologies such as Jaws and WindowsEyes. Additional meta-tag information for images and text-alternative versions of public-facing websites are also common requirements that must be included in enterprise architectural planning, to ensure that future-state solutions will be in compliance.

Managing Risk

Formal business continuity, disaster recovery, and continuity of operations planning and management skills are vital when architecting an extended enterprise network. Risk control and management starts with the lowest levels of operational readiness, such as power, telecom, and network availability. This planning includes technical considerations such as data center management solutions and technology replacement agreements, as well as physical security and data center planning measures.

Applying Formal Risk Management Practices

Many of the "alphabet soup" legislative articles include regulations that affect business continuity requirements for certain industries and settings, while operational guidelines may add to the complexity of risk management mandates. Selection of primary vendors with an established track record and future-state viability will factor into implementation planning, while emergency contact procedures and backup site testing may require the introduction of new solutions during an enterprise modernization project. A formal risk management process is necessary for every technology, service, or datum deemed critical to organizational operations. Performance of a formal risk review and creation of the risk register should be implemented early in the project planning process and updated regularly to address emerging issues identified during further planning and implementation efforts.

Note: A trait known as risk homeostasis can act to reduce the effect of risk management strategies. This is the theory wherein a change made to reduce risk can cause people to act in a more risky manner and offset the intended reduction. This was illustrated by a German case study involving taxicabs equipped with antilock braking systems. Because drivers felt safer, they engaged in riskier behavior and ended up being involved in more accidents than before the introduction of the "safer" braking systems. Clear and regular reminders of the purpose of security measures can offset this effect somewhat, but the tendency remains.

Targeted Threats

Risk management practices involve four possible strategies that may be used to address an identified threat

1. **Avoidance.** The risk may be avoided by selecting an alternate option that does not include the same element of risk, or by a decision to terminate the business process that creates the unacceptable risk.
2. **Transference.** The risk may be transferred to another responsible agency, often through outsourcing or insurance protections. While risk management and liability can be transferred, responsibility remains with the organization and can produce negative results in the "court of public opinion" that may not be easily overcome.
3. **Mitigation.** The risk may be reduced to an acceptable level by including additional protections or by altering the parameters producing the risk. Risk mitigation often comprises the bulk of risk management effort and cost.
4. **Acceptance.** The risk may be identified, examined, documented and formally accepted, provided the impact is fully understood and recognized.

Targeted threats such as viruses, worms, spyware, and other malicious code provide an elusive and varying level of risk that can be difficult to address. Blended threat code and viral programming agents designed to attack multiple operating systems and vulnerabilities can be created using simple downloadable GUI-based utilities. Microsoft's popular Windows platform draws the greatest attention because of its position as the leader in total number of systems, but virus developers are increasing attacks on Linux and other up-and-coming platforms as their market share increases.

Just as Sun moved its popular Java programming language into the open-source arena, Apple moved its OS-X platform out of the open-source community in order to protect the code from deep inspection that could reveal vulnerabilities to potential attackers. Vulnerabilities can also exist across the spectrum of available applications, such as the JavaScript Key vulnerability that posed a threat to dozens of different Web browsing clients on Windows, Linux, and Macintosh systems. New threats targeted at virtualization hypervisors may be developed in the near future, as virtualized data centers become more common.

It is not always possible to avoid or transfer risks completely and there are many risks that simply cannot be accepted because of regulatory or legal mandate. The CIO can add value to an architectural project by including risk-mitigation considerations to benefit the future-state enterprise, and by including contingencies and contingency reserves in project planning.

Beyond the End

Before beginning an architectural realignment project, the lead architect must work through and decompose all aspects of the update process from the high-level strategic vision down to the specifications necessary for evaluation and implementation of each element. This planning does not stop at a completed solution, however, because the end of a technology life cycle does not always provide a clean terminus.

Planned Obsolescence

Decisions must be made regarding lease agreements versus outright purchase before procurement can begin. Retirement strategies must be identified for solutions that are being phased out, while media and hardware disposal strategies need to encompass many types of media and destruction mechanisms. Legacy equipment may be maintained because an alternative does not exist or has been deemed too costly to acquire. The worst-case scenario here is that a large segment of the enterprise might be rendered obsolete as a result of changes in technology. One example of this involves the evolution of video connectivity from older VGA standards to DVI and HDMI standards, causing enterprises to extend tech refresh to include existing monitors and extended video cabling replacements due to the change in onboard workstation hardware standards. Effective long-term enterprise planning should include cyclic modernization of hardware, software, and media throughout the enterprise to ensure that obsolescence is managed in a planned manner.

Hidden Obsolescence

The emergence of service-oriented architectural programming methods has given new life to legacy systems near the end of their life cycle. By providing an XML-based Web service wrapper and securing these systems behind more modern technologies, the lifespan of legacy technologies and old "big iron" systems could stretch out almost forever (or until the last RLL or MFM drive is consumed). This attenuation of the technology life cycle provides time to transfer services to more modern alternatives, but it should not be accepted as a permanent long-term strategy.

Hardware replacement, service patch and update, expanding maintenance skills, and even data center facilities requirements can become risks to continued operation when legacy systems are maintained beyond obsolescence. A CIO must identify these systems and plan for their retirement in a controlled fashion, before they retire themselves through lack of suitable replacement parts or other similar unplanned event.

Good Enough Architecture

The enterprise architect should keep in mind Pareto's 80/20 rule whenever confronted by the full expanse of an enterprise network. It is not always possible to impose 100% solutions, such as a completely standardized workstation hardware and software package used by every person in the enterprise. Enterprise architectural projects become nearly impossible when they aim for unattainable goals, and so the strategies presented here should be considered when aiming for the first 80% of the desired solution. Once that has been attained, then planning can begin for 80% of what remains in turn.

Summary

Value in an enterprise must include not only monetary, but also regulatory, legal compliance and recoverability measures for the enterprise and the organization it serves. A network enterprise can be considered "good enough" for the first update cycle when the "low-hanging fruit" projects have been harvested and the defenses have been shored up. Cyclic modernization practices aid in future-state management, because what is good enough today will not be good enough tomorrow or the day after. The practice and process of architectural governance must be continually refined to fit the ever-evolving specifications unique to each organization.

In the chapters that follow, we will examine the elements of an enterprise network in greater depth. The guidelines presented up to this point should be comfortable and familiar before these elements can be effectively applied to extended network architecture. Before throwing out the old broom, it may be worth sweeping at the corners one more time to see what hidden value may be revealed.

Chapter 5

Managing Identity

In This Chapter

- An examination of the options for access authentication
- Considerations for access control planning
- Implications of directory service integration across the enterprise

In William Shakespeare's classic tragedy, Juliet asks of Romeo, "What's in a name? That which we call a rose / By any other name would smell as sweet." Her question concerns the feud between the two families that keeps the lovers apart, but it bears another, important meaning in terms of enterprise architectural planning today. Juliet poses the question of fundamental identity: What makes a rose a rose, and not something else? Certainly, the name alone does not define all of the qualities that make roses desirable.

Within the network enterprise, the issue of identity is fundamental to access and security. Without the basic requirement of unique identification, accountability and access control measures cannot be implemented. We will examine the process of identification, authentication, and authorization as they apply to the process of identity management. Identity management will play an important role in later chapters, where data storage and network resource access depend on authorization measures applied to individual and group identities.

This is the first chapter in which we conduct a detailed examination of the critical elements that are necessary for architectural planning, an endeavor that will continue through the remainder of the book. It is important to keep in mind the strategic aspects of enterprise governance and management presented in the earlier chapters while reviewing their application throughout the remainder of the text. Some chapters will develop more fully topics mentioned earlier, but the chapters need not be read sequentially in order to gain value from the information provided.

The Many-Walled Garden

Imagine a garden in which fruits, vegetables, and flowers are cultivated. Without a wall around this garden, small animals and unauthorized people could easily wander in and destroy the value present within the garden. This garden is the enterprise network, where barriers must be erected to protect resources from threats such as viruses and intruders.

At the garden gate, guards stand watch to ensure that only properly authorized people may enter to enjoy the flowers or gather the food. The guards must recognize each individual who approaches to establish their identity. Identity, then, is independent from authorization to enter or be denied entrance to the garden. The same is true for an enterprise network, in which a user or service account must first be identified and then granted or denied authorization for access to electronic resources.

Once inside the garden, pathways and fences ensure that an individual gathers food only in certain areas, to avoid trampling the plants growing elsewhere. Authorization protocols within the network provide similar guidance by allowing access to certain resources while protecting others. Without policies and access control measures, errant wandering could occur within either the garden or the enterprise.

Imagine now a large garden spread over much land, in which each area is walled apart from the others. Within each area, different rules are used to organize where fruits, vegetables, flowers, and animals are arranged. Different rules are also applied to control how and where these resources may be gathered. Guards at the gates between areas must each keep track of all individuals who may seek entrance, identifying each and authorizing or denying entrance without communicating with guards at other areas.

This many-walled garden poses difficulties for gatherers, hunters, and those who merely come to enjoy the flowers, because they must stop at each gate to negotiate entrance. Passing from area to area, different rules may cause inadvertent accidents when gathering food or hunting. Take this image now, and label each of the smaller areas with names such as Microsoft, Novell, IBM, and Red Hat, or with functional segment names such as Accounting, Shipping, and Human Resources. Within each vendor's offerings or isolated resource silo, identity management and directory services identify users, computers, and services that are allowed or denied access to enterprise resources within that segment.

Enterprise solutions that employ a single authentication base share much in common with a simpler single-walled garden. Enterprise solutions that include two or more authentication directory solutions become many-walled gardens, creating frustration for users and the potential for accidental or intentional misuse of networked resources, because too many walls can make users work against security.

A better solution in the many-walled garden might employ an accompanying document or representative able to authorize passage from one area to another more easily, in which federated identity management solutions provide the same service within an extended enterprise. Before examining these solutions, let us first gain an understanding of the process of identity management.

Identification

Identification within the network enterprise consists of some method by which the user or service identifies its unique identity to an authentication service. Typically, all of the various methods for identification can be classified in three general categories:

- What you know
- What you have
- What you are

Single-factor identification solutions depend on only one of these checks, while more complex multifactor solutions might employ a combination of checks for both what you have and what you know. Automated teller machine (ATM) systems use such a two-factor identification system by requiring both an ATM card (what you have) as well as a keyed Personal Identification Number or PIN (what you know) in order to manage funds within the linked bank account.

What You Know

Identification of this type includes personal identification numbers, log-on identifiers, and passwords. The log-on/password combination is perhaps the most widely used identification system, because it can be easily applied to many different environments and applications and is accessible by any user interface able to generate keystroke responses. Even eye-blink-readers and other forms of assistive technology can be used to provide keystroke responses for log-on and password identification.

Because of its utility, the log-on/password combination is a popular choice for identifying user and service accounts in many network enterprises. Because both factors fall within the "what you know" category of identification, however, such solutions are subject to guessing and brute-force attacks in which automated tools are used to test all possible combinations of characters sequentially. The relative "strength" of a log-on/password combination is affected by several factors:

- **Length.** The minimum length of a password determines the minimum number of tests that must be performed before all combinations have been attempted. If only alphabetic characters are used (A–Z), then a single-digit password would require only 27 tests to check all possible combinations (a null or empty password being an option unless prevented by security policies). A four-character non-null alphabetic password would require over 450,000 tests, while an eight-character password would require almost 410 billion tests. With gigabit bandwidth, teraflop processing power, and distributed attacks employing tens of thousands of attacking systems, even very long passwords can only slow down the time required to gain unauthorized access.
- **Complexity.** Like length, the complexity of a password can also improve its strength. By using uppercase (A–Z), lowercase (a–z), numbers (0–9), and special characters (such as ~, `, and !), each character within the password requires almost four times the number of tests before all possible combinations have been tried. A complex

eight-character non-null password will now require over 6 quadrillion (6 million, billion) tests in order to check all possible combinations. Complexity capability is limited in some cases by the available character sets, in that legacy systems may only use 7-bit character sets instead of the more common 8-bit systems. Using extended 2-byte character sets for complex passwords, however, can allow complexity to expand brute-force testing requirements by several orders of magnitude.

- **Age.** By imposing rules on how long a password may be used, brute-force attacks on complex lengthy passwords will not conclude all possible tests before a new password is selected. Limits on the minimum age of passwords, such as one user-originated change per day, can help to curb the tendency to change passwords back to well-known settings even when a history of the last few attempts is put into place to avoid password reuse.
- **Obscurity.** Strong passwords are not derived from easily guessed information, such as the names of family members or pets, important dates, or common nicknames and interests. Because automated hacking tools can rapidly test passwords against word dictionaries, strong passwords should not be based on standard words in the local language. The use of an easily remembered pass phrase can help in recall of longer, more-difficult-to-guess password combinations.

Note: The specific standards for minimum acceptable password strength vary from one organization to another, and additional requirements may be imposed on service and administrative accounts with elevated privileges. I recommend as an absolute minimum the following settings:

1. Passwords must be at least eight characters in length.
2. Passwords must not be null.
3. User passwords should expire regularly and automatically. The interval between password expiration processes should be considered during authentication planning. Whereas brute-force password guessing was once a weakness best overcome by regular exchange of passwords, modern enterprises must rely on automatic account lockouts and attack detection systems to remain effective in the face of supercomputing power on the attacker's desktop. Short password change cycles cause users to write down new passwords or to use

simple variations on a standard theme, such as "N3wPa55w0rd1," "N3wPa55w0rd2," and so on.

4. The minimum time between user-originated password change in highly secure environments should be 1 day, to avoid users rapidly expiring history tables by repeated resets.

5. The minimum history of past-used passwords in highly secure environments should be at least 25.

6. Passwords should be complex and contain at least three of the four possible character types: uppercase (A–Z), lowercase (a–z), numeric (0–9), and symbols (ex: ~, !).

   Pass phrases can also be used to improve security by making lengthy passwords easier to remember, so that users will not be as likely to keep written copies. An easily memorable phrase such as "Open says me" can be turned into a strong password by substituting characters (3 for e, 5 for s are common) and including case changes and special characters: "Op3n5ay5M3!"

Unfortunately, all tests against combinations of single-factor identification based on "what you know" can eventually be guessed with sufficient processing power, bandwidth, and time. Other forms of identification may be required in more secure environments or where alternative methods of identification are required by policy or technology.

What You Have

Identification based on the possession of a specific item is as old as the key lock and the signet ring, if not older. Knights and merchants once carried patents of nobility and specially crafted symbols in order to prove their identity. Even the Bronze-Age merchants known as the "beaker traders" employed specially crafted chalices for identification.

Keys are still widely in use today, particularly when paired with physical security measures. However, electronic access rights are more commonly coupled with tokens that must be present to identify the possessor, including the following types:

- **Tokens that are applied directly.** Such tokens provide identification directly, by proximity or presentation. Access cards, "smart" tokens with embedded circuitry, and radio-frequency identification

(RFID) tags are all examples of this type of token. When used in proximity-detection systems, these tokens can be employed for both electronic and physical access management. RFID-based tagging systems were originally used on animals, but they have since been applied to inventory management, vehicular toll tags, and even human identification systems using small implantable chips. Access cards and passive electronic tokens used to unlock terminal access are also common in critical infrastructure and governmental networks.

- **Tokens that provide information.** These tokens provide information that is employed in a secondary identification mechanism. Time-synchronous pass code and one-time-password generators may be used to supply log-on identification credentials that cannot be divulged by simply writing down a log-on and password, because the token is also needed in order to provide part of the required "what you know" information automatically. Synchronized identification is also used widely between electronic endpoint authentication and data transport agents, as with the time-synchronized Kerberos authentication protocol or the public-key-validated Secure Sockets Layer (SSL) transport mechanism. Active-content "smart" tokens can also provide information of this type, responding to interrogation with an appropriate calculated response message.

Single-factor identification solutions that employ the "what you have" test can be circumvented by theft of the token, accidental proximity to sensing elements, or outright forgery of the identifying token. Some automobile manufacturers employ key-fob RFID tags in order to unlock cars and trunks, and even to start up the vehicle's ignition in some models. Because the current generation of RFID authorization systems does not employ stronger encryption such as Advanced Encryption Standard (AES) or other more secure protocols, they are subject to certain forms of hacking that can provide a means for physical access and theft of the protected vehicle using nothing more than a transmitter and a laptop computer able to generate counterfeit RFID challenge/response information.

What You Are

The ultimate proof of identification essentially becomes a test of the "what you are" form of identification. In theory, each person is the only one who matches all of his or her own characteristics. Even in the case of identical twins who share the same DNA pattern, developmental differences result in variances in fingerprint, hand geometry, motion kinematic, iris, retina, pore, and blood vessel patterns. Effective measurement and analysis of these characteristics may provide the best means for personal identification, once the technologies involved have matured from their current state.

Tests of "what you are" are generally referred to as biometric tests, in that they measure specific biological characteristics against a previously identified value. Because biology changes, biometric measurements must be updated regularly in order to remain at peak efficiency. Performance of biometric identification systems is measured in terms of two primary metrics:

- **False rejection rate (FRR):** A measure of the number of times a valid identification fails, also referred to as the type I failure rate.
- **False acceptance rate (FAR):** A measure of the number of times an invalid identification succeeds, also referred to as the type II failure rate.

Biometric identification systems may use direct identification or behavioral tests, depending on the type of biological assessment employed. Examples of direct identification systems include the following:

- **Palm-print systems.** Palm-based biometric systems employ a scanner able to measure and identify the patterns of ridges and valleys of the palm. Like an enlarged fingerprint reader, this solution identifies unique characteristics on the palm; however, it can generate false rejections because of injury or mis-positioning of the hand within the scanner. Like all solutions that involve direct contact with the reader, palm-based security systems may also be opposed by some users fearful of contagion.
- **Hand geometry.** A second full-hand biometric system employs the unique patterns of growth in the bones to provide identification. By placing the fingers against pegs at specific locations in the reader, finger length and joint configuration can be identified. This solution is subject to an elevated potential for false response because finger length may be matched through accident or surgical manipulation,

while accident and injury can cause rapid changes to bone alignment and joint size. Advanced hand geometry systems also include thermal mapping of major blood vessels to reduce the chance of false acceptance results.

- **Iris.** Biometric identification using optical systems can identify unique patterns in the colored portion of the eye around the pupil without requiring contact with the scanning system. Because pupil response can change as a result of illness, light conditions, and certain medications, this system relies on a complex set of information to identify the specific patterns and color variations at different levels of pupil dilation. This type of identification requires storage and transport of a larger set of data than other forms of biometric identification.

- **Retinal.** A second form of ocular biometric identification employs a camera that is able to examine the pattern of minute blood vessels at the back of the eye. This system has a very low false acceptance rate, but the need for close proximity or direct contact with the scanner eyepiece creates barriers to user acceptance. Medical conditions such as cataracts can also render this solution unusable for certain individuals.

- **Fingerprint.** Perhaps the most commonly available form of biometric identification employs the unique pattern of ridges found on each fingertip. Optical fingerprint scanning systems are readily available as aftermarket identification add-ons, and can even be found embedded in some laptop, PDA, and flash storage devices. Fingerprint biometrics are inexpensive to implement, but they can be impaired by injury or dirt on the fingertips. This type of identification requires direct contact with the reader, and may be paired with skin conductivity, thermal, and blood-oxygenation sensors to ensure that the fingertip identification is authentic.

- **Facial geometry.** One of the more politicized forms of biometric identification makes use of measurements of key facial geometries, including the spacing and position of eyes, ears, nose, and mouth. Because these underlying characteristics remain unchanged by attempts at disguise, this type of identification system is being developed for terrorist identification in areas such as government buildings and airports. Facial recognition systems have the highest user acceptance rate in use, because they can operate without requiring physical contact or proximity. However, they also have elevated false acceptance rates compared to other solutions, particularly when attempting to discriminate between twins or siblings with similar facial features or in the identification of facial geometries from an oblique perspective angle.

Other biometric identification systems employ behavioral analysis, including the following:

- **Gait identification.** Analysis of the movement patterns of a walking or running individual can be used for identification. Such systems are limited in use, because of the need for movement within the identification area and an unobscured view of the subject.
- **Signature recognition.** Signature-based identification systems are being used increasingly and include digital signature images along with credit card point-of-purchase information. More robust versions can identify the rate, stroke patterns, and level of pressure throughout a signature in order to discriminate between authentic and counterfeit signatures that may match visually but differ due to tiny variations of bone length and musculature in the hand. This solution can be concealed under the target writing surface, but it is also subject to an elevated false rejection rate compared to other biometric identification methods because of variances in handwriting due to illness, injury, level of attention, use of initials, or other variable factors.
- **Voice recognition.** Voice-recognition analysis is one of the most readily accepted forms of biometric identification. It involves the identification of patterns in pitch, timbre, and tonal qualities in a spoken pass phrase. Improvements in acoustic recording technologies may affect the viability of voice recognition for the purposes of identification, but voice-recognition systems are being found increasingly in automated telephone applications such as the 4-1-1 information look-up service, available in most areas of the United States. Background noise, changes in vocalization as a result of illness or growth, and other factors can negatively affect the performance of voice-recognition systems.

An additional form of "what you are" identification might be better referred to as "where you are" and employs location-identifying information, either of a logical (network locale) or physical (GPS) nature. These forms of identification are suitable for integration with other forms of identification, but they are not sufficient to provide positive identification alone. Location-identifying systems include:

- **Callback system.** When a user requests network connectivity by initiating a dial-up telephonic connection, the host modem system disconnects the requesting connection and then redials a previously assigned number associated with the requesting identity. Only by responding to this callback can the user then connect to the network for authentication and authorization.
- **Virtual Private Network (VPN).** An installed VPN client application running on the requesting system establishes an encrypted connection to the requested network and establishes a virtual presence within the protected network. This connectivity allows secure encrypted communication over a public network segment, while also providing identification as a "local" system to other resources within the protected network segment. Some VPN clients make use of public-key certificates in order to digitally sign all communications, providing an additional identity check for each activity through a "what you have" identification using the issued unique key.
- **Global Positioning System (GPS).** Properly equipped systems can make use of Global Positioning System data together with public-key digital signature hashes to provide identification of the current physical location of the requesting system. Restrictions can be implemented to allow connectivity only to systems identified as being in designated physical locations. This type of identification can be problematic if the requester is underground or inside an electronically shielded physical location and unable to receive signals from the GPS satellites.

Multifactor Identification

Because each single-factor form of identification has its own strengths and weaknesses, network environments with enhanced security requirements may implement multiple types of identification together. As in the case of the ATM card/PIN combination, multifactor identification systems are more difficult to bypass through brute-force or counterfeit means.

Some forms of identification also require extensive secondary solutions to provide synchronized token values or unique public key sets for "smart card" systems. These secondary systems may have their own additional requirements for key management, certificate authority integration, and key distribution only to properly identified and authenticated token sets.

Authentication

Once a unique identity has been established, the process of authentication can begin. Authentication is a process used to determine whether a specific request for information or service access is valid. Like the garden gate guard who lets in only those on the list of approved townspeople and turns away all others, an authentication solution relies on some type of directory or database against which each identity is checked. Unlike authorization, authentication merely checks the identity requesting access against a listing of known identity credentials to determine if the identity is recognized as valid.

The Authentication Directory

The database containing information on valid identities is often referred to as a directory. Many different directory solutions exist, including Microsoft's Active Directory, Novell's NDS and eDirectory, IBM's Tivioli, Sun's IPlanet, OpenLDAP, and many other similar technologies. Most of these directories support the X.500 or Lightweight Directory Access Protocol (LDAP) standards, providing a means for authenticating against a database of known identities.

TIP: A common error in planning LDAP-based authentication solutions is the expectation that the final result will provide access control. LDAP and X.500 are protocol standards used to validate an identity; they provide no inherent access control restrictions. Such restrictions must be built into the consuming application in order to restrict what the validated identity may or may not do with a requested resource.

Vendor solutions such as the common Microsoft Active Directory merge both authentication and authorization functions, and should not be confused with standalone LDAP authentication-only services during enterprise planning.

External Authentication

Authentication can also be performed against an external source using public-key cryptographic digital signatures, which employ a trusted certificate authority such as Thawte or Verisign, in order to validate a request that has been digitally signed using the requestor's private key. When a signed request is made, the requested service validates the public signature with the certificate authority. The certificate authority, in turn, identifies the request as valid.

Authentication Standards

Many different protocols and standards exist for network authentication. These standards may employ internal or external databases of known identities, or they may make use of network information or other endpoint data to validate requests for service connectivity. Many different vendors provide their own proprietary authentication solutions, but most solutions conform to one or more of the common standards:

- **Lightweight Directory Access Protocol.** Derived from the X.500 standards, LDAP is a commonly adopted authentication protocol in solutions up to 500,000 identities per database. Free and open software (FOSS) and commercial off-the-shelf (COTS) directory services expose LDAP interfaces in order to facilitate system interconnectivity and LDAP management is critical to efforts at developing heterogeneous service-oriented architecture solutions and many single-sign-on (SSO) services. Unless LDAP is implemented in a blended fashion, as in the Microsoft Active Directory, it is solely an authentication protocol and does not include access control mechanisms.
- **X.500 Standards.** The X.500 suite includes several directory protocols, such as the Directory Access Protocol (DAP), Directory System Protocol (DSP), Directory Information Shadowing Protocol (DISP), and other similar protocols addressing fundamental or large-scale

authentication requirements. The X.509 authentication framework provides the standard for public-key certificates used in SSL, Secure Shell (SSH), and other types of public-key infrastructure (PKI) authentication.

- **Password Authentication Protocol (PAP).** PAP is a legacy form of authentication that utilizes unencrypted password transfer. Although it is still supported by authentication services such as RADIUS and DIAMETER, it is considered an unsecure authentication protocol that is no longer suitable for enterprise use.
- **Challenge-Handshake Authentication Protocol (CHAP).** CHAP is a form of authentication used in establishing Point-to-Point Protocol (PPP) connections between remote systems. The authenticating system sends a "challenge" message, which the receiving system translates using a one-way mathematical function into a unique "hash" value that is returned to the authenticating system. If this value matches the value the authenticating system calculated internally, the connection is validated.
- **Extensible Authentication Protocol (EAP).** EAP is an authentication protocol standard that is widely used in PPP and wireless connections. The WiFi Protected Access (WPA/WPA2) standards implement EAP to ensure interconnectivity between wireless networking manufacturers' products.
- **IP Security (IPSEC).** IPSEC is a standard for TCP/IP network communication that can encrypt and authenticate all IP packets transmitted between interconnected systems. The Authentication Header (AH) protocol ensures integrity and authentication, while the Encapsulated Security Payload (ESP) protocol supports authentication, confidentiality, and data integrity. This standard also includes the Internet Key Exchange (IKE) protocol used for public-key distribution, facilitating key-based authentication solutions such as "smart" cards.
- **Kerberos.** Named after the three-headed dog that guarded Hades' realm, the Kerberos protocol is a time-synchronized protocol used for authenticating two endpoints against a trusted third source. Unlike public-key encryption solutions, the Kerberos protocol utilizes a symmetric-key algorithm to calculate values exchanged between the authenticating systems and relies on a common time synchronized with the authenticating agent. Kerberos is commonly used in Microsoft and Linux networks, and forms the basis for some enterprise single-sign-on solutions.

Single Sign-On

Single sign-on (SSO) refers to a single authentication that provides access across all network resources and is sometimes considered the "holy grail of networking." In a SSO solution, a central authentication source provides authentication to each element within the extended enterprise. By using a central authentication solution, each element of the network must address only authorization and authorization limitations within its resources.

Central Authentication Services

Central authentication solutions can be implemented using a range of technologies, including the Central Authentication Service (CAS) standard, Microsoft's Windows Live ID (formerly known as .NET Passport), or Security Assertion Markup Language (SAML) implementations provided through the Liberty Alliance or the Internet2 Middleware project known as Shibboleth. Central authentication systems rely on an identity provider for authentication, returning validation responses to the requesting CAS-enabled application. While legacy solutions may be coupled to a specific authentication mechanism, this type of authentication can provide access to a wide range of resources, provided they all share the same central authentication mechanism.

Federated Authentication

A federated identity management solution can also be used for single-sign-on authentication. These solutions are populated with authentication credentials, coupled to a single authentication against the identity management system. When a user or service requests resources from within an authentication boundary, the identity management system provides the appropriate set of credentials from its encrypted store on behalf of the already-authenticated identity. Because of this caching of credentials, the user has to enter log-on credentials only once for each authentication boundary. After the initial entry, the identity management system asserts credentials on behalf of the authenticated identity.

This solution is very effective when coordinating a single log-on with resources from a wide range of authentication locales. Legacy systems can be provided with credentials automatically, so a user needs to log-on only once to a central authority or information aggregation site to gain access to all of its resources. Portal solutions commonly implement some form of SSO identity management system, so that individually configured portlets or web parts may be coupled to disparate resources without requiring the user to provide multiple sets of log-on credentials at each log-on. The aggregate collection of all identities and related credentials is sometimes termed a metadirectory.

Because the metadirectory acts as an authentication proxy, it can serve as a vulnerability subject to exploitation through access to the metadirectory server. If it is not specifically prevented by the chosen solution, administrative or physical access to this service can allow an individual to associate his or her own credentials with stored credentials from another user. This association can allow unauthorized access to enterprise resources, which must then be identified through a later review of access logs as a reactive rather than proactive security measure.

Password Synchronization

One other method used to improve authentication transparency involves the use of a service that synchronizes accounts and passwords across multiple authentication domains. Transparent password synchronization solutions accept a password change within one authentication boundary and replicate that change to all other associated accounts within other authentication boundaries. Provisioning password synchronization systems rely on a central location for password update or change, such as a secured website, and then apply the new changes to all registered accounts associated with the authenticated log-on used to conduct the change process. Variation in password complexity, length, and other constraints between vendors can present difficulties for password synchronization systems, which must restrict password selection based on the minimum length, complexity, and other factors present across all authentication systems.

Pluggable Authentication Modules

Some technologies, such as FreeBSD and OpenBSD, can consume authentication provided by lower-level components known as pluggable authentication modules (PAMs). Higher-level applications do not have to implement their own authentication solution, calling the exposed application programming interface (API) of the PAM component instead. The PAM can be configured to authenticate against any desired form of authentication service, returning identity validation to the calling application.

Authorization

Authorization is the practice of providing access to specific resources based on the rights allowed or assigned to an authenticated identity. Access rights to files and database information can include read, edit, write, or change capabilities, while service access rights may also include log-on, shutdown, and administrative management functions beyond simple change control settings.

Authorization involves comparison of authenticated identities against established security policies such as time-of-day and point-of-origin restrictions, as well as application of the principle of least privilege. This principle involves granting only the minimum level of access needed in order to perform assigned tasks, and restricting all other access. By preventing users from logging in using administrative accounts for daily access, accidental compromise of a user's session remains a local matter, thus not exposing elevated privilege or access rights to compromise. Similarly, database and file access can be restricted to the least information and access capability required to perform legitimate operations.

Access Controls

An identity may be authorized to access a requested resource using many different criteria, including:

- **Anonymous.** Some resources are available to any request, regardless of the requestor's identity. Public-facing websites are an example of this type of access, which require no form of authorization. In some settings, generic "guest" accounts provide a specific identity that is available anonymously for access.
- **Rule-based.** Resources may be available only during working hours, or only to requests made from particular terminal locations. Rule-based access restrictions are typically coupled with additional forms

of authorization, but they may be implemented on anonymously provided resources as well, to prevent connections during update or system maintenance cycles.

- **Explicit.** Explicit authorization or denial includes those connectivity rights that are assigned directly to an identity. In some authorization systems, explicit access may override implicit or inherited causes for access denial, while in other solutions, any denial always wins.

- **Implicit.** Implicit authorization or denial includes those connectivity rights present due to default or unassigned privilege. Default share permissions and exposed services may allow access to default identities such as the *Everyone* pseudo-identity, allowing implied access rights to be provided to all accounts except those that have been restricted through other assignment.

- **Inherited.** Inherited authorization or denial includes those connectivity rights assigned to an identity as a result of membership in a group or role. Because inherited access rights are passed from one group or role to subordinate ones, inherited rights can become complex and difficult to troubleshoot without careful planning and documentation. Role-based access control solutions make use of inherited rights and restrictions.

- **Mandatory.** Mandatory access controls (MACs) are applied using a set of classifications and categorizations applied by the security administrator to the requesting identity and to the requested resource. Only when the requesting identity has the necessary level of access in both classification and category will the requested resource become available. Highly secure network environments use this system of access control, which requires a great deal of management over the assignment and maintenance of classification and categorization labels for all resources and identities.

- **Discretionary.** Discretionary access controls (DACs) manage resource availability based on the resource owner's preference. This is the most commonly used form of access control in corporate environments, where file ownership allows direct assignment of access rights and restrictions to other identities or identity groups. Because ownership allows the assignment of rights to further assign access rights, DAC solutions can quickly become very complex and risk exposing resources to unanticipated third parties unless there are strong policies and careful segregation of resource pools.

Note: Discretionary access controls make use of an access control list (ACL) associated with each identity and resource to enforce privilege and access limitations. ACLs can become very complex, configured to control access over file and data resources, network shares, services, and port availability with fine-resolution control over specific rights such as change and delete capabilities.

Identity Management

The overall management of security principals and effective assignment of access rights and controls together form the practice of identity management. Without unique identification of user and service activity, many aspects of network security become difficult to maintain. Shared user accounts present a particular difficulty when attempting later to assign responsibility for unauthorized changes, system misuse, or discovered contraband data. Shared and anonymous log-on credentials should never be used for secured access to enterprise resources, due to the inability to later associate specific responsibility for account use and access actions.

Regulatory Mandates

Many legislative articles include specific requirements for identity management and access control logging in order to meet regulatory compliance mandates. Financial penalties and legal implications provide strong business drivers for the adoption of identity management practices to meet these guidelines. Federal legislation that requires identity management for responsibility and privacy controls includes the following:

- Gramm-Leach-Bliley Act (GLBA)
- Children's Online Privacy Protection Act (COPAA)
- Fair Credit Reporting Act (FCRA)
- Family Educational Rights and Privacy Act (FERPA)
- Federal Identity Theft Assumption and Deterrence Act
- Health Insurance Portability and Accountability Act (HIPAA)
- Sarbanes-Oxley Act (SOX)
- Aviation and Transportation Security Act

- USA Patriot Act
- Enhanced Border Security and Visa Entry Reform Act

In addition to these federal acts, many additional requirements derive from state and local legislation as well as regulatory mandates applied by specific industries. The Cardholder Information Security Program (CISP) and Payment Card Industry Data Security Standards (PCI DSS) are examples of industry-mandated practices involving identity management.

Business Drivers

In addition to regulatory compliance, many additional business drivers may affect the decision to implement an identity management solution. Effective identity management practices and technologies provide a number of advantages that may hold value for stakeholders and decision makers:

- **Security.** Border control, asset protection, and data exposure controls rely heavily on effective identity management. Fraud, misuse, and internal access management rely on the ability to distinguish acting identities and to assign responsibility for use. Unique identity assignment ensures non-repudiation of logged events by establishing the acting identity involved.
- **Cost.** User access provisioning and password management solutions can reduce the amount of administrative overhead required to create, update, and retire user identities to meet changes in employment and organizational structure.
- **Productivity.** Improved transparency between authentication boundaries can increase user productivity and acceptance by eliminating unnecessary reentry of identifying credentials when accessing remote resources. This is critical to the functionality of service-oriented architecture (SOA) distributed application development and data consolidation solutions such as intranet portals.

Identity Management Elements

Identity management solutions differ from identification, authentication, and authorization systems. Identity management systems may include services that provide credentials management, authentication, and authorization. These solutions may even provide federated delivery of credentials across a range of authentication pools. However, formal identity management solutions also provide management and administrative support to the infrastructure that delivers identity services, including:

- **Account provisioning.** Identity management systems provide automated tools for creating, updating, and retiring security identifiers. Examples of this type of functionality include application services that access human resources data to create user log-on accounts for new hires, update information fields based on departmental assignment, and suspend or deactivate log-on accounts upon termination or dismissal. When implemented in high-turnover environments such as food-industry or higher-education enterprises, automated provisioning of user accounts can provide tremendous time and administrative cost savings over manual management methods.
- **Permission assignment.** Identity management solutions may assign group membership and access rights based on departmental assignment or organizational role (such as an accountant or manager). By automating permission assignment, there is less opportunity for accidental access assignment or delayed revocation of rights following employment separation procedures.
- **Password management.** Identity management solutions provide mechanisms to control password strength, re-use, and other aspects of a credential's lifecycle. This may include automatic regeneration and assignment of public-key infrastructure (PKI) certificates, expiration of password values, and similar processes necessary to ensure the security and viability of provided security credentials.
- **Self-service.** Identity management solutions frequently include utilities to allow users the ability to update public information associated with their log-on identity, such as contact information and status. Other solutions provide password reset capabilities without requiring administrative assistance, or may allow a user to request access to a protected resource without having first to identify the resource owner (DAC environments).
- **Workflow.** Identity management solutions may include provisions for automating workflows, performing such sequential tasks as first passing resource access requests to management for request

authorization and then transmitting the authorized request to the proper resource owner. Once approved, the workflow system applies the necessary access control list (ACL) changes and then notifies the requestor of the new access rights assignment or denial. Obviously, workflows can become much more complex where resource access involves multiple data owners or when operating across organizational or authentication boundaries.

- **Audit reporting.** Formal identity management systems include support for compliance audit, logging, and reporting. These features may provide very flexible reporting options, or they may involve packages tailored for the reporting requirements of specific regulatory statutes. Preformatted audit reporting tools can greatly simplify legislated compliance reporting requirements by ensuring that standardized format guidelines are met.

Identity Management Providers

Many different solutions providers have created identity management applications and suites, although most solutions implement one or more standards for identification and authorization in order to provide enterprise interoperability. Examples of identity management providers include:

- CA (eTrust Admin)
- Hewlett-Packard (OpenView)
- IBM (Tivoli)
- Microsoft (Microsoft Forefront Identity Manager)
- Netegrity (IdentityMinder)
- Novell (eDirectory and Nsure Identity Manager)
- Sun (Java System Identity Manager)
- Oracle (Oracle COREid)
- Quest Software (Vintela)

These solutions offer a broad mixture of features for both enterprise and federated identity management requirements. Some solutions may be more applicable to enterprises with an established technology base, such as the Microsoft Forefront Identity Manager for Microsoft Active Directory solutions or Tivoli for WebSphere integrated networks. These utilities have the advantage of a common interface for administration within their technology envelope.

Identity Management Strategies

In this chapter, we have provided an overview of the functions involved in managing and consuming identities within the enterprise network. A number of strategies apply to these solutions, providing enhanced resource availability, reduced operational costs, and improved regulatory compliance.

Implement Strong Identification

Passwords should be strong and changed regularly. Multifactor authentication solutions provide better protection against unauthorized use and credentials counterfeit than single-factor alternatives. Combinations of "what you know," "what you have," and "what you are" are much more difficult to fake than single-factor means of identification such as the predominant textual log-on/password combination.

Although biometric and token-based solutions may provide improved security over log-on/password combinations, it is important for the enterprise architect to keep in mind physical accessibility requirements that may restrict their use. Beyond the obvious difficulty of users who may not possess the appropriate "bio" being "metered," many conditions and ailments restrict the ability to use such methods of identification.

Combine Authentication and Authorization

Authentication solutions such as LDAP, CAS, and Kerberos provide only identity validation. Applications that authenticate identities against a service such as LDAP must also include their own mechanism for authorization and access control. Enterprise architects must identify whether these functions should remain separated or if they can be combined in more well integrated enterprises.

By consuming a merged authentication and access control solution, application developers will not need to write and maintain separate own access control systems. This improves security by ensuring that the same standards are applied across all development projects, that the skill of the programmer does not affect the level of security provided, and that changes made to an identity and its access rights are more rapidly propagated to all resources.

An example of this involves the development of portlets and Web parts designed to operate within a portal's authentication and authorization umbrella. Such applications can be rapidly created, tested, certified, and deployed because there is no need to develop authentication and access control code for each applet. The portal hosting application provides all security and access control functions using a central authentication solution.

Assign Rights to Groups

Effective enterprise organization supports efficient rights assignment. Rights and access restrictions should be assigning to groups and roles rather than directly to individual identities. This simplifies rights management and avoids accidental conflict and rights management complexity. Nested groups and roles can produce complex fine resolution access rights using easily maintained configurations. Each level of organization and rights assignment subsumes all levels of higher-order inheritance, improving troubleshooting and problem identification in larger enterprises. This practice ensures that access controls are correctly changed upon role transfer or reassignment.

Employ Identity Management Solutions

Identity management automation saves time and can quickly pay for itself with direct benefits in terms of time, effort, user acceptance, and regulatory compliance. These solutions require careful planning to ensure integration across an extended enterprise. A simplified authentication landscape will improve management ease, while workflow and automated provisioning can enhance resource availability across varied authorization domains. These solutions are most appropriate in medium-to-large enterprise environments, though they are also used in smaller networks in order to support legacy authentication systems or self-service needs created by a highly mobile workforce.

Simplify the Garden

Authentication and access control provide the key to all resources distributed throughout the enterprise and its affiliated partners. This is the most fundamental technology decision made in planning an enterprise reconfiguration. Identity conflict across multiple authentication boundaries and mis-configured authentication proxies can create complexity and user access difficulties throughout the enterprise. The only segregation of authorization domains should be due to specific mandate or legislated controls. This may prove unpopular with departmental administrators used to having full control over their own local identity management solutions, but it is critical to avoiding conflicts, sharing resources, and ensuring that adequate controls are maintained in all areas.

Each authentication boundary represents additional complexity for user interaction and federated access management. In order to answer the question of whether a rose by any other name still smells as sweet, we must first be able to navigate the garden to find that rose. Unnecessary walls create inefficiency and difficulty without gain. Simplify the authentication boundaries to provide the most effective user experience in the garden, whether gathering food, hunting, or simply stopping to smell the flowers.

Summary

A rose by any other name may smell as sweet, yet be granted far different access permissions in a modern extended enterprise. Planning for effective authentication, authorization, and access control strategies is critical to both enterprise security and utility. Overly complex or difficult solutions tend to encourage users to find "workarounds" that may weaken the enterprise's usefulness or its defenses. User provisioning and access control assignment should be integrated into employee hiring and termination procedures, contract negotiation with business partners and external consumers, along with other elements of the business the enterprise supports. These practices should be reviewed regularly and updated as needed to address the ever-changing user environment. Elimination of isolated resource silos should be a primary consideration in any enterprise architectural planning, to simplify access controls, promote resource sharing, and facilitate enterprise-wide auditing of resource access and use.

Chapter 6

Sharing Information

In This Chapter

- Examining the value of communications mechanisms
- Detailing common communication mechanisms in the enterprise
- Considerations for groupware combinations of communication streams

The sixth-century military strategist, Sun Tzu, identified communications as a critical factor in successful conflict engagement. The tools available in his time may have been somewhat primitive in comparison to today's globe-spanning Internet, but their application reflects the same value now. Sun Tzu noted: "At night, use torches and drums; during the day, use flags and pennants. Drums, gongs, flags, and banners unite men's eyes and ears." Just as in the sixth century, different means of communication can unite people around a common task or goal today. Combining these means into a cohesive collaborative solution can aid an organization in defining and implemented directed action across widely distributed operations, just as drums and flags did on the sixth-century battlefield.

Technology-mediated communication extends throughout the modern network enterprise, providing synchronous and asynchronous modes of information exchange. As bandwidth and technical maturity increase, these modes are beginning to extend to remote personal interaction through telepresence and virtual space integration.

This chapter will examine the value of collaborative solutions, as well as introduce many technologies that are already present and a few that are currently emerging. While reviewing this information, keep in mind the groups and roles in your organization. Collaborative technologies provide a ready means to control, coordinate, communicate, and integrate the business structure through directed alerts, shared workspaces, and other modern versions of the gong and banner.

The Value of Communication

Wolves howl in order to coordinate movements of the pack across many miles of territory while tracking prey. Armies have used complex horn and drum patterns to control troop movements across similar distances since King Minos's time. Modern warfare solutions are built atop an interwoven mesh of data collection and information distribution channels, in order to make better use of communications to direct participants under the most dire conditions. Fortunately, most organizations will only fight their battles with business rivals or purely electronic attackers, but the need for communication and effective information sharing is just as vital to effective business engagement as for physical conflict.

Communication Systems

Mathematician Robert Metcalfe expressed the value of a communications network as proportional to the square of the number of users of the system. This means that as the number of users increases, the value of the mechanism for communication increases significantly (see Figure 6.1).

David Reed extended Metcalfe's law to include social networks, noting that the value of a social network contains all possible channels of communication for the primary group as well as those present within each possible subgroup. This value is the foundation for social networking sites such as Facebook and MySpace—the more connections that can be expressed in a social network, the greater will be the level of communication and community that results from participation.

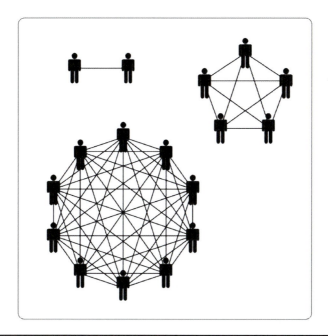

Figure 6.1   Metcalfe's law states that the value of a means of communication increases significantly as the number of users increases.

Note: MySpace, Facebook, and blog entries are sometimes used by employers when evaluating applicants for suitability within the organizational framework. Because of the way Web content is cached and may be copied elsewhere, caution is appropriate when posting to such venues. It is not always possible to take back what has been posted for online consumption, because that information may have been copied, referenced, or otherwise transferred to other locations.

Social networking may even compromise privacy through alternative channels, such as when a third party tags a photograph with a user's identification in a way that will be visible to others. This type of cross-identity exposure can create very negative results, as in the case of the Olympic athlete tagged in a photograph of him performing an apparently unlawful act. Potential for information misuse increases as social networks weaken privacy measures through automated association processes and real-time tracking of current location or locales recent visited.

Network of Trust

Beyond purely social interaction, network solutions such as LinkedIn focus on the professional value of trust created by links between individuals and others they are willing to vouch for professionally. By following the chain of trust from one individual to another, the initial level of expectation and trust between two parties can be greater than when meeting someone without prior introduction. This is akin to the practice of providing a letter of reference, but the chain of trust expressed between members allows a more personally validated level of trust by creating a virtual introduction between the linked parties, illustrated in Figure 6.2.

Collective Intelligence

Social networks exemplify the ability of well-coordinated groups to produce a more effective or efficient outcome than the individuals can produce without communication. A common phrase for this type of synergy is that "the whole is greater than the sum of its parts." Coordinated synergies exist in many forms of collective intelligence, from the selec-

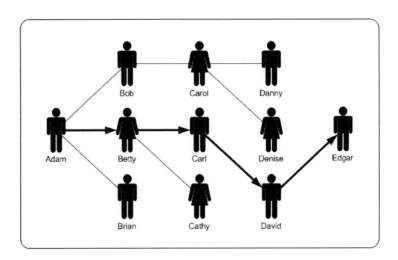

Figure 6.2 Network of trust between Adam and Edgar. Here, David vouches for Edgar, Carl vouches for David, and Betty vouches for Carl. Because Adam trusts Betty, the chain of reference extends through the intervening members to produce a higher level of initial trust for Adam toward Edgar.

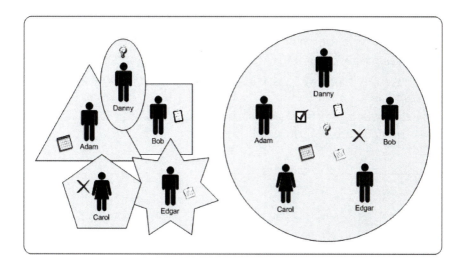

Figure 6.3 Individuals possessing different skills, preferences, and experience can create collective intelligence synergies through coordination and communication.

tion of a 12-person jury for legal evaluation to the implementation of a change control board for project management oversight. These solutions seek to eliminate personal bias and achieve a higher level of reasoning by including multiple viewpoints, skill sets, and bases of experience in the decision-making process (see Figure 6.3), although some concerns exist that collective decision-making processes suffer from domination by the vocal minority and support the status quo over change, so that new ideas may be crowded out by participant majority opinion before consideration is even possible.

The effectiveness of collective intelligence systems will vary based on the level of interaction, coordination, and communication between its members. Technology-facilitated collaborative intelligence is a specific concern for the architect, who has a wide array of tools available for collaborative enterprise solutions.

Communication Technologies

An architect must be familiar with the tools available for communication, collaboration, and virtual teaming within an extended enterprise.

Very small organizations may find simple groupware to be adequate to their needs, while more extensive enterprise solutions may require more robust systems to facilitate mobile, remote business operations. Within these solutions, there exist three primary categories of technology, as seen in Figure 6.4.

Each form of communication balances speed of communication and consensus against disruption and impact on other activities:

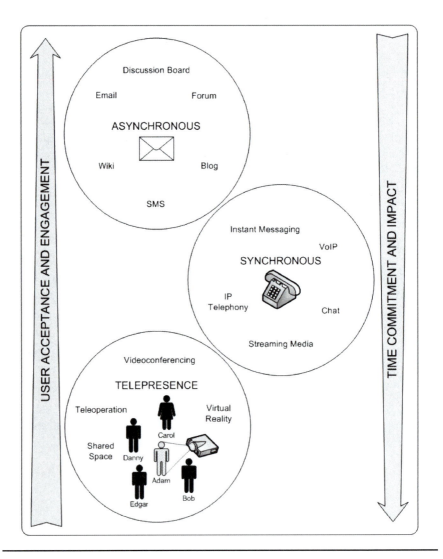

Figure 6.4   Primary categories of communication technology.

- **Asynchronous.** Asynchronous technologies allow participants to engage in communication through delayed response systems. Because users may review, respond, and interact with other members whenever time is available, these technologies have a high level of user acceptance and a low level of intrusion into scheduled activity and operations. These forms of communication are subject to a high degree of latency in transmission, because each participant may not receive a message or respond until time has passed since its initial transmission. Asynchronous communication systems form the communication backbone for operations that are distributed across widely disparate time zones, because participants need not even be awake at the same time in order to conduct an ongoing discussion.
- **Synchronous.** Synchronous technologies require users to coordinate participation, reducing latency at the cost of convenience. Because users are actively engaged in communication at the same time, corrections and amplifications address misunderstandings very rapidly. These technologies experience a lower level of user satisfaction for some users because of the potential for disruption of other activities to attend synchronous engagements.
- **Telepresence.** The most interactive forms of synchronous communication involve the ability for parties to share information beyond simple text or vocal communications. These systems allow groups to share common whiteboards or desktops, engage actively in face-to-face remote video conferencing, and even control and manipulate remote physical systems directly, through tele-operation. On the very edge of technology, some organizations are beginning to blend real-world and virtual world spaces in order to extend services and access to participants who would otherwise be unable to interact with their remote peers. Linden Labs' popular Second Life environment is one such shared-presence venue, allowing real-world and virtual-world interaction in real time. Because these solutions involve technology-mediated face-to-face communication and other forms of direct interaction, they produce the greatest impact on performance and operations, because participants are actively engaged in the communications medium and cannot typically perform other tasks simultaneously, while all communications are dependent on availability and bandwidth availability, which is not necessary for synchronous in-person meetings.

Asynchronous Communications

Asynchronous modes of communication employ store-and-access forms of information interchange. These technologies include standalone applications such as e-mail and Wiki servers, or as components in more complete business groupware solutions that couple functionality such as calendaring and task management with basic messaging, threaded discussion boards and other forms of stored communication. Remote consumers, interested parties, business partners, and internal users may all make use of asynchronous communications to conduct business with an organization—making this one of the most effective means for information transport.

Electronic Mail

Electronic mail (e-mail) is arguably the most prevalent form of electronically mediated communication. The simplicity of its interface, durability of the transport mechanism, and global availability has expanded the once-simplistic means for systems administration staff to pass messages between servers into a near-mandatory component of modern business in a globe-spanning market. The inexpensive nature of e-mail allows businesses to use this means to contact millions of customers and interested parties with little more effort than sending a single message.

Note: At the time of this book's writing, no charge is currently billed per e-mail message except for mobile-device textual Short Message Service (SMS) transfer charges. Many "e-mail tax" solutions continue to be examined, however, and may be imposed in the future in an attempt to limit the volume of unsolicited "junk" e-mail (spam). If a per-message charge is imposed at some point, the architect should have a good grasp of the various uses of e-mail in an organization, in order to ensure that directed and targeted transmission can be isolated from wideband e-mail distribution.

Origins of E-mail

The basic e-mail transport protocol is the Simple Mail Transfer Protocol (SMTP). This standard is an element of the TCP/IP protocol suite that has been extended to include support for file attachments beyond simple ASCII text, sender/recipient authentication, and transport-layer security. Very early forms of e-mail evolved as a means for systems administrators to leave one-another messages, and the SMTP protocol's evolution reflects this origin.

The first e-mail systems operated exclusively within a single mainframe computer, although the development of network connections between mainframe systems was rapidly met by a network-capable version of the messaging system. Because early networking was not always-on, transfer of messages from one node to the next required a messaging protocol able to queue a message for transfer the next time that network connectivity was available. This type of transport is known as "store and forward" transfer. It was also necessary for messages that waited too long for transfer to be reported back to the originator as undeliverable.

Early forms of e-mail did not enjoy the automatic routing provided by the Internet's hierarchical Domain Name System (DNS) and were instead directed from one node to the next by the message sender and system administrators along the transmission path. An early e-mail address might have been: *bob.admin!bobscomputer!joescomputer!bettyscomputer*, so that the message would be sent through each server in turn until it reached its intended recipient. If a node in the specified path remained unavailable, this form of routing could not adapt and redirect through an alternate path.

The SMTP protocol is more robust than the early forms of e-mail routing, allowing an e-mail message to travel along any available route. If a node fails along the path, the previous SMTP server can simply retry along an alternate route, as shown in Figure 6.5.

E-mail in Critical Communications

Electronic mail transfer is very durable and is able to overcome temporary network changes. This same durability, however, affects its use in time-sensitive or content-sensitive communications. Emergency notification systems in particular cannot rely solely on SMTP transport, because durability of transmission does not equate to urgency of delivery. Timeliness suffers in SMTP-based notification systems, requiring additional mechanisms for urgent alert notification.

E-mail is very valuable in providing continuity of operations during disaster recovery efforts or during other times when the workforce is

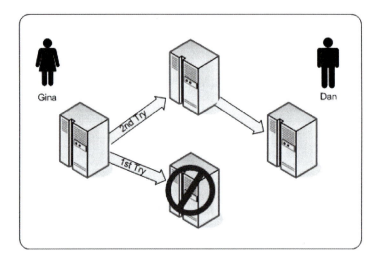

Figure 6.5   When Gina's message to Dan fails on its first attempt, the SMTP protocol can route through an alternate network path to reach Dan's server.

highly mobile. However, access to e-mail relies on many transfers of each message from one server to the next, and an ongoing delivery attempt may take several days before the last SMTP server determines that a message is ultimately undeliverable. During this time, the sender knows only that a message is in transit, and the recipient has no way to know of its pending arrival unless alerted through other means. Additionally, users may only check targeted e-mail addresses on an infrequent basis or may receive such a volume of messages as to obscure an important item in the midst of hundreds or thousands of offers for mortgage rate improvement, physical enhancement, and other forms of common spam.

Note: The term "spam" refers to the electronic equivalent to junk mail. Analysis of network traffic identifies more than half of all electonic messages as falling in this category, with some studies showing this to be possibly as much as 90% of all e-mail or more. The term "spam" was coined from a humorous skit by the British comedy troupe, Monty Python, in which Norsemen kept drowning out the principal conversation by chanting "spam" over and over. The association was made because the volume of unsolicited e-mail has become a problem for servers that must store these messages and for users who must wade through thousands of unsolicited messages to access items with desirable content value. The architect must include planning for filtering, storing, and managing this constant flood of e-mail.

Because e-mail transport may follow any available path, content is vulnerable to interception and possible modification en route to its intended recipient. Sensitive information such as financial or personal data should never be sent using e-mail transport without additional protections to prevent unauthorized access or modification. Encryption and digital signatures are often used to improve the security of information transferred using the SMTP protocol and its derivatives, and the architect should identify areas where these functions are required for business operations.

Because of its durability, the SMTP protocol is also used by some proprietary technologies in order to transfer non-email information between distributed nodes. Almost any form of data can be encapsulated and transferred using the basic SMTP protocol, and architects should identify where these protocols are implemented in order to ensure that e-mail and other SMTP-transport protocol management policies and firewall settings can be maintained and updated separately.

Mailing Lists

A single e-mail message can be redirected to one or more e-mail addresses through an e-mail mailing list application, sometimes referred to as a "listserv" after the popular mailing list application. An e-mail sent to *allusers@somecorp.com* can easily reach all of the e-mail addresses associated with this address by relaying a copy of the message to each member of the mailing list audience. Mailing lists are used for many purposes (see Figure 6.6):

- **Announcements.** Mailing lists can be used for one-way communication to a large audience or other group of e-mail accounts. Typically, access rights to send to these mailing lists are restricted to a single individual or authorized source. Announcements are transmitted in a one-way fashion, with all ReplyTo responses returned to the sender or dropped into a discard folder, depending on the mailing list configuration.

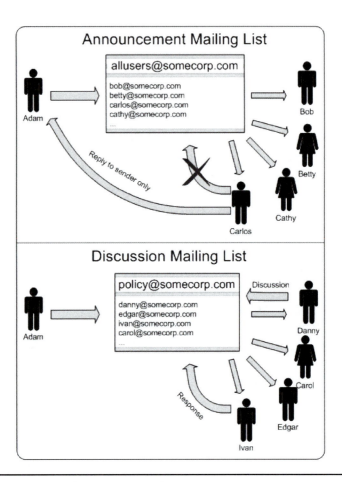

Figure 6.6   Mailing lists can provide one-way announcements or two-way discussion.

- **Discussions.** Some mailing lists allow anyone to send e-mail messages to all recipients. These mailing lists allow discussion among members and may include the ability for outside parties to inject e-mail messages targeted to the included group. Because discussion lists can include two-way communications, they can aid in rapid participation from multiple group members collaborating on a task or project. This quality can also lead to virtual arguments conducted by rapid back-and-forth e-mail messages in what is essentially a public forum. The very ease and speed of e-mail communication, coupled with the emotional anonymity of interaction with technology rather than face to face with another individual, can lead to impassioned arguments termed "flame wars." The architect might consider enacting a mediation function or transmission delay to reduce this potential by allowing a cooling-off period between messages.

- **Moderated lists.** To manage content submitted to a mailing list, particularly discussion lists, a mailing list can be configured for moderation. E-mail messages sent to a moderated list address are forwarded to an assigned moderator, who must approve the message before it is retransmitted to the mailing list audience. This imposes some delay in the relay of e-mail messages and can impose a heavy time cost for the assigned moderator of an active list.
- **Common point of contact**. Lists may also be used to provide a common point of contact, such as *sales@mycorp.com,* which can then relay customer communications to the proper individual recipients. This simplifies routing of communications to targeted operational recipients.

Mailing lists have several advantages over manual transmission of e-mail to a large number of recipients. Through careful planning, an architect can leverage this functionality to target focused audiences both within and beyond an organizational network enterprise. Properly planned and organized mailing lists provide additional advantages as well:

- **Stable contact.** Because the membership of a mailing list is easily changed, mailing lists provide an opportunity to establish standard contact points for an organization's various functions. An e-mail can be sent to a common or easily remembered address such as *helpdesk@somecorp.com* without requiring knowledge of the e-mail addresses of users assigned to helpdesk response. If the mailing list application is capable, e-mail messages sent to the common address will reroute to different groups automatically, based on criteria such as time of day or e-mail source. Point-of-contact lists ensure that key contact operations are not affected by changes resulting from employee turnover, mergers and acquisitions, and disaster recovery requirements.
- **Secure identities.** E-mail messages sent to mailing lists are retransmitted to each audience member without including the addresses of other audience members. Unlike e-mail messages sent manually to multiple recipients, each recipient can reply only to the list itself or

to the original sender. This protects the identity of list membership and ensures that members of moderated groups must reply through the list rather than directly to all members individually.

- **Access mechanisms.** Almost any type of criteria can be used to specify e-mail mailing list membership inclusion, creating both a powerful mechanism for business communication and the source of so many spam messages. Mailing lists can be created by assignment, through elective subscription, or automatically through criteria for automatic inclusion of accounts based on group or role assignment.

- **Assignment.** List management can become very complex and time-intensive without adequate planning and control to maintain and update list assignment. A communications strategy and governance council should be developed early in the planning phase of any enterprise architectural project, to ensure that adequate resources and controls are in place before they are needed.

- **Subscription.** Elective subscriptions can allow users to receive e-mail messages sent to listings created for specific purposes or topic areas, based on their own choice and without requiring action on the part of the central information technology personnel.

- **Automation.** Mailing lists can be automatically populated from database sources to target an audience based on whatever criteria are desired. Recruitment, sales, and customer management functions can automatically target groups of e-mail addresses based on past purchases, location, and other identifying qualities. Operational mailing lists can be populated automatically, with all members assigned to a particular group or role within the organization.

- **Information Archival.** Mailing list archives can provide a rapid means for users to identify responses to common questions or requests. They also create a living history of published communications and announcements, which is automatically updated as new messages are transmitted, improving information access and topic awareness. This body of data should be included as part of the organizational process assets (OPAs) used in future project planning actions.

Tip: Archiving of electronic communications, both asynchronous and synchronous, is a growing issue for enterprise networks. Storage, management, control, retirement, and the ability to provide access to archived communications must be considered during capacity and network planning. Legal subpoenas for communication archives have become more common, as in the case of electronic communications reviewed during the legal actions against Enron. An architect must identify retention mandates, archival policies, access mechanisms, storage requirements, and the legal implications of electronic communications throughout the enteprise.

Because of its pervasive nature, e-mail is the most fundamental and widely accepted—even demanded—means for asynchronous communication within the modern network enterprise. E-mail creates a number of potential security issues and vulnerabilities, however, because the protocol is designed to allow data to enter into a protected network from external sources without requiring specific authorization prior to connection. This offers a potential vector for a directed denial-of-service attack, which can be mitigated somewhat by separating edge-boundary SMTP transport from internal transfer between e-mail accounts within the same server.

Short Message Service

Short Message Service (SMS) is a second form of asynchronous communication that provides information directly to users. The protocols have evolved to transmit short text messages between cellular phones and other types of mobile technology, but have also become fixtures in the modern mobile communications suite and provide directed alerting from security appliances and services outside of e-mail transport that may be under attack and unavailable. The value of these devices is clearly underscored by concerns raised over the possible cessation of the popular Blackberry service during its patent engagement with a rival firm. Emergency services, governmental agencies, and large corporations expressed strong concerns that a termination of the service could have widespread negative effects, due to the vital role SMS messaging can play.

Modern SMS solutions can transmit other media content in addition to textual data. SMS connectivity can also be used for monitoring and telemetry between independent devices and is gaining acceptance in vehicle-tracking solutions along with cellular GPS tracking. Although it is not suited to transmission of sensitive information, SMS solutions are gaining widespread acceptance among emergency responders, following the success of their use in New York at the time of the terrorist attack on the Twin Towers on September 11, 2001.

Twitter

Similar to the SMS short message, Twitter is a particular technological solution that embodies development of immediate-post communication streams. Rather than directing a message to a particular recipient or list, Twitter users can send short text-based messages (called "Tweets") to their own Twitter site. Individuals who subscribe to the sender's Twitter feed are notified of the new message, in essence creating a "bulletin board" type of notification system, with advertisement capability alerting of new content. Underscoring the mass appeal of these systems, individuals have managed to expand their social network to over a million subscribers for a single Twitter feed.

Web Log (Blog)

The Web log, similar to a diary or journal, has become a popular form of social and professional interaction. Web logs, also known simply as blogs, are constructed by the author entering information segments of textual, graphical, or other content that is displayed with the most recent post first. As new content is added, older items are displayed later or archived in order to limit storage consumption (see Figure 6.7).

Blogs are accessed using Internet Web browsers and do not rely on specialized client software applications. This utility provides a ready mechanism for quick notations and other rapid communications to an open or secured forum. Many blogs are publicly viewable, while other may be secured in part or whole so that only registered members or specifically approved members can access Web log content. On social networks, blogs may contain deeply personal information that is often publically shared to any visitor with knowledge of the proper blog URL for access. Other Web logs provide an insight into the actions taken regarding a project or technology solution, creating a Web-accessible repository for testing and development actions.

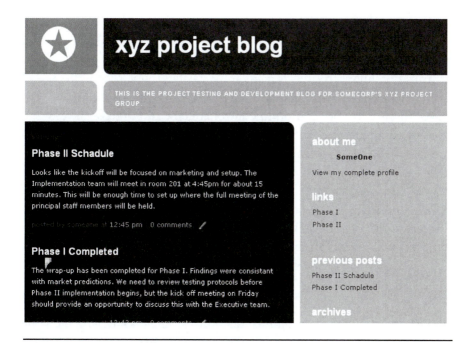

Figure 6.7 Blog for SomeCorp's XYZ Project Group posted by user SomeOne.

Free open-source software (FOSS) and commercial technology implementers, developers, and support communities make extensive use of blogging in order to identify solutions to commonly experienced problems in setup, configuration, or other aspects of implementation. Among development teams, blogs provide insight into the intent of testing and development choices, so that other members of a distributed team can better participate in the overall solution development—a distinct advantage for teams coordinating in geographically distributed or service-oriented development.

Forum

Web logs, handlers' diaries, developers' notes, and many other forms of professional content can be easily maintained using Web logs. However, blogging provides only a one-way mechanism to present information to its consuming audience. To facilitate two-way participation by multiple contributors, forums and electronic bulletin boards provide a medium for information submission and coordination.

These applications allow contributors to read and add content related to a particular topic. Each topic is arranged with subordinate topics, each represented as a specific thread of conversation between participants. This organization allows related threads to be easily grouped, combined, and cross-referenced by participants. Like e-mail discussion lists, forums can be configured for moderation to control content addition, or may be left open to all members of the contributing community.

Like Web logs, forums and bulletin boards are accessible using common Internet Web clients and can be open to all comers or restricted to only a select membership. These solutions have evolved from discussion boards implemented originally on dial-up bulletin board systems (BBS) before the rise of the Internet, and can be found addressing almost any topic from style and fashion to gaming and investment management.

Wiki

Because bulletin boards often include multiple threads covering the same topic area, members may find navigation and review of related items somewhat cumbersome. The wiki is a Web service developed to coordinate collective group topic content contribution by providing a single location for each topic.

Note: The term "wiki" comes from a common term from my homeland. The Hawai'ian term "wiki wiki" means to hurry very quickly. Its first identifiable use as a designation for this means of electronic collaboration was as an exchange of information between programmers, the WikiWikiWeb, created by Howard Cunningham.

Wiki contributors can review, add, edit, and modify content relating to a particular topic or project. This information is cross-referenced to other topic areas within the wiki to build a web of collective information. By harnessing the combined knowledge base of all participants, wikis seek to reach information convergence more rapidly than when individual contributors operate alone to produce documentation or research findings, as shown in Figure 6.8.

Wikis maintain a change history, so information that is accidentally lost or discarded during earlier edits can be returned to the active content

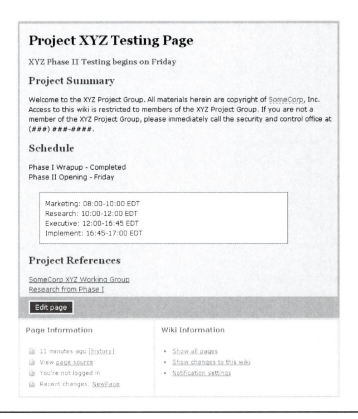

Figure 6.8   Wiki page for the Project XYZ testing group, showing editing controls and change history access.

page. This helps to reduce the impact of open-contribution vandalism and also allows teams to step back to an earlier project state if it turns out that the selected path of inquiry or development does not produce desired results. By rolling back to an earlier state, a project wiki can be used to "reset" research or development projects so that team members can move forward from that earlier familiar point more easily.

Contributions and changes can be made available to any user with an Internet Web browser and network access, or may be limited to approved content editors only. Project and product wikis may be implemented as a part of an organizational intranet, allowing access only within the organizational network. Wikis may be used to coordinate internal policies and guidelines, project development and testing, and almost any other form of community topic management in which the ability to add, edit, review, recover historical information, and cross-reference content is desirable.

Really Simple Syndication

Wikis, forums, and blogs are all very useful in creating content streams and repositories. A version of the newspaper headline is lacking in these modes of communication, which do not provide a rapid mechanism for directing

```
//* Example XML RSS Feed *//
  <?xml version="1.0" encoding="ISO-8859-1" ?>
- <rss version="2.0">
- <channel>
  <title>SomeCorp.com New Products</title>
  <link>http://www.somecorp.com/rss/newproducts/</link>
  <description>New information on the latest SomeCorp products.</description>
  <language>en-us</language>
  <copyright>© 2009 SomeCorp, Inc.</copyright>
  <pubDate>Mon, 01 Jun 2009 15:13:34 EDT</pubDate>
  <ttl>5</ttl>
- <image>
  <title>SomeCorp.com New Products</title>
  <link>http://www.somecorp.com/rss/newproducts/</link>
  <url>http://www.somecorp.com/rss/logo.gif</url>
  <width>144</width>
  <height>33</height>
  <description>New information on the latest SomeCorp products.</description>
  </image>
- <item>
  <title>SomeProduct</title>
  <link>http://www.somecorp.com/rss/newproducts/someproduct/index.html</link>
  <description>New SomeProduct - from SomeCorp.com</description>
  <pubDate>Mon, 01 Jun 2009 12:05:01 EDT</pubDate>
  </item>
- <item>
  <title>AnotherProduct</title>
  <link>http://www.somecorp.com/rss/newproducts/anotherproduct/index.html</link>
  <description>New AnotherProduct - from SomeCorp.com</description>
  <pubDate>Mon, 01 Jun 2009 03:19:06 EDT</pubDate>
  </item>
  </channel>
  </rss>
```

Figure 6.9 Example XML RSS feed.

consumers to only the most recent topics or those within a particular subject area. The concept behind the Really Simple Syndication (RSS) format is to create a method for publishing the electronic equivalent of headlines using the XML data standard. For an example, see Figure 6.9.

An RSS web feed might provide details on hot topics, user-interest stories, or even standard news headlines. Many popular news and information sites publish multiple RSS feeds, each targeted to a specific audience or topic area. Because these feeds provide only limited detail, a user can easily review a large number of potential items to identify those of specific interest for further inquiry. Within an organization, RSS feeds can be used to publish upcoming events, action items, changes to policy, and employee newsletter items.

Although RSS XML data is human-readable, an RSS feed reader client can present headlines for quick review and item access (see Figure 6.10). Clicking on a headline within the feed reader client will initiate a Web browser session with the linked Internet resource.

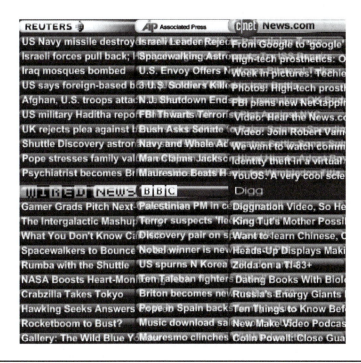

Figure 6.10   Various news source feeds are displayed using simple feed readers on the user desktop.

Podcasting and YouTube

A wide range of Internet Web resources can be published using RSS XML feeds, allowing users to identify topics of interest quite rapidly. This has led to the publication of a wide range of materials and media, by both commercial providers as well as individual hobbyists. Web broadcasters use improved audio compression, higher-bandwidth connections, and the RSS simplified means for publishing links in order to reach consumers with rich-content broadcasts on a wide variety of topics.

Media content is available on demand from many different resource sources, providing personal commentary, technology reviews, online educational course content, and even commercial news broadcasts for download to mobile media players. Podcasting gained its name from the Apple iPod media player, which was popular during podcasting's initial emergence as a means for content publication. Podcasting and the use of shared-media services such as YouTube have become popular ways to provide rich media content to an increasingly mobile audience.

Within an organization, this technology can be used to provide access to audio and video commentary from chief executives, project meetings, and even live events. Commercial and public feeds also include market-watch details, news events, and shows dedicated to emerging security issues and new technologies.

Synchronous Communications

Asynchronous electronic communications have existed since well before the advent of the Internet, in the form of dial-up BBS systems and electronic messaging between systems operators on pre-network mainframe computers. Most of these technologies mirror the functionality of similar physical communication mechanisms, such as mail and bulletin boards, and so are easily accepted by users in the modern workplace. However, they share some of the same issues as their physical-world counterparts, because they lack a live-interaction component between participants.

Synchronous means of communication build more rapid and efficient mechanisms for teamwork and collaboration, because participants can quickly correct misunderstandings or amplify unclear information. Feedback is immediate, allowing convergence of understanding much more rapidly than is possible through asynchronous connectivity. Subtle nuances in language use and inflection can produce enhanced understanding when synchronous systems include voice and video content, while simple chat interfaces and instant messaging allow managers to respond to emerging issues rapidly, without having to miss other events requiring their physical presence.

Instant Messaging

Like e-mail and RSS feeds, instant messaging (IM) relies on a specialized client application that coordinates textual communication between two users acting in real time. Because there is little or no lag in this communication, it is much closer to a conversation than is possible using asynchronous means. Like a face-to-face conversation, similar social conventions are used for IM communications. Users take turns "talking," and most clients display some form of indication to the other party when a user is typing a new entry, so that the discussion does not become too fragmented.

Instant messaging systems make use of a client application at each end of the communication, connecting through a service provider. These systems have proliferated, including commercial providers such as AOL, Yahoo, MSN, and Jabber. Other servers can be implemented exclusively within an organization, such as the popular ICQ service that is commonly implemented for communication between helpdesk staff members.

Instant messaging can provide a means for rapid communication between organizational members, particularly when implemented with some form of state awareness (examples: away, busy, on the phone, available). Instant messaging clients can also be used in an asynchronous manner, akin to leaving a message for someone that will be received when that person is next online. As with e-mail, instant messaging communications may require logging and archival in some enterprises, because of regulatory or legal mandates.

Chatrooms

Chatroom systems extend the instant messaging capability for back-and-forth communication to a larger audience. Typically, these solutions are implemented as Web-accessible systems, although there are enhanced standalone chat clients for enhanced security and integration with webcams and other types of interactive communication. Like forums, chatrooms can be coordinated into topic areas and configured for public or controlled access.

Chatroom systems provide the primary means for real-time social community interaction, and are implemented in many social networking solutions to allow public textual communication between members in real time. Some chatrooms also include voice communication and other forms of media enhancement to improve participant interaction. Enhanced applications of chatroom solutions are employed in distance education, online training, and social network sites, although commercial and noncommercial users worldwide still commonly use the text-only Internet Relay Chat (IRC) system.

Tip: Chatrooms have gained attention as venues for illicit communication and other antisocial behaviors. As a result, chatrooms may gain additional legal requirements for archival and legal discovery, like those imposed on e-mail and instant messaging communications now.

Voice Communication

Improving connectivity and available bandwidth has allowed person-to-person communications to include real-time audio feeds. In chatroom systems, these are used to participate in open-forum or private communications between members with properly equipped systems. Instant messaging clients have been extended to include enhanced voice communication between users as well. This functionality has been extended into fully integrated voice communication systems that replace traditional telephony with telephone-like interfaces operating entirely over TCP/IP connectivity on data networks, such as the Ventrilo group audio service commonly used by online gamers for coordination and communication among participants.

Voice-over-IP (VoIP) systems provide standard telephonic device communication between individuals without requiring telephony service connections or per-call long-distance fees associated with the use of a public switched telephone network (PSTN) connection. A common example of this technology is the popular Skype service, which allows telephony-style audio communication from a Skype-enabled computer or dedicated Skype phone handset.

Because these systems share bandwidth with data communications, care must be taken to ensure that converged data and voice networks do not saturate network capacity both within an organization as well as through its external ISP connection.

Note: Voice-over-IP systems do not provide exactly the same functionality as PSTN connections, even though the appearance and use is very similar. Lack of Enhanced 911 location identification, latency due to Internet routing, and a variety of incompatible VoIP protocols may complicate implementation projects. VoIP should never be the sole means for emergency communications during disaster recovery operations, because the network itself may be unavailable or saturated by traffic generated during denial-of-service or viral attacks.

Streaming Media

The same bandwidth expansion that has allowed voice communications between two parties also allows rich media to be streamed to consumers using standard Internet Web clients. Streaming media services allow Internet access to audio and video content of both live and on-demand content. Organizations may implement streaming media services in order to provide remote access to recruiting videos, rich-media training materials, and archived footage from live events. Live feeds can allow remote participation in public events and meetings, particularly when coupled with remote user response interaction through a simultaneous chatroom interface.

Streaming feeds from webcams are used for a wide variety of purposes, from security to monitoring of meeting-room availability. Feeds can provide managers an easy way to verify employee presence, while external cameras can alert employees to weather and traffic conditions. Highly secured operational environments may even employ outside cameras and interior displays configured as "windows," to allow employees an opportunity to "look outside" without requiring an exposed physical portal.

Shared Whiteboards and Desktops

In addition to media and textual content, synchronous technology can also allow remote participants to share a standard area in which additional content can be added in real time. Taking the name of the popular white drawing board used in organizational and educational settings, electronic whiteboards can be used by participants to present text, images, and hand-drawn details exactly as if all were physically present at the same location and able to access a physical drawing board shared by all. By color-coding each participant's input, managers can more easily identify individual contributions and assess project engagement by all members, even though the team members may not share geolocality or even a standard language across all participants.

Shared whiteboards can be used to allow participant interaction, or as a means for shared presentations using functionality similar to slide shows and overhead projectors, so that the moderator can control who may make notations or amplifications in the display space. When integrated with shared desktop applications, technology and software demonstrations can be conducted remotely in real time without requiring special equipment. Participants may also make use of VoIP or PSTN connections, or chatroom systems, to ask questions and interact with the presenter. Some of these systems allow remote users to take control of the keyboard and mouse input to the remote display desktop, allowing a virtual "test drive" without needing equipment, software installation, or even personnel to be present at the client's site.

Telepresence

By looking for opportunities to leverage remote access technologies, architects can extend opportunities for remote participation, demonstration, and engagement. These synchronous solutions do not come without a cost, because participants must still coordinate time, and network capacity must be adequate. However, the benefits in terms of participation, engagement, and accessibility can provide tremendous value in an increasingly global arena of consumption.

As network bandwidth increases, so too does the volume of information shared among remote locations. The progress of synchronous communications is just starting to reach the level of sophistication necessary for true remote participation. Two-way communications combining voice, data, video, whiteboards, desktops, and other types of information can create a virtual engagement among remote sites in which all participants gain similar advantages to being physically present. This form of electronically mediated participation, known as telepresence, includes everything from videoconferencing to virtual-reality interaction. Telepresence offerings provide opportunities for greater community involvement, as well as substantial cost savings through reductions in travel and lodging costs necessary for physical participation in meetings at remote sites.

Videoconferencing

By transmitting video and audio between two locations, a virtual "window" can be shared between participants. Videoconferencing systems allow organizations to span the globe and still conduct real-time "face-to-face" meetings between key stakeholders without requiring constant travel. Personal videoconferencing systems can be used to communicate directly with traveling staff members and between family members living far apart, using commonly available Web conferencing software and standard IM clients. Videoconferencing systems have also been used successfully for medical diagnosis of patients located in inaccessible or remote locations, and for remote assessment in dangerous or hazardous environments.

Because participation requires little preparation and only minimal specialized equipment, videoconferencing can improve efficiency in an organization by eliminating the time normally spent in travel for physical meeting attendance. Participants can also attend videoconference meetings without concern over local contagions, common workday timing, and all of the other details that make coordinating meetings troublesome over long distances. These systems are widely used in distance education to allow classroom participation by remote or geographically isolated students.

Tele-operation

Remote users provided with the means to control local technologies remotely can participate in a more robust manner than simple videoconferencing. Remote operators have successfully performed training, system management, and even medical procedures. Supervisory control and data acquisition (SCADA) systems allow operators to control large, complex equipment and devices located in geographically disparate or inhospitable locations, including everything from pipeline controls to water treatment facilities and nuclear power-generation systems.

Medium- to large-scale enterprises make broad use of remote management utilities to maintain and support hundreds or thousands of distributed computers. By sharing control of remote desktop interfaces, helpdesk personnel can provide direct user support without requiring a visit to the supported user's location. Virtualized desktops can also protect against potential data loss by retaining all information on a protected system, while the remote console provides only video, audio, mouse, and keyboard interchange. We will review this type of virtualization in greater detail in later chapters.

Virtual Reality

Virtual-reality simulated environments extend tele-operation and telepresence into an environment that exists entirely in the electronic realm. Virtual reality simulations provide an excellent venue for training, entertainment, and social interaction, because the environment can be tailored to meet any desired need. Participants interact with virtual worlds through a specialized client application, which synchronizes the actions of their virtual representation (known as an "avatar") with those of other participants in the electronically generated landscape.

Virtual reality simulators, originally developed for flight training, have also been implemented as law enforcement and diplomatic training systems using specialized virtual simulators. Some chatroom systems implement a simplified virtual space so that avatar proximity can reflect private or public conversation with other participants. Virtual reality systems can provide an environment available to only a single user or to literally thousands of simultaneous users.

Popular multiplayer games support cooperative game play in a shared environment, while educators are beginning to employ virtual environments to allow students to interact directly with the learning environment and with other students. Harvard's River City and the Whyville project shared virtual environments are examples of the application of virtual reality in an educational setting. Educators are also developing classroom labs and training settings using the Second Life University virtual space created by Linden Labs.

A popular coffee shop in New York had a virtual representation fashioned in Linden Lab's *Second Life* virtual world. What makes this interesting is the two-way communications configured between the physical-world coffee shop and its virtual aspect. A webcam and microphone in the physical shop provides information to a wall in the virtual setting, while the virtual world is displayed through a monitor and speakers in the physical setting. Patrons of the coffee shop who travel extensively can "stop by" using their avatars while on the road, sharing in the discussions and other daily events of the shop through this interface. Virtual-only patrons now stop by and take part, occasionally visiting the physical shop when visiting New York. Strangers living in disparate parts of the world become friends, and friends can keep "in touch" wherever they travel.

Current team-building exercises and challenge courses require participants to travel physically to the training location. Virtualized versions of these social environments can be used to develop cooperation, improve participation, and create team bonding experiences without requiring physical proximity. Many opportunities exist for customer interaction, virtual meetings, simultaneous real-world and virtual-world presentations using these newly emerging virtual-reality simulated environments, where literally anything is possible.

Combined Collaboration

Obviously, a wide variety of technologies is available for communication and collaboration in both local and highly distributed network enterprises. Individually, these technologies can provide opportunities for information sharing, group discussion, and other forms of electronically mediated interaction. Linked together into coordinated communication suites, the various elements can create useful synergies.

Groupware

E-mail systems are commonly linked with other functions supporting shared calendaring, task assignment, instant messaging, and document sharing. Such solutions are known as groupware, and include systems such as Microsoft's Exchange platform and Novell's Groupwise. The specific features included in each groupware platform may vary slightly, such as the inclusion of functionality supporting access through Internet Web clients or easy identification of free time for event invitees. These features can greatly extend the availability of messaging resources for mobile users or those who may not always access network resources from the same computer.

The Virtual Office

Groupware solutions have created the concept of a virtual office space. By abstracting communication mechanisms so that users can interact with their peers from any location, organizations can make use of human resources located anywhere in the world. In addition to home-office tele-commuting and off-shoring, this functionality can allow organizations to reach into new territories without the expense and delay required to obtain a fixed physical location. Using a laptop equipped with a cellular data link, staff members can set up shop with full access to centralized resources almost anywhere in the world.

Portals

With so many technologies available to users, an organization may find it necessary to create a central point of contact. Internet and intranet Web portals provide users with a single point of contact that carries both general and personalized content, as shown in Figure 6.11.

Portals and business intelligence dashboards provide information aggregation as well as access to a wide variety of communications mechanisms. Specialized applications can be created and deployed automatically within the portal environment using accepted standards for portlet and Web part construction. Large support communities exist for many portal technologies, increasing the availability of already-tested solutions for common requirements.

In addition to commercial products such as Microsoft SharePoint, Lotus Domino, and IBM's WebSphere Portal, a wide variety of FOSS portal solutions exist as well. Before investing in commercial solutions that fully integrate with user productivity suites, architects should consider creating

Figure 6.11 This portal example was created using Microsoft's SharePoint system for the fictional Contoso corporation.

a test portal using a FOSS solution such as DotNetNuke. This will enable users to provide input on desirable content, interface layout, and content organization while IT support staff members develop policies and protocols for document storage, archival, and information aggregation.

Portals can include many different features, with new functionality easily added through portlet development and database integration. A few of the more common features of enterprise portals include the following.

- **Collaborative technologies.** Enterprise portal solutions include many of the collaborative tools detailed earlier in this chapter. Discussion boards, forums, Web logs, wikis, chatrooms, polls, and messaging components may all be found within an enterprise portal.
- **Personalization.** Personal information, contact details, and links to managers' and subordinates' own portal sites allow the user sites of a portal to replace operational charts and phone lists, which are often out of date by the time they are distributed. This information can also serve to aid in virtual team building, particularly when cultural differences separate individual team members. Information on background, training, education, and other details presented on the public side of a user's site can aid in gaining a more personal level of trust for other team members. Users can also arrange many items

within their portal interface in order to place elements to suit their specific preferences.

- **Information feeds.** Channels of information, portlets, alerts, and other functionalities can be targeted to a specific group of users or available for portal user subscription. RSS feeds, podcasts, links, and action items can provide information to users based on their organizational roles, personal preferences, or duty assignments. Access restrictions can also be placed on certain feeds, so that only authorized members may have access within the portal environment.

- **Content management.** Information presented in portals can be highly customized to meet requirements for specific audiences or based on specified criteria such as time of day or day of the year. Many portals include functions supporting information creation, approval, version control, and publishing schedule. When integrated with other messaging functions, a new announcement can be authored by a contributor, the portal alerts an editor about the pending approval, and the approved content is published on specified days only, while users subscribing to alerts in that area receive notification of a new item in their area of interest. This type of content management and integration makes portals much more efficient for information expression than simple static websites, whose content must be changed directly.

- **Document control.** In addition to content management, many portals include document sharing and version control mechanisms. These systems allow collaborating users to check out documents so that only one editor makes changes at a time, as well as allowing participants to roll back to a previous version of the document if desired. Some portals also include robust workflow engines that can automatically perform notifications or other functions based on content in a document or data in a form. Because portals are designed for remote access through Internet Web clients, documents stored in a portal are more accessible to remote users than those stored on file servers and local system storage devices.

- **Navigation.** Beyond simple aggregation of information, portals also support access to a flood of options through site navigation and search functions. By searching an entire portal or a particular site area, users can rapidly identify content of specific interest—and will see only matching items for which they have been granted access. Navigation between portal sites can also provide a more readily available body of data, which can be cross-linked and referenced within any hierarchical structure appropriate to an organization's needs.

- **Authentication.** By leveraging a portal's built-in authentication and access control systems, developers can create portal applications without having to create their own access control systems. Many portals extend this authorization through a single sign-on (SSO) system, automatically providing additional authentication details to secondary data sources. This functionality allows portals to aggregate information and access components from within other authentication boundaries, improving the transparency of data access and value as a single point of contact for all organizational functions.

Educational Portals

Portals may also include features such as user assessment and training materials, leveraging the power of the portal to train users in its own use or for other training purposes. Portals can serve as robust training environments, including content presentation and user response coordination. Many distance education solutions use portals to coordinate classroom participation, discussion, and project management.

Business Intelligence

In addition to information aggregation, portals provide a mechanism for knowledge management and collective decision making. Decision support systems, balanced scorecards, and other forms of information analytics can be presented as customized portal applications and coordinated dashboards. By properly configuring thresholds, executives can see at a glance whether their department is all green or whether there are urgent issues requiring attention. Through item drill-down, a specific alert can be rapidly identified and dealt with. Similarly, individual employees can be alerted to new action items or projects that are nearing key milestones using customized business intelligence elements. Because the uncontrolled flood of information can rapidly become unmanageable, dashboards and other business intelligence solutions can turn the portal into a robust window into an organization's entire operation. This requires careful planning, as well as capacity management and access control.

Beyond the Boundary

The many forms of electronic communication benefit an organization, but without careful planning and control, they can also create impediments to operational requirements. Remote access to documents may require specific controls on content availability or encryption requirements for accessing devices, while overly antagonistic discussions boards may require moderation. Attempts to pour every possible element of data onto a user's portal interface can rapidly obscure any value present in the data through sheer volume overload. Planning for summarization using dashboards or other controls is essential to making complex information available for rapid review and assimilation. These technologies represent opportunities for growth in new areas for some organizations, while others may find themselves relying on videoconferencing and remote access simply to sustain operations in the event of a transportation halt or a widespread pandemic.

Summary

The very nature of communication technologies mandates that their planning and coordination be included in any form of enterprise architecture. Although we may have put aside the drum and the gong, communication is still necessary to keep everyone's eyes and ears focused on the same goal. After considering authentication and access control, the architect must consider all collaboration solutions before moving forward. Many communication solutions will be used during the project planning and implementation phases, so these must be established as early as possible in the planning phase of an architectural project.

In this chapter, we have identified common communications mechanisms that may be present in a modern enterprise environment, as well as groupware aggregations of these communication streams. The enterprise architect must consider not only the current systems in use, but also emerging solutions whose inclusion may alter resource requirements and access control mechanisms in mid- to long-term enterprise strategic planning.

Chapter 7

Storing Information

In This Chapter

- An examination of file storage mandates in an extended enterprise environment
- Considerations for storage policy planning
- Examination of the need to plan for data storage management through end of life and disposal

Calculating mechanisms have existed for centuries, from the venerable abacus to Charles Babbage's difference engine. The Antikythera mechanism was an analog computing device dating from early Greek culture. Calculating mechanisms such as these were limited by the inability to access programmatic information and store results for later processing. Joseph Jacquard is credited with the earliest recognizable form of automated machine programming, having created a loom that could adapt color patterns based on a series of hole-punched cards passing through the loom. Earlier paper-tape looms required manual tape entry, as would many more recent reel-to-reel forms of magnetic storage.

Although Jacquard's loom was not technically a computing device, his system of punched cards was adopted in early electronic computing devices to store and input reusable programmatic code. Paper punch cards gave way to paper tape, magnetic media, optical storage, and newer mechanisms with increasing storage density and greater access speeds. Gordon Moore is credited with the famous Moore's law, which identifies an effective doubling of computing power every 18 months. Mark Kryder is credited with an extension to Moore's law explaining the doubling of storage on roughly the same 18-month cycle.

This chapter focuses on data storage solutions and techniques for dealing with Kryder's law in the modern enterprise network, where terabytes of data can be found on individual desktop computers and multigigabyte flash drives are embedded in phones, watches, pocket knives, and even coffee mugs. Rich content media and expanding databases mandate careful planning so that capacity remains ahead of demand, with a watchful eye toward security and recoverability.

Everything in Its Place

The earliest personal computers had 4 kilobytes (4k) of RAM and were loaded using audio tape recorders. A 4k program such as *Haunted House* took only 15 minutes to load—assuming everything worked just right. Hard drives have existed for some time, storing electronic data in large disk packs that were once mounted manually into drive systems the size of small refrigerators. The times before that are dark indeed, when data was stored on magnetic tape reels that required large, carefully controlled storage areas and huge reel-to-reel systems for media access and storage.

Looking farther back, paper tape reels and punch cards were the medium of programmatic data input. At 40 bytes per card, a single 3-minute MP3 file would have taken up 75,000 punch cards; and if a card jammed halfway through the file input, all cards to that point would have to be collected and resorted before replacing the damaged punch card and starting the input process again. I can well remember the excitement of completing an entire program and data set on punch cards, submitting the run to computer technologists who then went into sealed, chilled areas to feed my hard work into hoppers to processed data into early mainframe systems. This was typically followed by the disappointment of being told that card #4031 had jammed in the reader and needed to be re-punched (and re-sorted along with cards #0000 through #4030 that were jumbled together in the output hopper).

File Storage

File size has expanded to meet the growing capacity of computing systems, storage devices, and transmission mechanisms. Individual overhead presentation files commonly include embedded media content and graphics, while databases swell to massive proportions as data warehousing and data mining systems attempt to coordinate information and transactional data compiled from millions of objects. Streaming media and on-demand entertainment systems can send hours worth of audio and video content in a single transmission, all of which must be stored for consumption at merely human rates of review.

With multigigapixel still-image and digital high-definition video cameras embedded in cell phones and watches, image data alone has expanded enormously—and all of it may be automatically uploaded to file servers when users synchronize their iPhones with their desktops. The proliferation of rich content can choke older storage systems unless care is taken in planning expansion and availability updates to meet requirements that so far have seen no upper limit in file size and complexity. Nowhere is this more clearly evident than in research and health care networks, with radiographic and photographic images extending resolution to microscopic scales in an environment in which loss of resolution is simply not an option and availability can literally be a matter of life and death.

Logging

Legal mandates such as HIPAA and Sarbanes-Oxley include requirements for access logging and log archival for multiple years. At the same time that such requirements are being implemented, the sheer volume of information available for logging is expanding. Always-on, high-bandwidth connections allow for constant connections by both local and remote users, while service-oriented and distributed processing architectures mandate process tracking in real time. E-mail and instant messaging traffic may also require logging and archiving to meet regulatory statutes and retention mandates—and every item of spam and *LOL* text message can take up space for years.

Logging and archival storage systems can seriously affect performance and storage throughput, while extending capacity requirements by an order of magnitude or more. The architect must always balance regulatory and operational mandates against the maximum amount of data that can possibly be logged and maintained. Logged information is a two-edged sword, in that it can be legally subpoenaed as evidence but consumes network, CPU, storage, and media resources faster than a college student with a gigabit line straight to the campus DVD collection.

It is very important for the architect to identify meaningful data to be logged and stored, because logging cannot be performed after the fact. If an attack has already occurred, turning on network access logging will do as much good as letting horses out of their stables after the barn has already burned down.

E-mail

E-mail presents one of the most volatile data storage requirements in a network enterprise. This information, which is vital to operational control and communications, must be available at a moment's notice yet be protected against viruses, spam, and unauthorized access. E-mail messages can contain attachments of additional content, from funny background images of ducks and bunnies to viral programs or architectural diagrams. Without imposed per-message size limits, entire movies can be attached to individual e-mail messages. If someone e-mails a copy of the latest company picnic video to *allstaff@somecorp.com*, the storage requirements can skyrocket in a moment's time as a thousand copies of the video flood into the mail server's file storage.

E-mail can originate both locally and remotely, or it may be destined for other locations and remain resident on an SMTP host only long enough for its next route to become available. Individual organizations may receive millions of e-mail messages every day, consuming huge amounts of storage just to facilitate e-mail processing queues. Individual users may also decide to keep interesting messages ("interesting" often meaning "all messages ever received") until the end of time, causing a never-ending cycle of continually accelerating storage expansion as file sizes continue to grow according to Kryder's law.

Repositories

A similar cycle of expansion affects user file storage, nowhere more so than in file repositories that allow for version control and recovery.

Individual files can take up storage capacity quickly, but storage within a versioned file repository can expand fantastically when each version of a saved file is maintained separately. Portal systems that include document management features for version control provide a much more versatile mechanism for collaborative communication than simple shared folders with a single copy of a living document, at the cost of a vastly expanded storage requirement to store new copies of a file every time the file is checked back in or changes are saved. Similarly, file storage that includes automated backup and recovery options must also include adequate storage to meet whatever recovery threshold an organization establishes. The longer the backup recovery period maintained (say, up to two weeks back versus up to a month back), the finer the resolution for recovery (once an hour versus once a week), and the speed of recovery (full backups each time versus a single full backup and multiple incremental backups) all affect the total storage required for file recovery and disaster recovery support. We will review specific backup solutions later in this chapter.

Virtual Computers

As virtualization mechanisms become more prevalent, the storage requirements for virtual systems and processes continue to grow. Chapter 9 will focus on the benefits of virtualization in the network enterprise, but an architect must ensure that adequate storage capacity is available not only for the virtualized system but also for the source system images, spawned duplicates, differencing files, and other system copies maintained for disaster recovery, testing, and load balancing. Because a virtualized computer is nothing more than a large file, the ease of virtualization can lead to significant requirements for additional storage on virtualization hosts.

Storage Policies

Storage capacity faces a constant threat posed by the ever-increasing flood of information pouring into local and central file stores throughout a network enterprise. Before planning can begin for physical storage requirements, the architect must identify all existing mandates and develop basic data storage policies. It is simply not reasonable for all users to have an open-ended storage quota when connected to a network able to provide continuous streams of new content at a rate of tens of millions of bytes of data every second, 24 hours per day, 7 days per week, 365 days per year. Saving every joke-of-the-day, advertisement, and e-mail from family must also have limits, or an organization will face storage and backup requirements that far outpace even Kryder's predictions.

Scouting the Land

The architect must identify existing storage mechanisms and practices before attempting to create cohesive storage management policies. This practice should be as obvious as the need to survey a physical location before beginning construction of a building, but some information technology planners may attempt to apply one-size-fits-all industry practices or personal favorite storage solution without understanding the impact on resource availability and capacity. The storage survey should include both internal and remote access requirements, with special attention to challenges presented by external partnerships, regulatory mandates, and service-level agreements for disaster recovery time objectives.

The majority of this chapter addresses the various storage technologies and configurations found in the modern enterprise network. An enterprise architect must have at least some familiarity with each, in order to plan for current support requirements as well as future upgrade and expansion. An initial storage survey will also aid in identifying isolated authentication and resource silos that may expose issues of perceived ownership and control so they can be addressed and resolved. Channels of communication and collaboration established during this phase of enterprise planning will also aid in the distribution and review of emerging policies for storage and other operational procedures.

Areas of Interest

Storage management policies cover a wide range of technologies. The architect should have an understanding of each type of technology and its resource requirements. Lacking this understanding, seemingly unrelated processes can negatively impact others and reduce efficiency overall in the storage, transmission, and consumption of data.

Note: Network security practices identify three primary areas of focus, which should be kept in mind when planning resource management configurations. These three areas are referred to by the acronym C-I-A, reflecting the following concepts:

- **Confidentiality**—Ensuring that information is not disclosed through unauthorized access
- **Integrity**—Ensuring that information is not lost, manipulated through unauthorize means, or corrupted
- **Availability**—Ensuring that information is accessible and available for authorized use

Networking

For obvious reasons, network utilization and capacity directly affects resource availability in a distributed environment. Centralized resources, service-oriented architecture Web services, and network applications all depend heavily on network availability for basic operations. Network capacity can also affect local storage access by slowing authentication and access control validation, adding latency between distributed processes, or creating bottlenecks in replication and backup operations.

Identification of slow, intermittent, or demand-only network islands will be useful in planning storage and capacity, as well as future-state network upgrades. Private-address (not publicly routed) networks dedicated to replication, backup, and application-specific connectivity can greatly improve overall performance, reduce bottlenecks, and address network saturation issues by removing this traffic from the production network. Remote and mobile users may also have special connectivity requirements related to the device, service, and application structure consumed during remote access.

Data Storage

It is necessary to develop an understanding of the types of files being stored and managed before attempting to address storage format and organization solutions. User files often make up the bulk of personalized data storage, although the ability to send file attachments in e-mail messages has led to a blending of these personal storage requirements. Static files that do not change often, such as photo galleries and previous-version file copies, take up space without affecting daily backup requirements except when a full backup is required. Shared files and files that are constantly accessed by applications consume storage and backup resources daily, as these files are always changing. Virtual machines exist as very large files that change constantly while under operation.

File Versioning

Automatic file and mail archiving systems can help to distribute the storage load somewhat, but the increasing ability to roll back to previous copies through file versioning can hold multiple older copies of individual files in "active" storage areas. This type of functionality has been present in mainframe operating systems for many years, such as the VAX/VMS architecture that saves a file using a numerical designation for each successive copy. PC-based operating systems have started to enable the same type of versioning control as storage capacity increases, including Microsoft's "Previous Versions" option in workstation operating systems starting with Vista, taken from the Windows Server operating system functionality.

File Repositories

Repositories are very prone to file storage bloat, particularly in shared storage areas where individual changes are retained as full separate file versions within groupware systems. Because portals and other online file repositories store file data within a database system, the impact on overall storage caused by long-term file retention can be masked or hidden by normal database and transaction log expansion. Careful planning is crucial when creating file repositories, to ensure that adequate storage capacity is available to users without creating a bottomless pit of iterative file retention. Database backups involving file repositories can also be larger than file-level backups in operating system file stores, so planning is important to avoid overrunning backup and recovery service levels.

Databases

Databases have become the backbone for many different business applications, from inventory control and accounts receivable tracking to advanced data warehousing and customer-response management solutions. Storing this information and the log of transactional changes requires attention to storage capacity requirements as well as network capacity and availability for authentication, application access, and backup processes. Active Web content, reporting services, XML Web services, and other forms of interconnectivity rely heavily on access to information stored in database solutions, and any plans to move or consolidate these types of file storage systems must be carefully tested to avoid isolating data from its consuming agents.

Log Files

Database transaction logs are not the only form of rapidly changing log files that may be found in an enterprise environment. Many access control logs, including log-on attempts, file and service access, change control, and other forms of information tracking may be mandatory for an organization, depending on legislative and mandated reporting requirements that apply. As an example, HIPAA's patient information access logging extends the storage requirement for access log data to include almost a decade of audit capability, affecting not only capacity and backup planning but also archival and long-term storage practices such as archival media aging and environmental controls.

Organizations that track and mine customer and website navigation data will find that storage capacity as well as log file access speed can greatly affect customer satisfaction. The lead architect planning data center consolidation projects that will affect such systems must balance logging resolution against hardware, software, and networking capacity before making changes or introducing new functionality into the network.

Virtual Servers

Server virtualization is rapidly changing data center organization, leading to tremendous gains in resource utilization ratios while significantly reducing air conditioning and power consumption requirements. We will examine the extension of data center operations to a virtualized state in detail in Chapter 10. In the most simplified view, a virtualized server represents an entire computer, including operating system, applications, storage, and communications stack, all of these elements wrapped into a set of files stored on the virtualization host computer. In most cases, multiple virtualized servers will be supported by a single powerful host system or by a cluster of systems that share a storage area for high availability.

These files are easy to copy, allowing rapid creation of multiple servers using a standard basic configuration, or facilitating rapid disaster recovery by simply starting up a copy of the lost system on another host server. Virtualized systems rely on storage in many ways, and often employ dynamically expanding virtual disks for internal operations. Without coordination, expansion of multiple virtualized disks can rapidly overrun available host storage capacity. Because virtualized systems can include databases, user accounts, and other forms of protected or sensitive digital information, these systems may require specialize handling and storage to meet regulatory demands. This becomes problematic when a single file can easily exceed 100 GB or larger, and any use of the virtualized server will be reflected as a recent change to the entire file set. Backing up virtualized systems can consume available resources quickly if the same strategies for backing up file servers are used for managing virtual host backups.

Rich Media

Raw ASCII text and other basic file types take up very little overhead beyond the actual file content. Modern word processing documents, spreadsheets, and presentation files can include huge amounts of additional information for formatting and rendering as well as image, audio, and active media content. Recent developments point toward 100-Gbit/s networks and 50-TB workstation drives in the near future, in no small part due to the rapidly expanding demand for rich media content.

With streaming audio and video podcasts, dynamically updated webcam feeds, and multigigabyte movie clips embedded in overhead presentations, the mandate for data storage and transfer continues to expand at an accelerating rate. An enterprise architect should develop strategic policies on total user file storage and acceptable file types, but should also remember that these policies must remain living documents in order to meet the requirements of emerging forms of information exchange. Increasing complexity in media, security key data such as biometric measurements, and dynamic presentation content all contribute to a constantly growing need for more space.

Storage Configuration

As enterprise networks become more extensive and well integrated, storage policies must address this evolution to gain increased economies of scale as well as improved resource utilization ratios. Local storage resources (DAS) attached to individual client systems can be aggregated to centralized network storage (NAS) solutions to improve resource availability and backup capacity. Centralized network attached storage solutions can be aggregated into dedicated storage area networks (SAN). Ultimately, distributed file systems (DFS) can aggregate resources of all types into a seamless body of storage accessible through virtualized resource allocations, as seen in Figure 7.1.

High-performance storage solutions such as the GridFTP protocol extend virtual file systems to include storage distributed throughout the enterprise into a large, redundant, temporary file storage area. By accumulating unused space on the local storage devices across a large number of workstations, for example, a huge pool of storage can be created for temporary sup-

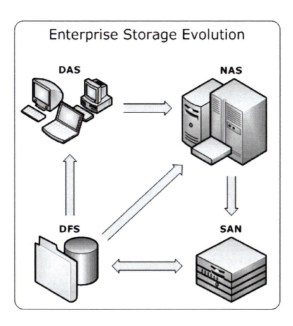

Figure 7.1   Enterprise storage policies can act to aggregate local storage to centralized systems that in turn can be aggregated using dedicated storage networking. Ultimately, all storage resources in an enterprise can be enabled using distributed file solutions and storage virtualization systems.

port of very large data sets. Sufficient redundancy across multiple devices ensures that storage remains viable even in the event of individual workstation reboot or shutdown in these distributed storage systems, although care must be taken to avoid overwhelming network capacity.

Direct Attached Storage (DAS)

The most rudimentary storage configuration involves storage devices and arrays connected directly to a client computing system. This includes both internal and external devices, attached via a wide range of interface technologies. Thin client systems lack extensive direct attached storage, consuming remote resources for storage and operational capacity. Direct attached storage is generally the most difficult to expand, due to hardware constraints on the maximum number of drives that may be connected.

Network Attached Storage (NAS)

Backup and access audit control can be greatly improved by relocating data to centralized networked storage locations and dedicated network attached storage devices. This is the first step towards a coordinated enterprise storage solution, and requires careful planning to ensure that adequate resources and connectivity are present for all consuming client systems. NAS solutions should be considered when planning migration from client to centralized server storage if an intermediary storage solution is required before a central data entry storage system can be fully implemented. Placing network attached storage arrays at departmental-level data closets can begin the process of data abstraction from DAS standalone configurations.

Storage Area Network (SAN)

Unlike network attached storage solutions, which use software and hardware to provide networked resource access across standard network interconnectivity, a storage area network employs specialized high-performance network transport protocols and dedicated network connectivity to aggregate storage and consuming systems into a more cohesive high-speed mesh. SAN solutions allow greater control over resource allocation and management, thus facilitating data center storage consolidation efforts. SAN solutions should be considered for consolidation and when very-high-density servers preclude large direct attached server storage arrays. Many blade server implementations include SAN elements for storage aggregation and provisioning external to the high-density server blade chassis. Organizations with sufficient networking capacity and through-put can integrate SAN storage pools and host agents across numerous well-connected locations, allowing enterprises to take advantage of sepa-rate cooling efficiencies for server data and data storage centers.

Distributed File Systems (DFS)

Distributed file systems allow access to storage resources through access virtualization. By aggregating storage capacity on DAS, NAS, and SAN elements of the enterprise, DFS solutions allow the highest resource utili-zation fraction possible. Managed by both software agents and dedicated hardware, DFS solutions also allow transparent data replication and pref-erential resource access based on connectivity, security, or other architec-tural factors. In addition to capacity aggregation, storage virtualization also allows transparent media substitution. As an example of this func-tionality, virtualized hard drive–based storage systems can be accessed using standard tape storage access protocols and tape-aware backup appli-cations as if they were connected directly to a tape media device.

External Interaction

In addition to virtualized distributed storage solutions, other file system constraints can affect storage policy planning in extended enterprise net-works. Authorization systems may be integrated with file and share-level access control, requiring logical network proximity to authentication ser-vices and adequate connectivity to ensure availability. Encrypted file sys-tems may be required for mobile devices, or in solutions storing sensitive or protected information. Point to point transport encryption and other forms of data protection may also be mandated by legislative controls or operational guidelines, requiring segregation of certain bodies of data or transport control limitations that must be included in storage policy development and data center planning efforts.

Interface Technologies

Before storage policies can be developed, the architect must identify existing interface technologies being used for data storage. Rather than differentiating different types of data storage (such as optical versus magnetic), the interface format each storage device uses affects which devices may be physically aggregated and the rate of data transfer possible for each. These interface solutions may be configured for parallel or serial data transfer, making use of local or network-capable transfer protocols.

Parallel ATA (PATA)

Modern parallel ATA (PATA) storage devices evolved from earlier modified frequency modulation (MFM) and run length limited (RLL) interfaces and include technologies such as the common integrated development environment (IDE) interface. PATA devices are almost always found in client computer systems rather than in servers, which employ serial attached storage devices for higher transfer rates and resource aggregation. PATA devices may be connected directly to a controller channel, or they may be configured to share connectivity, with two or four devices per channel in some cases. Although PATA devices require no path terminator, they may be configured for dedicated master/slave relationships to set device preference and boot order. These devices employ parallel data paths, requiring wide cables that are unsuited to long distances and that can increase thermal control issues in a data center environment.

Serial Attached Storage (SAS)

Data center server systems often employ serial attached storage solutions such as small computer system interface (SCSI) and serial ATA (SATA). These technologies allow for higher signal throughput and greater access speed. The SCSI interface has multiple versions that are not directly compatible, as they vary in signal and voltage standards. Care must be taken when planning SCSI storage consolidation to ensure that all devices in a stack follow the same standard.

SCSI devices can be connected in series, typically with up to seven devices per channel, and require a terminator to identify the end of the signal path. Because serial signals can be transmitted over long distances,

SAS installations can have cable management issues in crowded data centers when cabling is extended between widely separate storage devices. Storage policies and data center standards must be established to limit this potential source of difficulty.

Serial advanced technology attachment (SATA) devices have replaced many older interfaces such as integrated drive electronics (IDE) and SCSI as the standard in both personal computers and data center storage arrays, because each device enjoys a dedicated high-speed serial data path connected directly to a control channel, allowing for "hot swap" replacement and configuration without path termination. The narrow cable medium for SATA connectivity also allows for improved thermal management over older, ribbon cable interfaces.

ATA over Ethernet (AoE)

Serial ATA protocols are also being extended to allow connectivity between devices using standard Ethernet transport. Networked storage devices using this protocol do not require specialized interface cabling between the storage repository and a consuming system, only standard Ethernet connectivity. Because this standard does not employ the full TCP/IP stack, AoE transport cannot share public routed Ethernet transport and requires a separate data-only network. This technology is not in wide use, but it may be found where wide-bandwidth network storage protocols are too expensive or when evaluating the potential for storage area networking before purchasing iSCSI or Fibre Channel hardware.

iSCSI

The Internet SCSI (iSCSI) standard is a robust TCP/IP-based storage area network protocol that is common in small to mid-sized data center SAN solutions. It allows SCSI connectivity across TCP/IP transport. It is slower than a similar-speed Fibre Channel storage networking because of the overhead imposed by the TCP/IP abstraction process, but iSCSI is an effective alternative to Fibre Channel SAN networking. Dedicated transport endpoint acceleration can aid throughput for an iSCSI storage network, though network saturation and transport latency can limit the effectiveness of the acceleration.

Fibre Channel

Fibre Channel connectivity, the standard for enterprise storage area networking, allows high-bandwidth connectivity between storage and consuming devices. Fibre Channel connectivity employs wide-area network (WAN)-type protocols for rapid data transfer, requiring host bus adapter (HBA) connections on each device and specialized SAN-aware applications for backup and resource management. Fibre Channel connectivity can be arranged as a point-to-point connection, in an arbitrated loop configuration, or in a switched fabric that allows large-scale integration of multiple storage and consuming devices.

The theoretical device limit in switched fabric installations exceeds that of other SAN solutions by a wide margin, allowing more than 10 million unique port designations within a single fabric. Fibre Channel protocols have been extended to include TCP/IP-based transport (Fibre Channel over IP and iFCP), though these derived protocols carry similar limitations to iSCSI storage area network transport methods due to the TCP/IP abstraction overhead.

Data Protection

Because of its value to the modern enterprise, stored data represents a vulnerable business asset in need of constant defense and protection. Confidentiality must be addressed by transport and storage security measures, access control systems, and other mechanisms we will examine in greater detail later in this book. Integrity relies on adequate change controls and fault-tolerant storage technologies. Availability requires all of these factors, in addition to adequate capacity for storage access and network transport. When one or more of these factors fails, an effective backup strategy becomes a critical factor for continuity of operations.

Backups

As enterprise storage capacity increases, so too must the capacity of any backup solutions used to capture point-in-time copies of important data stores. Application-specific backup solutions may be required to facilitate fine-resolution item recovery from within large databases, e-mail stores, or file storage areas. Other backup mechanisms can duplicate entire storage areas, even creating a copy of all system parameters needed for bare-metal recovery in the event of total hardware loss. Virtualized server recovery extends this capability to a hardware-agnostic level of abstraction, allowing recovery of virtualized systems to any other platform running the same virtual hosting protocol by simply copying the necessary virtual system files to a new host and reactivating the virtualized server.

Media Retirement

Storage media is only pristine until it has been used to store actual data. Once this has occurred, it may be repeatedly reused, overwritten, and erased, but it will never again be entirely free of all traces of the information that was stored in it. Because this information has value as an asset, and may represent a liability if accessed by unauthorized means, its eventual retirement must be included in storage policy planning.

Media Erasure

Because file deletion and even drive reformatting may only remove file storage entries, secure erasure should be the minimum standard for retired media. Secure erasure utilities employ successive overwriting of data, using all 1's, all 0's, and random information to effectively eliminate or mask previously stored magnetic data. Very powerful magnets may also be used to saturate the magnetic media, erasing not only the surface data but also randomizing magnetic potentials deep within the media substrate as well. The latter method of erasure requires dedicated equipment, but it can be performed on drives that no longer operate. Erasure of rewritable optical media can also be performed through secure overwriting, though the chemical changes used to write information can still be used to reconstruct overwritten information from discarded media.

Physical Destruction

A better solution for optical media involves physical destruction of the media itself. While some shops may use a microwave oven to destroy the metallic layer on optical disks, this yields incomplete media destruction and releases noxious gases that present a health risk. A better solution for optical media involves cross-cut shredding through a device rated for optical media destruction. This same technology works well when destroying floppy disk media, though removable semirigid magnetic media such as Bernoulli drive storage platters may require more rigorous destructive measures. Certain highly secure environments go so far as to require physical destruction through a grinding process, with even the resulting dust then stored in a plastic suspension and the resulting material protected against physical access. This may be well beyond the security requirements of most enterprise networks, but it remains an effective concept for media retirement in high-security environments.

Because electronic data storage technologies can retain residual information markers, retiring flash drives should also include media destruction when possible. Physical destruction of hard-drive devices is more difficult, making high-powered magnetic erasure a more popular option, but destruction is possible when dealing with media used to store protected information, trade secrets, and other data of a highly valuable nature.

Note: While some administrators may find it enjoyable to attempt media destruction at the local rifle range, penetration damage may not fully protect against unauthorized data disclosure, even though the results may appear spectacular.

Summary

Like children, enterprise data storage requirements continue to grow daily. As network bandwidth and storage capacity expand, so too do the formats and types of information made possible by the enhanced availability. Mark Kryder's observations ring true when measured against the 10,000-fold increase in data storage that has occurred over the past decade, with technologies in prototype able to extend the same rate of growth into the foreseeable future. Through careful planning and storage policy development, the architect can ensure that this growth is met with adequate capacity and ready management mechanisms.

In this chapter, we have reviewed many of the options for storage and some policies that may need to be put into place to manage the ever-growing body of information produced and consumed by the enterprise. Individual entities may have special requirements for storage and retention, due to legal or functional mandates. The enterprise architect must take these into account in planning for the entire data storage lifetime, to ensure that data is maintained in a secure, available format and properly eliminated at end-of-life to avoid undesirable exposure.

Chapter 8

Making Connections

In This Chapter

- An examination of the evolution of Web technologies
- Considerations for search and availability
- Identification of varying types of networking that may be present

I was recently contacted via instant messaging by a reader of one of my certification-related texts. We discussed the certifications he was working toward and possible avenues for progress in his professional development. During this discussion, we also talked about the weather, recent news events, and other details that allowed a fair degree of comfort in our communication. This conversation is otherwise unremarkable save that neither of us spoke the other's language—he speaks only Portuguese, whereas I speak only English fluently. By avoiding colloquialisms and idiomatic terms, we were able to hold a lengthy discourse though technology-moderated translation software that is freely available on the Internet. Using simple sentence structure and reflecting information back to one another, we were able to converse while ensuring that the translation packages were yielding an effective avenue for communication—using the Internet as an automated "Rosetta stone" to bridge our separate languages.

Development of the globe-spanning Internet has created opportunities to address a worldwide marketplace, to foster virtual communities, and to bridge geopolitical and linguistic barriers that once kept peoples from one part of the world isolated from their peers elsewhere. This chapter focuses on the use of Internet technologies to build communities and value in the extended enterprise. The use of portals, intranets, extranets, and shared virtual environments pose opportunities, challenges, and new mechanisms for community development in an increasingly geographically distributed workforce. Services built in this environment have the potential to reach thousands or even millions of users from all corners of the world.

What Came Before

Leonard Kleinrock, a researcher at MIT, published his doctoral thesis, "Information Flow in Large Communication Nets," in 1961, which established the fundamental process of data transfer and routing between interconnected computing systems. In 1963, a sociologist named Ted Nelson, working on creating a user-friendly computer interface coined the term "hypertext" to refer to embedded links between two textual elements. Following the Russian launch of the *Sputnik* satellite in 1957, the U.S. Advanced Research Projects Agency (ARPA) was formed and given tasks including research into command and control uses of computers.

By the end of 1969 the early ARPA Network (see Figure 8.1) was in place, and sharing of data between research nodes had begun. During the 1970s and early 1980s, the ARPANET project defined internet working protocols for voice and data communication, including TCP/IP (Transmission Control Protocol/Internet Protocol) and Packet Radio Network (PRNET).

As the ARPANET was extended, user communities emerged between system administrators, starting with the USENET user's group. Multiparticipant virtual environments also emerged at the end of the 1970s, with the introduction of early text-based Multi-User Dungeon (MUD) gaming environments. By 1981, combined transfer services including e-mail, listserv, and directed file transport were available for BITNET clients (BITNET was an early research network originally created between CUNY and Yale and later expanded to other universities), while military

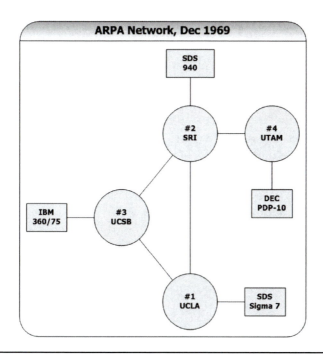

Figure 8.1   Early four-node ARPA Network, circa 1969.

network components had been removed from ARPANET and transferred to the separate but also IP-based MILNET.

The 1980s provided the introduction of the Domain Name Service (DNS), allowing human-readable computer names to be resolved automatically to routable numeric IPv4 addresses. Availability of personal computers and dial-up modems saw the development of bulletin board services, creating pools of communication between private citizens instead of only between governmental and educational sites. During this same time, the National Science Foundation created the NSFNET to link multiple countries throughout North and Central America, Australia, and Europe.

The early 1990s produced services designed to search and access resources across multiple remote computer systems, including the WAIS and Gopher services. Meanwhile, MIT professor Sir Timothy Berners-Lee established interconnections between systems using the new HyperText Transport Protocol (HTTP) and established what he called the "World Wide Web." Researchers at the U.S. National Center for Supercomputing

Applications (NCSA) developed Mosaic (see Figure 8.2), the first graphical user interface (GUI) with widespread distribution.

The mid-1990s saw the emergence of Internet talk radio, the first gopher space search tool (Veronica), and early examples of Internet telephony. Since that time, the world has seen an explosion of services that bring together extensive communities of users who no longer need to share geolocality in order to participate in shared online events. Fiber optic, satellite, and other forms of data interconnection technologies now connect almost all parts of the world into a unified whole, allowing commerce and productivity to reach everywhere. E-mail can be sent from polar research stations, and astronauts can Tweet while in low-Earth orbit (LEO), extending the Internet beyond the boundaries of the planet. When mankind reaches outward to the moon and beyond, the same solutions can be extended to include asynchronous communications with the same facility as my conversation across the world.

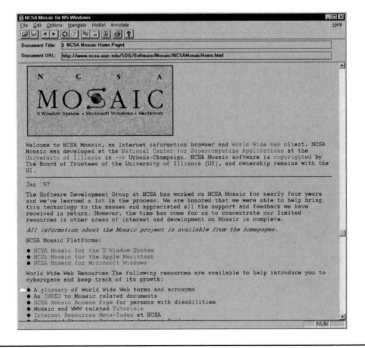

Figure 8.2   Early example of the MOSAIC version 0.6 graphical user interface. (Courtesy of NCSA/University of Illinois MOSAIC image archive.)

Note: As an example of the extended community reach of the Internet, the international youth World Organization of the Scout Movement has conducted a World Scout Jamboree On The Internet (JOTI) since 1996, including thousands of Boy Scouts, Girl Scouts, and Explorer Scouts from countries on all continents save Antarctica.

The World Wide Web

The TCP/IP-based ARPANET became the common Internet link between research institutes, businesses, and individuals at home. The World Wide Web (WWW) soon lived up to its name. Today, many telephones have Web browsers and client applications that offer a rich panoply of media and services anywhere. Because of this expansion, the governance of the Internet has grown into an international matter, leaving U.S. government control in 2009.

Recent developments include the use of non-English-language character sets for domain naming and the rapid extension of the original hierarchical namespace of .com, .gov, .edu sites. The evolution of the WWW is considered to have occurred in several stages, marking the evolution of content, availability, and offerings.

Web 1.0

The earliest WWW expression included static content pages, similar to physical publication of information. Web 1.0 pages were often unchanging and rapidly outdated. Visitors to Web 1.0 pages generally had no mechanism for modifying or adding to the content presented. The Web 1.0 spectrum of applications and proprietary information interchange maintained a balkanization of early WWW efforts, separated into pools of vendor-specific or browser-specific offerings.

Web 1.0 technologies were often tied to software licensing that prevented development of complementary applications without paying for access to APIs and proprietary standards. The Graphics Interchange Format (GIF) image compression that was popular with CompuServe users in the late 1980s is a perfect example of this, where issues over software patents caused the emergence of the newer Portable Network Graphics (PNG) standard.

Web 2.0

The World Wide Web 2.0 extended earlier work without displacing it, including active content, user interactivity, and a more tailored interactivity suited to a personalized consumption of data. Read-only content was transformed into community-developed content in Wikis, together with shared communication in blogs, threaded discussion systems, and community portals (see Figure 8.3). Communication streams ceased being pull-only content accessed by directed action, evolving instead to push-form alerts and announcements from subscriptions in Twitter, friends in Facebook, or reputation referrals in LinkedIn.

Web 2.0 technologies include all of Web 1.0's capabilities but allow consumers opportunities to tailor their information feeds and to search more efficiently using large data aggregation engines such as Google, Bing, and AltaVista. This is the realm in which my conversation with the Portuguese individual becomes possible, because Web 2.0 technologies facilitate user-responsive data expression and a more interactive environment for interchange.

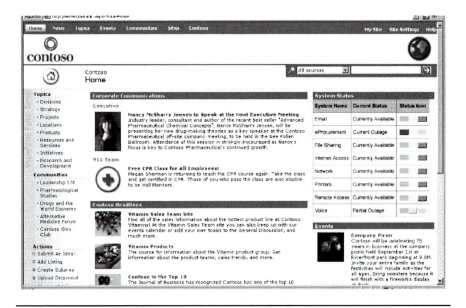

Figure 8.3 Sample information portal presenting dynamic content from the fictional Contoso corporation.

Web 2.0 marks the evolution of more fully integrated access solutions. The "browser wars" of Web 1.0 fame calmed, as proprietary formats gave way to open standards. This is not to say that Silverlight versus Flash arguments have left the IT shop, but users today can make use of both as they choose.

Tip: When building Web-based solutions, it is best to pick a standard methodology and avoid content that involves downloading unfamiliar add-ons. Many forms of malware use this technique, and an increasingly sophisticated consumer base is wary of downloading additional applications to view content. Common add-ons include familiar Flash players and Adobe PDF readers. A custom-built applet called "FriendlyCursor-Manager" might easily be mistaken for adware like the old Gator Corporation (now Claria) suite offerings (eWallet, GotSmiley, Screenscenes, etc.), spamware, or worse. Clients revisit sites with active, updated content that they trust. Alerts about additional unknown downloads can rapidly drive away customers.

Browser-specific issues in Web 2.0 tend to be in the mechanisms that different browsers use to render displayed elements, such as padding variations, or between desktop and mobile browser variations. As one example, the Apple Safari browser on the Macintosh desktop allows media content delivery from popular sites such as Hulu and YouTube, while the mobile Safari browser on the popular iPhone does not support Hulu's format and allows only limited YouTube content through a secondary application with a limited set of media from the full YouTube collection and not available within the Safari browser itself.

Web 3.0

The emerging near-future World Wide Web 3.0 continues to include static content from Web 1.0, dynamic content from Web 2.0, and adds further personalization and "smart" content delivery to aid consumers in filtering the enormous volumes of data into a manageable stream. Current development of sites like the Amazon.com online marketplace include early elements of this type of filtering, offering ratings derived from input of past consumers together with recommendations based on past purchases related to the item under consideration. In this way, the likes, dislikes, and affiliated history of past consumers can rapidly aid customers in their consideration of an item or related items for purchase.

The Web 3.0 is also becoming more "mature," with tools such as phones disappearing from view even as they grow more ubiquitous. Once, telephones were installed centrally to a house in an obvious position as a mark of status, while today phones are everywhere and take forms more akin to art (remember the "Hot Lips" phones from the 1980s?) or so utilitarian they essentially disappear, as in the case of today's mobile phones hidden in a pocket or bag. Web 3.0 technologies extend interactivity to Web-enabled appliances, automobiles, and even buildings. Embedded computers can take advantage of the Internet for coordination, control, and reporting in almost any environment, making Web 3.0 much more service-oriented than earlier forms of the Web.

Web 3.0 offerings include real-world interactivity, allowing content to be delivered based on GPS/GIS coordination or through entirely virtual mechanisms. The Yelp application on my phone allows me to call up restaurants near my location (see Figure 8.4). As I pan the phone around, I see which restaurants lie in a particular direction, their distance from me, and details such as past client ratings and menus. Other solutions can react to changes in the environment, routing commuters around accidents or notifying parents to pick up their children at an alternate location due to weather conditions. Web 3.0 will continue this trend, becoming responsive to all manner of data inputs.

Web 3.0 also includes physical-to-virtual components. Consumers interested in a new home can build the home of their dreams online, conduct a virtual walk-through with virtual furnishings matching their own, arrange to purchase the home and negotiate financing all entirely online and self-service. Online marketplaces showing two-dimensional photographs of goods can be extended to three-dimensional interactive environments like the Second Life virtual world, where paintings, clothing, and many other items can be experienced virtually before arranging for physical-world purchase and delivery. Even virtual currency exchange will be a part of Web 3.0, where today's multiplayer gaming environments such as Entropia Universe allow direct transfer of real-world monies into in-game currency, whose value can then be withdrawn at a physical-world ATM by the in-game virtual recipient's player.

Figure 8.4   Yelp application showing augmented reality based on my location and the direction I am facing. Supper awaits just a short walk away from my office.

Note: Virtual currencies and virtual environments involve many legal issues that are just beginning to reach the courts, from virtual infidelity to virtual property theft, ownership, and inheritance. Businesses with virtual representations may face issues of virtual vandalism or consumer dissatisfaction in the form of a virtual picket line. Legal matters such as slander and libel are being tested against real-time expression of information through Tweets and Facebook posts. Control over official use of Internet communication mechanisms is a crucial part of near- to mid-term enterprise planning.

Culture

The static, dry informational content of Web 1.0 still exists in today's vibrant evolution of the Internet, because there remain many reasons for publication of read-only content. Interactive elements of Web 2.0 allow communities to form and disband, re-form, and evolve to meet the whims of their creators and their consumers. "Smart" aspects of Web 3.0 and the blending of physical and virtual realms offer mechanisms for community involvement at an ever-increasing rate.

Figure 8.5 illustrates an emerging Web 3.0 add-on interface called the Web of Trust (WoT), in which standard search results from a Google search of the term "test" are given additional red/yellow/green visual rankings based on the prior experience of visitors to each site. Beyond simple

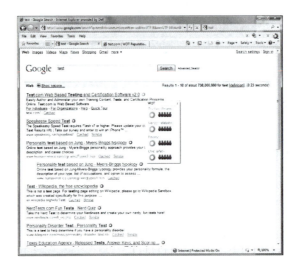

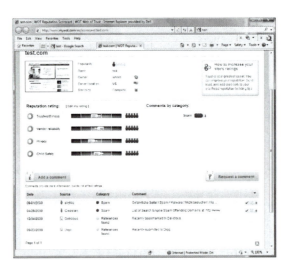

Figure 8.5   Web-of-Trust integrated Google results for the term "test," with an expended view of the rankings for "test.com."

measures of hit rank, each site is characterized by aggregated subjective values for trustworthiness, vendor reliability, privacy, and child safety. These values alter a user's browsing experience using a WoT-enabled browser based on subjective input responses from prior visitors.

Early Web 1.0 groups of sites sharing a similar theme once created cross-linked "Webrings," while Web 2.0 linked blogging sites into "Blogrolls." Web 3.0 offers the opportunity to link people, places, and even ideas in totally fantastic created settings. While a virtual help desk might not improve an enterprise today; in Web 3.0, clients may look for virtual interaction as much as they look for a website.

Enhanced reality already plays a part in enterprise operations today, where instant messaging client status can be used to see if it's a good time to walk down the hall and talk to a co-worker. Social networking provides word-of-mouth advertising and personal referrals from existing clients. Without extending advertising into new areas such as "augmented reality" listings, a business can easily see its customers finding their way to more tech-savvy competitors.

Enterprise clients, too, are changing as they become more comfortable with constant access to information and peers. College students no longer give up their friends back home, maintaining close ties to family, friends, and their extended virtual social groups. Streaming media content reduces the impact of traditional advertising mechanisms, where broadcast media are displaced by play-on-demand video and Pandora Internet radio feeds. Millions of people routinely engage in competitive and cooperative engagement with fellow guild mates via online gaming environments, creating a 24/7 stream of focus 365 days each year.

In the face of this evolution, organizations must:

- Plan for more creative socially integrated mechanisms to reach their clients, who are increasingly isolated by the same flood of information that ties them together.
- Provide more interactive and "live" up-to-date information for visitors to their websites, including mechanisms for referrals and feedback to aid those who travel the same path later.
- Recognize the value of trust, interest, and ease of access for members of extended groups of interconnected clients.

Enterprises must also focus on the value of continued access even during extreme events such as power outages, natural disasters, and other wide-scale issues. An auxiliary Web server located in a distant geographic location that says only "We are down due to <problem X> and expect to return to operation shortly. Please check back in a few hours for updates" can decrease client loss to competitor services. Such sites can also play a critical role in disaster recovery by allowing communication between displaced elements of the business during recovery efforts. I will discuss these and other disaster recovery/business continuity (DR/BC) opportunities in greater detail later in this book.

The Needle in the Haystack

The sheer volume of information present on the World Wide Web (versions 1.0 through 3.0) is simply staggering. This content reflects advertising claims intended to sway customers toward a product or away from competitors. It reflects personal opinion, political agenda, or may be entirely fabricated to suit no obvious purpose at all. Finding useful information in this vast sea of data requires automated tools to find, identify, categorize, and return references to information that may be useful to the searcher. Even simple search queries can return hundreds of thousands of individual sites that might or might not contain the desired information. This is searching for the needle in thousands of haystacks, many of which are not even written in the same language and some of which have been crafted to be deliberately misleading.

From the early Gopherspace search engines predating the World Wide Web, search engines have become increasingly robust and focused in the materials they return. Search engines such as Google and Bing attempt to regularly index large portions of the Internet, identifying key terms and presenting subsets of this data to users based on terms provided by the user. A good query might return a few hundred references, which can then be reviewed by the client for relevant details. A bad query might return tens of thousands of potential sites, references to sites no longer in existence, or unrelated sites that have malformed search tags.

Ranking

Most search engines display returned results based on an internal ranking system, attempting to provide the most useful, most common, or most relevant results first. Some search engines include paid "content promotion" services, placing advertised sites first or in highlighted areas. Others search engines place the most commonly searched sites first, effectively isolating newcomers by relegating them to the end of the list.

An organization needs to make sure that:

- Sites are identified to search engines.
- Public sites are accessible to the indexing services.
- Access logging and network bandwidth planning include overhead for search engine access.
- Proper keywords are included in site meta tags to ensure visibility.

An organization should routinely review its placement in search engine results and consider changing tags to meet evolving business functions and to address changes in search order ranking.

Caching

Search engines frequently cache copies of indexed content, to ensure availability in case the indexed server is unavailable and to provide a reference of when the site's content was last indexed. Visitors can examine content from previous indexing operations, which can lead to difficulties if the published content has been changed or purposefully removed. Accidental release of sensitive information is a common issue for businesses without formal policies to prevent customer data from being made available via public websites. Once it is indexed, this information becomes very difficult to remove from future searches.

An enterprise should have data release mitigation plans in place that include search engine cache redaction notification procedures, along with the proper format and contact information for each major search engine. Organizations should also include scheduled reviews of search engine content return following site updates. Some search engines can be prompted to re-index a site to reflect new data, while larger organizational sites may wish to use XML site mapping tools provided by the search engine vendors to ensure that all desirable content is properly identified.

Bogus Information

Search poisoning is an all-too-common practice used to attract browsers to unrelated sites, or to turn search results away from competitors' sites.

The most common form of this involves the inclusion of unrelated terms intended to place a site in the list of references returned from a keyword search. Organizations should regularly search brand name or trademarked terms to ensure that their use in external website search results remains in accordance with licensing and copyright protections. Organizations should also have policies in place for routine review of keywords tagged in provided Web content, to ensure that malware or directed action has not modified these terms.

Note: Popular websites are often targets for attempted malware infection or modification of presented content in support of a particular polical message. Such "hacktivism" has been seen providing antigovernmental messages, spouting propaganda, or merely displaying embarassing, crude, or other types of unsavory content. Because of this, organizations should develop, test, and regularly review defacement recovery plans, including search cache mitigation strategies.

Name Squatting

The term "name squatting" evolved from early pioneer practices of simply taking up residence on a piece of land and claiming ownership. Such "squatters" were given protection from landowners who remained absent too long and otherwise failed to take care of their lands, assuming that the new tenants would take better care than an absent landlord. Today, the practice of "name squatting" involves the registration of a Domain Name Service (DNS) entry that matches a product, service, or protected term owned by or affiliated with another entity.

When the hierarchical naming system used for Internet name resolution contained only a few root domains (such as .org or .com), businesses in disparate locations often ran into naming conflicts when both attempted to register the same term for their Internet site—"Bob's Pizza" in Buffalo and "Bob's Pizza" in Sidney could not both own "bobspizza.com" in the global marketplace.

Generally, the first entity to register a name with an Internet Registry service and pay the appropriate fee was allowed to own the Internet name. However, many individuals realized the economic potential for this practice and rapidly registered names for all manner of goods and services, including trademarked terms, celebrity names, and generic terms such as "love," "sex," and "money". Name squatters then offer to transfer the desired name registration in return for substantial sums of money. Legal tests of these squatting cases have led to requirements that the domain be used in a manner related to the term in order for the registration to be considered valid, while other cases involving trademarked terms have been prosecuted by copyright owners to every site that makes use of the term or any derivatives across the globe, as in the case of the Disney franchise and all of its related imagery, themes, names, and other content.

Recently, the expansion of root domains (such as the added .net root) has created new pressure for trademark holders and well-recognized entities to pay for name service registration in each new domain. With the potential for non-English-language sites now emerging, this problem becomes much larger for international corporations that may find their trademarked terms translate into something more common and already registered to other entities by the time translations are completed.

Holding all sites with a particular name across all possible domains will become increasingly difficult. This allows companies without a Web presence to extend into previously controlled generic naming opportunities, but offers a substantial cost that should be included in line-of-business operations within a business entity interested in protecting its name recognition.

Typos and One-Offs

A common practice for unscrupulous websites involves the registration of commonly mistyped versions of popular website names. As one example, the pornographic website whitehouse.com made use of the common .com registration of the highly trafficked U.S. government website designation, whitehouse.gov. Others have made use of transposed digits, dropped characters, alternate spellings, alternate domain entries like the example provided, and many other minor variations intended to draw unwary browsers to sites offering services, malware, or other content to inadvertent visitors.

Organizations with lengthy, difficult-to-type, or commonly misspelled domain names should examine opportunities to register these sites as well, configuring automatic redirection to the organization's main site so that any bookmarks will return users to the proper Web location. This process can be costly or difficult to perform for small businesses, and is typically necessary only when protecting well-known trademarked terms or a highly trafficked Web presence. However, it must managed from an early stage, because it is difficult to go back later and acquire names that may already have been registered by other organizations, even when they are copyrighted or otherwise registered and protected.

Name Service Poisoning

An organization's availability and profitability throughout the Internet depends on successful resolution of the human-readable name (bobspizza. com) to its registered numeric IP address, used by computers to identify a particular destination. The Domain Name System (DNS) is a service that provides this translation, with root domains (.com, .gov) resolved by central servers that point to secondary servers responsible for subsets of the overall namespace. If bobspizza.com is registered, the .com registry includes an entry for the address of the server that supports any names within this namespace. This server, in turn, ensures that www.bobspizza. com can be directed to the website for Bob's Pizza, while hiring.bobspizza. com can be directed to Bob's human resources portal.

Compromise of the registration service entry can result in traffic being redirected to an undesirable location or outright loss of access to the desired Internet resource. An organization should include the regular re-registration of any owned namespace entries as part of the yearly budget cycle, with technical and administrative contact information updated with the registrar upon personnel change or termination. Access to authentication credentials to change an organization's DNS entry should be carefully controlled, to prevent undesirable redirection of Internet traffic.

Organizations should also arrange for regular testing of name service resolution from different regions to ensure that all attempts resolve to the same location. DNS entries can become corrupted through accident or attack, with such changes "poisoning" later requests for name resolution. Following any change in service hosting, IP address space, or server/ service transfer, name resolution should be tested again to ensure that updates to the registration are propagating to all DNS servers properly.

Due to the practice of locally caching name resolution results, a change in IP address of an organization's servers or service hosts may take several days to be reflected in all subordinate DNS systems. Users may also have to flush their local name resolution caches to clear outdated service entries following a change. Changes to network name resolution, address space, and other functions throughout the enterprise should be fully tested, with adequate time planned to allow cached name resolution entries to expire before legacy access mechanisms are removed. This is particularly important for remote elements of extended enterprise networks.

Inter, Intra, and Extra

The World Wide Web continues to evolve, including new elements and extending connectivity to an increasingly mobile population. Before I address mobile computing in greater detail in the next chapter, it is best to first examine the nomenclature used to define regions of interest in the extended network.

Terminology for networking often derives from the type of connectivity used to communicate between nodes and the scale of integration within the network boundary. Common network connectivity categories include:

- Local Area Network (LAN)—A network comprised of closely connected nodes using smaller packets, facilitating greater numbers of individual nodes sharing the same transport media. This is typically the largest level of integration in small- to mid-sized enterprise networks, with logical addressing across a single or very small number of subnets. Smaller companies may find cost savings by licensing a limited number of publically routed addresses and using an internal private address space, with some type of network address translation (NAT) device providing connectivity across the edge boundary. Networks of this type avoid having to pay for large numbers of publically routed addresses; typically, only services exposed for public consumption, such as Web servers, virtual private network gateways, and locally hosted DNS services, need external addresses.
- Wide Area Network (WAN)—These networks span large geographic areas using large data packets to facilitate exceptionally high throughput across very-high-speed connections. Organizations of mid- to large scale may employ connectivity across WAN links between remote sites, but typically this is handled by the Internet service provider (ISP) without direct management within the enterprise. When using public Internet WAN connectivity, end-

to-end transport encryption may be mandated for communications and data access of sensitive data types.

- Metropolitan Area Network (MAN)—Large-scale networks supporting a limited extended area of coverage, such as a university or corporate campus, may be categorized as a MAN. This level of connectivity is more nonspecific, in that both WAN and LAN protocols may be mixed within the same MAN. Organizations with sufficient scale to employ this mixture should plan high-speed WAN backbone paths with branching LAN connections covering the "last mile." Network devices should be included in planned upgrades, and require regular review for firmware updates.

- Storage Area Network (SAN)–WAN protocols have been adapted to storage systems, producing very-high-speed connections between nodes and remote (though often physically proximate) storage devices. These dedicated networks allow external storage to be consumed as if connected directly to the consuming host. I will discuss this function in greater detail later in this book, when looking at virtualized storage and backups.

Obviously, there are many more types of connectivity, from personal area networks (PANs) comprised of all interconnected devices worn or carried by a particular individual to wireless local-area networking (WLAN) connectivity for mobile devices and in locations where wired connectivity is difficult to arrange or otherwise undesirable. Any time wireless solutions are employed, data transfer should include encryption and strong authentication mechanisms to protect against inadvertent data disclosure or compromise of the connection.

Internet

Simply put, the Internet is the collection of all TCP/IP-based systems connected to the public address space that has emerged via the World Wide Web. Internet connectivity makes use of publically routed addresses identified by DNS services supporting a limited number of root domains that are directly controlled by the Internet Corporation for Assigned Names and Numbers (ICANN). In late 2009, this agency was separated from U.S. government control and made an international body to reflect its scope in the global Internet. Whenever referring to the globally accessible public network, the term Internet can be applied.

Intranet

An intranet is also generally a TCP/IP-based network, but it does not necessarily include publically routed network addressing. Private addressing, such as the 10.0.0.0/8 subnet originally reserved for BITNET, is often used internally to provide cost savings on lease of public address space. An intranet's purpose is to support an organization and its operations. Local DNS may be used to give internal addressing user-friendly names, including nonroutable naming using additional roots not part of the ICANN-moderated public namespace (such as the common .local root).

Internal file storage, collaboration solutions, and other forms of interconnectivity have a place within an organization's intranet. Intranet defenses typically involve gateway security and internal authentication mechanisms for access control. Formal change management procedures should be put into place for control over intranet resources to ensure continued function in the face of updates and network evolution.

Extranet

Similar to an intranet, the extranet is a privately accessible set of network resources available for organizational operation. Extranets extend the same functions as intranets but include external partners, suppliers, customers, and other authenticated computing resources outside the organization's internal network space. Because of the rapid emergence of mobile devices used for business purposes, the line between intranet and extranet is increasingly blurred. Extranet security may involve stronger authentication mechanisms, such as two-factor log-ons, together with transport encryption strategies to secure data traveling over public network segments. As with intranets, formal change management procedures are mandatory for continued extranet function in the mid- to long term.

Summary

This chapter has focused on the evolution of Internet connectivity, from the earliest days of the ARPANet through Web 1.0, 2.0, and beyond. Enterprises must consider the global nature of the Internet when securing online naming and when competing for attention in the worldwide online marketplace. As enterprise networks become increasingly extended, challenges will arise for control and management of content and name resolution services that are critical to operations depending on Internet connectivity. The next chapter will examine the extension of extended enterprise networks to facilitate anytime, anywhere computing.

Chapter 9

Anytime/Anywhere Computing

In This Chapter

- An examination of the expansion of remote network solutions
- A review of accessibility considerations for remote service availability
- Considerations for securing remote and mobile resource access

Miniaturization and high-density batteries have placed more raw processing power in my cell phone than was available for the *Apollo* space program. This small device makes available e-mail and social networks, media content and maps, communications and data exchange. The sheer volume of data available through my mobile window to the world is staggering, empowering my ability to access every element of enterprise network resources from anywhere at any time. The curse of this flood of information and connectivity is that I am never truly away from the office unless I take action to shut off that window.

Applications and data extended in this manner require care to ensure that mobile access is secure, meaningful, and available via limited bandwidth.

Physicist William Pollard once noted that unless information is organized, processed, and available, it becomes a burden rather than a benefit.

Mobile Technologies

Technology continues to shrink in size while increasing in power. Figure 9.1 illustrates this evolution clearly, comparing my first portable computer (a Tandy TRS-80 model 4P) alongside the MacBook, iPad, and iPhone devices that currently extend my workplace anywhere I choose to travel.

This chapter will focus on the use and integration of mobile technologies within the extended enterprise network, an area that you will likely find very challenging because of the rapid pace of change and adoption of both new platforms and entirely new products.

New Technologies

Personally acquired mobile devices are the most common pain point for mobile access integration, due to the sheer variety of options and configurations available. Policies should be put in place to provide guidance for users who will expect that the newest, latest, and greatest device can automatically provide access to e-mail, calendars, portals, and remote-accessible applications. Training for helpdesk support technicians is also

Figure 9.1   A comparison of portable computing devices. On the left is the TRS-80 model 4P (portable) that was my first portable computer, while the right displays Apple's slate of technologies including the MacBook notebook, iPad tablet, and iPhone devices. (Photo of Apple technologies provided for public use at http://commons.wikimedia.org, courtesy of Mr. Jon Mountjoy.)

critical to facilitate emerging mobile technologies, as the interface can be very different between devices. This is also true of application development, where a testing emulator for each device can aid in the identification of mobile access issues. Figure 9.2 demonstrates this functionality, which can allow testing of applications across a wide range of common mobile devices before deployment.

New devices often present challenges for the network due to unforeseen interaction with existing technologies. When the first generation of iPhone was released, a remote user with local desktop administrative privileges installed a beta version of the iTunes media player in order to better manage a music collection—arguably not a work function, but common enough among tech-savvy users in enterprises that enjoy "incidental use" permissions. A glitch in the beta software caused an instant 100% load on the network to the e-mail server because the desktop hosting the iTunes software was attempting to poll the user's mailbox and calendar for updates continuously. That one user unintentionally created a denial-of-service attack on the internal e-mail system, affecting users across the enterprise. Such situations can be magnified a hundredfold or more when highly anticipated devices like the popular iPad are finally released and users immediately introduce them into the enterprise.

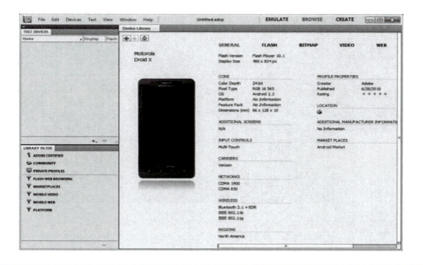

Figure 9.2   The Adobe Device Central emulator displaying a Motorola Droid.

Network Connectivity

Mobile access will typically enjoy lower bandwidth connections than wired workstations in the enterprise. Although newer wireless solutions continue to provide higher speeds of transfer, designers of applications for mobile access should keep in mind data transfer limitations as well as smaller display capabilities and limited haptic interface options such as the obvious lack of a mouse.

Figure 9.3 illustrates common public and private Wi-Fi options, including the high-powered outdoor access points used in many municipal systems, together with short-range commodity devices commonly used in small office/home office (SOHO) environments. The small square device is a mobile hotspot that I use when traveling. It bridges cellular data links (3G/4G) and a short-range connection for up to five Wi-Fi enabled devices.

Because wireless connectivity transmits data in all directions, it is possible for mobile users to expose sensitive information to unwanted interception. Encryption between the device and enterprise resources is necessary to avoid data disclosure through this access, while on-device encryption measures should be mandated by policy to ensure that the loss of a mobile device does not expose organizational data or intellectual property.

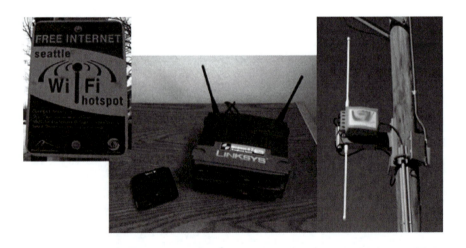

Figure 9.3 Wi-Fi access points can be found in many public locations, restaurants, office buildings, and homes. Network access points can be secured to require a password and configured for automatic encryption of data transmitted between the access point and a connected device.

Extending the Enterprise

An inventory of mobile devices in use within the organization should be conducted regularly, to ensure that enterprise resources are made available in an accessible manner. Apple's popular iPhone, for example, cannot be used to access Flash-based Web content. If an enterprise application or Web portal relies on Flash, it becomes inaccessible to a very popular device type.

Information aggregators, dashboards, and Web portals can aid the mobile user by providing a single target for accessing enterprise resources. Dashboards that consolidate information into simplified presentation can aid limited-bandwidth access, with additional detail made available through drill-downs and linked documents. Applications designed for server-side processing can reduce the on-device CPU impact, as well as the data throughput requirements found in many client-server desktop applications. Extranets designed for partners and supplies can aid in cross-functional data sharing by avoiding the need for application deployment or external-authentication data connections.

Accessibility

In addition to mobile device constraints, applications should be developed for availability through alternate-accessibility interface types. Section 208 of the Rehabilitation Act of 1973 (amended 29 U.S.C. 794d) provides guidelines for federal agencies to provide services and electronic information to individuals with disabling conditions. These guidelines have been implemented across many state, corporate, and industry interpretations, and can serve as a good reference for applications designed to meet accessibility standards.

Table 9.1 illustrates some options for addressing Section 508 guidelines. This is not an exhaustive analysis of all possible solutions for all required standards, but it should serve as a starting point for consideration.

Mobile and Remote Access

Many types of devices are currently enabled for mobile or remote access, including standard formats such as the laptop, netbook, tablet, and "smart" phone. However, increasing numbers of devices may also include mobile

Table 9.1 Some Options for Addressing Section 508 Guidelines

Section 508 Guideline	Application Design Solution
A text equivalent will be provided for every nontext element.	Every image, applet, Flash presentation, video or audio file, etc., will have a descriptive "alt" tag. Complex graphics will be accompanied by detailed text descriptions of the information and conclusions. "Alt" tag descriptions of hyperlinks should describe the link destination. Purely decorative graphics should have very succinct descriptive tags.
Text alternatives for multimedia shall be synchronized.	Video files should have captions, transcripts, or closed captioning synchronized with audio content. Audio files should have captions or transcripts.
Interfaces shall be designed to convey all data without requiring color discrimination.	Key information should be highlighted using a means other than color changes. Visually distinguishing characteristics of data representations should include captions for nonvisible review.
Text links will be provided for each active region of a server-side image map.	Textual hyperlinks with descriptive tags should be included for each hot spot in a clickable server-side image map.
Row and column headers will be identified in tabular data.	Data tables should have columns and rows identified using appropriate "alt" tags. Tables presented for side-by-side visual comparison should include descriptive tags detailing comparisons.
Frame titles must facilitate identification and navigation.	Frame "title" attributes should describe the frame's content or purpose, to allow rapid review before drilling down using alternate accessibility interfaces.
Content will not cause flickering between 2 and 55 Hz.	Highlights, active content, and other screen elements should not flash at a rate between 2 and 55 cycles per second, to reduce the chance of causing optically induced seizure.
A text-only equivalent must be provided when there is no other mechanism for compliance. This equivalent shall be updated along with the original.	Text-only alternatives must be provided when there is no other option, and must include the same information and functionality as the original content. Flash-based navigation systems are a common example, where a text-only navigation alternative will allow the navigation capability for alternative interfaces. The text-only version must be updated along with the original content version.

(continued)

Table 9.1 (*continued*)

Section 508 Guideline	Application Design Solution
A link must be provided to any additional element, plug-in, or other application necessary for presented content.	Whenever a plug-in, applet, script, or specialized content requires an additional download to present the content (examples: PDF or PowerPoint viewers), a descriptive hyperlink to the download's source will be provided.
Online electronic forms shall allow use by assistive technologies.	All form controls, field elements, and requirements for completion and submission must have descriptive text labels. All functions and data entry fields should require only standard keyboard or keyboard-emulation input.
Users must be allowed to skip repetitive navigation links.	Any lists of links or groups of information should include a descriptive link for skipping to the next section rapidly.
Users should be alerted to time requirements and provided sufficient time to indicate more time is required.	Automatic-progression or timed-response controls must include an option for user control over content changes. The option for extending or canceling timed actions must be presented early and allow sufficient time for the user to identify and enact the option.

connectivity and must be indentified and controlled through policy to avoid impact on enterprise functionality and availability. Cars, building environmental controls, and even jogging shoes may employ some type of wireless data transfer solution. Some devices, such as cellular phones, may also serve as mobile WiFi hotspots, allowing small workgroups to connect remotely to the Internet or to share information wirelessly between team members.

Mobile Limitations

In addition to constraints on wireless bandwidth and interface options available to mobile devices, the mobile user may encounter additional issues that are not present in a wired desktop office environment. As an example, power becomes a precious commodity for the mobile user. I have seen clusters of people around wall power plugs at airports and during conferences, all trying to recharge devices for continued use. I have personally found that a small external auxiliary power supply, shown in

Figure 9.4 A small power pack (the size of a deck of cards), which adds several hours of operation to my netbook, while charging various other mobile devices when I am on the road (it is shown here charging my phone).

Figure 9.4, is a fundamental working requirement for sustained mobile technology use.

Remote Desktops

I also recommend the use of remote desktop access and a very limited set of software on any mobile laptop or netbook when you will are traveling through security checkpoints. This can expedite the process of inspection and avoids the risk of data loss or exposure if a device is confiscated. A lightweight mobile computer with only an operating system, antimalware protection, VPN client, and remote desktop client provides little risk of exposing information if it is stolen or otherwise lost. No data, applications, or other functionality is present on the device beyond the applications necessary for configuring a secure connection back to the remote desktop host, which provides processing power while the mobile device only transmits keyboard and mouse input and returns video and sound to the user. Provided that remote desktop caching is disabled and files are left on the remote host, forensic investigation of the mobile device will expose little if any data to unwanted review. Remote desktops and other virtualized elements of the network will be examined in detail in Chapter 10.

Transport Security

Encryption is important for securing remote and mobile access. Many standards for encryption between devices and wireless endpoints do not provide adequate protection—for example, the common Wired Equivalent Privacy (WEP) protocol can be decrypted in a live setting. More recent protocols such as the WiFi Protected Access (WPA/WPA2) protocol provide greater device-to-node encryption, but they do not provide continuous protection against data interception elsewhere along the route. For remote Web connectivity, Secure Sockets Layer (SSL) transport is mandatory for protecting data in transit. For remote desktop and remote application access, the use of a virtual private network (VPN) system will allow a remote device to access local resources as if it were directly connected, but using an encrypted tunnel for data interchange.

Kill Pills

No matter how careful they are, users will occasionally misplace a mobile device or have it stolen. Encryption standards and policies will help to protect data, but they may still provide a conduit for e-mail and other data. Use of protective measures such as a remote data wipe option (sometimes called a "kill pill") can aid in rendering the lost device useless for ongoing data exposure. Systems such as Microsoft's Exchange collaboration platform include an example of a remote wipe service, allowing an administrator to trigger a mobile device's e-mail client to wipe the device when it next communicates with the server. This is highly useful in cases of theft, loss, or forced termination of an employee, but it can result in total loss of all data on the device, depending on the types of remote-wipe options available.

Device Interaction

Because wireless transmissions can overlap with similar broadcasts, users may find that interference between devices can affect mobile access. High-density areas such as office buildings can be particularly troublesome, because broadcasts from nearby offices or other floors may block access to an organization's own wireless nodes. Figure 9.5 illustrates the sheer number of devices found within a small residential neighborhood near my office, where more than 500 nodes were immediately identifiable by simply driving through the area.

It is important to perform a site survey of your organizational facility before attempting to add wireless connectivity, to ensure that device interaction is minimized and broadcast channel selection is optimized

Figure 9.5   Wi-Fi nodes broadcasting within a suburban neighborhood, with 33 nodes active within range of my truck on the street. Many of these nodes are open for access without authentication or encryption enabled.

to avoid other devices in the nearby area. Many devices such as mobile hotspots and WiFi-enabled cell phones enter and leave areas, requiring regular site reviews.

Signal Boosters

Your site survey may also identify areas where signals from two or more devices interact and cancel each other out, or where building construction or other environmental factors create areas of low signal strength. This is common in areas with heavy mechanical equipment, electrical motors, or steel-frame construction, and may only affect part of an area so it is not caught during general site surveys. Signal boosters or directional antennas may be necessary in certain areas to ensure that wireless connectivity is available continuously. Care should be taken in high-density environments to avoid boosting signal strength to the point at which it compromises access on the same channel nearby.

Policy Requirements

The prevalence and growing use of mobile and remote-access solutions creates a number of challenges for the modern network enterprise. Unless policies are put in place early and updated often, emerging solutions may compromise organizational capabilities or expose data to unauthorized review.

Required policies might include:

- **Mobile computing**—These are on-device requirements such as storage encryption, firewall settings, requirements for device antivirus software, and automatic patch management options. Liability for loss requirements should be signed in agreement, before equipment is transferred to the mobile user. A specific enumeration of allowable device types may be necessary in some organizations.
- **Remote access**—These are policies governing transport and access requirements, such as VPN configurations for remote access to enterprise resources, SSL mandates for portals, and preventing local retention of stored authentication credentials.
- **Wireless use**—These policies address the use of wireless connectivity within the workplace or at remote locations. These policies will include whether personal wireless technologies may be used and which channels they may consume within the organization's physical space, or what types of authentication and encryption must be used when using a remote wireless link.

Summary

This chapter has addressed the extension of network resources to an increasingly mobile consumer base. Kari Skoog, a spokeswoman at Intel, once said that the vision of future networking is to have access anytime, anywhere, and on any device. This presents challenges for the enterprise architect, who must manage the integration of rapidly evolving technologies into a sustainable enterprise environment. This potential requires care in planning, application design, information presentation, and network design. Without strong policies governing the facets of remote and mobile access, enterprise functionality and data security are at risk. In the next chapter, we will examine the impact of virtualization such as the remote desktop mentioned earlier in this chapter.

Chapter 10

Virtualization

In This Chapter

- Examination of many different types of virtualization
- Identification of scenarios that may benefit from cloud computing
- A review of best practices in virtualization

The Greek philosopher Plato formulated the *theory of forms*, which is based on the concept that the world of experience and sensation is merely a reflection or representation of a more fundamental abstract form of reality. The modern enterprise network embodies a form of Plato's theory, creating electronic copies of physical documents that can be duplicated and re-created at will or constructing entire virtual worlds with their own physics models and constraints. Even technology itself is becoming more a reflection of purpose and function, compared to physical systems dedicated to a single task or purpose.

This chapter will examine the virtualization of services and technologies within the extended network enterprise. While I will not attempt to rival Plato's work with a "theory of virtualization," it is worth noting the continued shift from physical representations of technology toward more fundamental abstracted forms that consume less power and provide greater flexibility than their physically bound predecessors.

Virtualized Services

Virtualization of services and functions is not a wholly new concept. Answering machines, for example, provided a virtual replacement for human answering services, and have since been replaced in turn by voice mail systems. Modern enterprise collaboration systems such as the Microsoft Exchange platform with its Live Communication Server option can even take a voice message, perform automated voice recognition, and transmit the resulting text and audio to an individual's mailbox for easy review on the recipient's device of choice.

Other services, such as virtual faxes, print spoolers, and virtualized data storage reduce the technology equipment footprint within the enterprise while extending access to consumers throughout the enterprise. A single automated fax service can serve the entire enterprise, providing electronic facsimiles of documents without requiring consumables such as paper and ink cartridges and without delays involved with distribution of physical document copies.

Automated monitoring and update services allow management of maintenance and security functions without requiring direct access to individual physical systems. Such virtualized services provide a mechanism for direct support of thousands of distributed systems by a handful of support technicians, gaining efficiencies in personnel costs and user downtime. Additional support functions rely on virtualization for management over very large numbers of systems that may be distributed across many sites in a global network. We will examine the use of support solutions such as automated system deployment using virtual system images in Chapter 11.

Virtualized Applications

Virtualization of applications involves the creation of an application package that is made available to users automatically or on demand. Applications can be automatically deployed to a user's system based on role membership, ensuring that the user's desktop experience remains the same regardless of which system is used to access the enterprise network. Coupled with virtualization of user file storage using a distributed file share and/or user folder redirection, users need never know worry about data and application availability. These services also allow rapid deployment of replacement or upgraded equipment, because the user experience is automatically applied to any system when the user first logs onto a new system.

Virtualized applications allow multiple versions of an application to be available simultaneously on the same system, ensuring continuity of operation for legacy applications depending on second-party add-ons or applications. For example, an older form of Java virtual machine (JVM) might be required for Application X to operate. Users could then automatically use the older browser and JVM when accessing Application X, but use newer versions of each during normal operations. Updates become easier in a virtualized application environment, by allowing an updated package to be uploaded onto the application virtualization server, which is then automatically downloaded to a user's system upon next use of the appropriate program or file type.

An additional efficiency provided by virtualized application environments is the potential to reduce software licensing costs by providing a reduced pool of concurrent licenses, which are claimed upon application access and freed up for reuse when the application is closed. Rather than installing an expensive application on each computer system across the network, or limiting application availability to a select group of workstations, users can be added to application virtualization groups to gain automatic package availability using a smaller pool of concurrent licenses.

Virtualized Desktops

The next level of virtualization involves the user experience to include the entire desktop, encompassing operating system and all other functions into a virtualized setting mirroring the experience of sitting at a dedicated workstation desktop environment. This is somewhat similar to older mainframe operations, when terminals provided keyboard input and returned displayed output from processes that ran entirely within the mainframe's CPU, memory, and storage resources.

Remote Desktop Clients

Client systems accessing virtualized desktop environments may use "dumb" terminals similar to older mainframe configurations or "thin" clients with only sufficient resources for input, output, and network communications. "Thick" clients may have local storage and applications to shift processing power from the server, while mobile computers with their own applications and configuration details may be used to access organizational services and data while limiting exposure.

Updates to a virtualized desktop environment occur at the host system, allowing rapid update to applications and system settings from a centralized data center. Remote desktop connections can be made to in-place dedicated systems for availability in mobile or remote settings, or may connect to one of many virtualized desktop sessions maintained on a powerful virtualization host residing in the data center. Virtual desktop infrastructure (VDI) implementations include additional services to facilitate user reconnection to virtual desktop sessions left in operation.

A virtualized desktop environment can allow continued use of legacy desktop hardware that is no longer able to run the most current applications, by allowing the older hardware to function as a thin or thick client for a remote virtual desktop running on hardware with sufficient resources to support more recent applications and services. Extending the life cycle of individual systems this way reduces procurement costs and the environmental impact of computer manufacturing and disposal processes.

Virtual Appliances

Virtual appliances consist of preconfigured virtual systems with their own operating system, applications, and settings. These systems can provide an excellent mechanism for distributing entire software environments without requiring installation of packages on a host system, beyond the virtualization service itself (called a hypervisor). Demonstrations of new applications within a preconfigured virtual appliance require only a copy of the virtual hard drive files and minor network configuration to be up and running on a client's test bed.

Virtual appliances and PC-hosted virtual machines can also allow a single workstation to provide access to multiple computing platforms simultaneously. The popular Apple Macintosh system includes the Parallels virtualization environment, allowing native Windows functionality within a virtual PC hypervisor. Newer forms of Microsoft's Windows platform include the Windows on Windows (WoW) virtual hypervisor for backwards compatibility in legacy applications. Use of a PC hypervisor such as the popular VMWare service can allow a single workstation to support as many different virtualized desktop configurations as system resources allow, together with options for capturing point-in-time snapshots for automatic rollback during testing and development. This can greatly reduce design time by eliminating the need to completely reload a test system each time a setting or application function is altered and by providing developers with multiple versions of operating systems, browsers, and application software suites with which to test the new application under development, without the need for individual physical hardware systems for each.

Virtualized Servers

Virtualization of multiple physical servers onto more powerful centralized hosts within the data center can provide significant cost savings in terms of hardware, energy, and cooling requirements. Since many servers can operate at a reduced level during off-peak hours, consolidation onto a smaller number of hosting machines can reduce the power consumed by idling systems. Each virtualized server is merely a collection of files, rather than a dedicated hardware platform with storage, CPU, and memory of its own, allowing more efficient utilization of available resources as well as portability across hardware hosts, as shown in Figure 10.1.

Automatic load balancing across hosting farms can ensure that spikes in demand are met with adequate resource allocation to individual virtualized servers. Resource management requires strict policies and attention to operational thresholds in order to protect against "virtual sprawl" in the data center and alignment of dedicated resources within each host to the needs of its virtual machines. Because virtualization allows separation of hardware and software refresh cycles (discussed in Chapter 11), policies must also be put in place to handle software update and retirement of virtual as well as physical systems in order to properly secure the network and to limit complexity in support requirements.

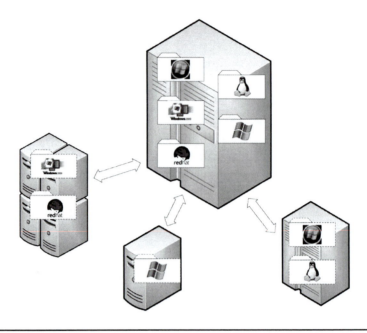

Figure 10.1   An example of the portability of virtual machines across multiple hosting hardware options. Host operating systems may also vary, provided the hypervisors are compatible across all hosts.

Virtualized Networks

Virtualization of networks beyond simple desktops and servers can afford an enterprise with opportunities for modeling, testing, and defense. Construction of a test network matching the full suite of applications and services within a large enterprise can be a very costly matter, while a complete virtualized network with identical configurations and settings might be managed using only a single powerful host. Each virtual system in the test network might have reduced processing power compared to its production equivalent, but can be easily rolled back to a previous snapshot in the event of corruption or failure during test. Virtualized networks can also be used for penetration testing without concern for disruption of the production network, while "decoy" networks with automatically generated traffic and network utilization can allow would-be network attackers an environment in which their efforts are encapsulated and recorded for later review of attacking methods. These decoy networks, called *honeynets*, appear to be valid, active network environments but are actually virtual sandboxes, separate from the production network environment with only simulated use and data files present for access by an attacker.

Cloud Computing

When the network, servers, and infrastructure are virtualized and resources are made available automatically from a pool of systems, the result is termed *cloud computing*. Cloud computing is a natural extension of distributed grid processing (discussed in Chapter 14) when combined with the virtualization of services and operating systems. A cloud computing client might be allocated up to 8 processors, 20GB of RAM, 300GB of storage, and up to four websites supported by 4 databases. Without needing to know the details of the location and type of these resources, an authorized user might request a new Web reporting application supported by 40GB of storage, 4GB of RAM, and 2 CPUs. Because these resource limits fall within the user's allocated constraints, the resources can be automatically provisioned without interaction with tech support.

Comparing Cloud and Traditional Application Life Cycles

Figure 10.2 illustrates a traditionally developed application, passing through the design phase, increased capacity requirements during testing, reduced requirements during rollout, and the highest resource need during it active life cycle. Pain points occur when escalating resource need exceeds available resources, requiring hardware upgrades or application migration to provide needed application host resources (represented by the dark gray boxes). Following end of life, applications retained for reference purposes continue to consume the same resources unless migrated again to other equipment.

Figure 10.3 illustrates application development in a virtualized or cloud computing environment. Cloud computing resources can flex as needed, allowing the easy scaling of prototype solutions through testing and up to production levels with nothing more than an automated request for additional resource allocation. If expected capacity far exceeds

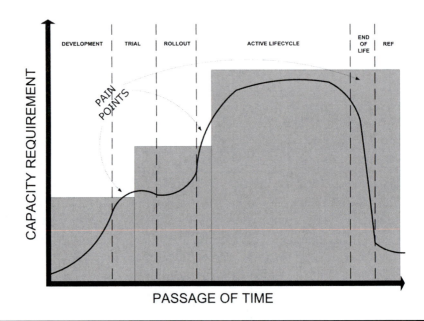

Figure 10.2 A traditional application life cycle, comparing system resource availability against application resource requirements. Note that insufficiencies must be met by hardware upgrades or migration to more robust equipment.

actual capacity requirements, resources can be scaled back and allocated to other purposes through the same mechanism.

Types of Clouds

Because the term *cloud computing* refers to the configuration of resource availability more than a specific configuration of hardware and software, there are several common types of cloud computing that may be employed by an organization.

- **Public clouds**—These clouds are hosted on publicly accessible systems, available for Internet access from anywhere in the world. Examples of this type of cloud include Google's Gmail and Microsoft Live Hotmail services. Most public clouds share host servers across multiple client cloud resource pools.
- **Dedicated clouds**—Like public clouds, dedicated clouds are hosted on systems available via Internet connectivity. Dedicated clouds isolate

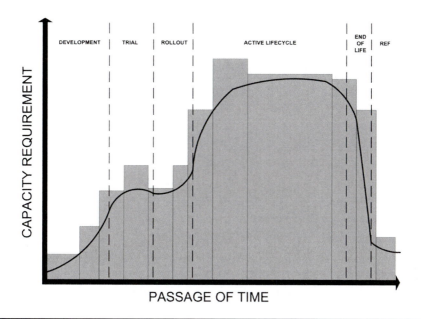

DEVELOPMENT | TRIAL | ROLLOUT | ACTIVE LIFECYCLE | END OF LIFE | REF

CAPACITY REQUIREMENT

PASSAGE OF TIME

Figure 10.3   A virtualized or cloud computing application life cycle, comparing system resource availability against application resource requirements. Note that incremental changes, both positive and negative, are possible through automated allocation, without requiring migration or hardware upgrade.

instances by restricting resource use by a particular client to a specific subset of hosting systems. Because the resources are dedicated to a particular client, these services are generally more costly than public cloud implementations.

- **Private clouds**—A private cloud is one that is typically maintained within an organization's own network, or isolated in some manner from external access. Cloud hosting services may place dedicated hardware within the organization's data center, or an organization might construct a private cloud using its own hardware.
- **Hybrid clouds**—Hybrid clouds may provide a mixture of dedicated, public, and private cloud resources. Management of disaster recovery (DR) functions, service-level agreements for resource and network availability, and other characteristics must be carefully negotiated in order to obtain the greatest value from a hybrid cloud configuration.

Cloud Flexibility

The flexibility of resource assignment within a cloud computing environment can be very attractive to operations that require a variable amount of resources. Examples of scenarios where this availability provides greatest benefit include:

- **The bump**—This scenario, illustrated in Figure 10.4, includes a sudden unexpected spike in activity. Examples include sudden surges in activity during emergencies or following the mention of a site on a popular news aggregator, causing a flood of interest outside normal access levels.
- **Cyclic surges**—This includes resources that are only necessary on a cyclical basis but are unused during other times, as shown in Figure 10.5. Examples include mandatory training just before evaluation periods and end-of-month or end-of-year reporting cycles.
- **Rapid growth**—This scenario includes any application access that expands rapidly beyond expected resource requirements, as illustrated in Figure 10.6. Prototypes placed into limited use may see rapid adoption enterprise-wide, or Internet information sites may experience sudden expansion of interest following initial exposure.

Best Practices

Due to the relative newness of cloud computing, best practices continue to emerge and evolve. A few of the more common practices include:

- **Setting standards**—Cloud resource hosting services, such as the Amazon EC2 or Microsoft Azure standards, do not work well between technologies. Selection of a cloud computing standard will ensure that developed applications and services interoperate well with other cloud resources and with in-place technologies in the enterprise.
- **Controlling costs**—Because cloud service vendors scale costs based on resource allocation and segmentation, enterprise cloud service hosting should be negotiated using the most economical model for existing and near-term requirements. Cost models include current levels of dedicated resource and bandwidth availability, longer-term contracts providing a set level of resources for a fixed cost, or resource pools that may be used across a variable period of time and

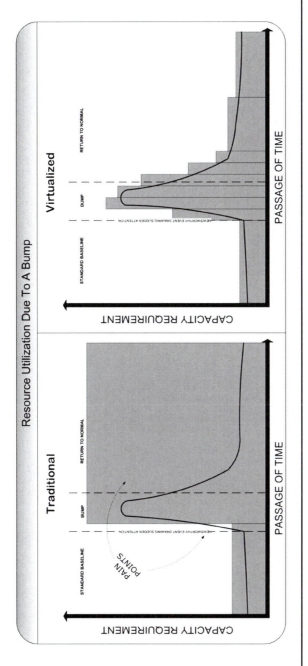

Figure 10.4 A comparison of capacity requirements due to a short-term unexpected bump in activity.

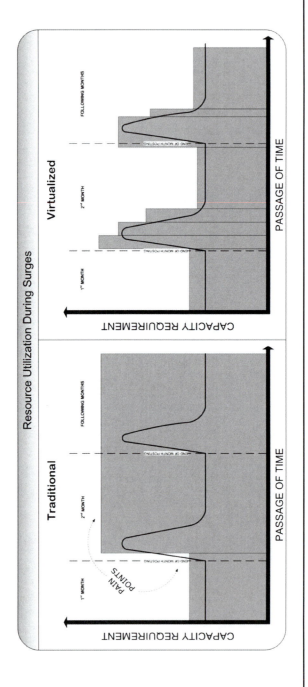

Figure 10.5 A comparison of capacity requirements created by cyclical surges in activity and access. Note that in virtualized cloud scenarios, capacity can be preprovisioned to meet expected need during successive cycles.

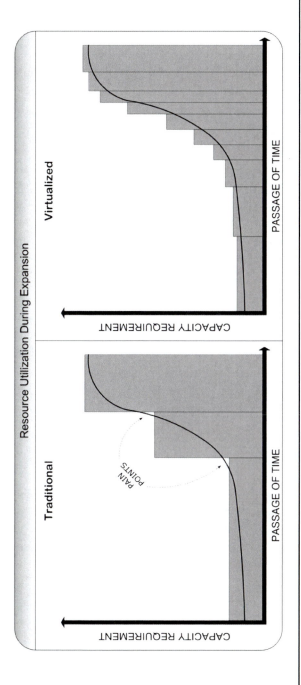

Figure 10.6 A comparison of capacity requirements created by an unexpectedly rapid growth in utilization. In virtualized and cloud computing scenarios, automatic increases in capacity could be established at a particular utilization level to account for varying rates of increase.

renewed when consumed. More complex hosting costs include per-transaction micro fees, upload/download transaction costs, incremental storage costs, and specialized costs for restrictions of data and DR backups to specific geopolitical boundaries.

- **Privacy requirements**—Contracting cloud services should include statements of where data will be stored, where DR copies may be made, and conditions for reporting when data is exposed or transferred to new hosting facilities. Because larger hosting firms may make use of environmental cooling by moving data center operations north during summer months, requirements for legal data discovery and open records requests may fall under different legal systems. Contracts should include details regarding reporting discovery actions and other forms of external data access.

- **Compatibility**— to best use available application development skills and tools, cloud computing platform standards should be selected to integrate well with existing enterprise technologies. Mid-migration between local and cloud-hosted e-mail services, for example, is much less problematic if both services are compatible and can interoperate transparently. Because cloud services trade off flexibility and customizability for protection against potential conflict with shared resource clients, some applications may prove to be unable to migrate into the cloud and so a standard for interoperability between cloud and local applications is mandatory.

Summary

This chapter has addressed the virtualization of services, applications, workstations, servers, networks, and migration of entire infrastructures into the cloud. Virtualization practices provide significant cost savings by reducing hardware, energy, and cooling costs. Virtualization provides reductions in support requirements, as well as ease of recovery following system loss or upgrade.

The steady migration of resources into the cloud reduces tech support requirements for new initiatives, and eases resource extension to meet growing or widely varying requirements. Care must be taken to ensure that virtualized resources are managed, updated, and retired just like their physical system counterparts. The next chapter will examine tech refresh cycles and strategies in greater detail.

Chapter 11

Enterprise Sustenance

In This Chapter

- An examination of Project Management Framework practices in enterprise maintenance
- Identification of common hardware update strategies
- A review of software update considerations

Several years ago, I was fortunate enough to present at a conference in San Francisco with sufficient spare time to travel about the wonderful city and take in its unique character. While experiencing the city, I was told by locals and visitors alike about the Golden Gate Bridge—how it was planned, constructed, and maintained continuously to stand against the elements as one of the most beautiful landmarks of a singularly fascinating city. While watching the suspension towers rise from the morning fog, I was struck by the splendor and functionality of this long-standing monument to engineering and found myself considering the continual effort to maintain the bridge's structure against earthquakes, storms, salt corrosion, and the many other threats to its existence.

A few years later, while hiking in the desert north of Tucson, Arizona, I found myself remembering the cool moist fog fondly. The stark beauty of the desert took my thoughts to the words of Percy Bysshe Shelley's poem, "Ozymandius," which tells of a magnificent creation of the past that had long since fallen to ruin: "My name is Ozymandius, king of kings: Look on my works, ye Mighty, and despair!" Nothing beside remains. . . . The lone and level sands stretch far away."

I was struck by the lesson inherent in that comparison—the contrast in imagery between the bridge, standing strong and beautiful, and the imagined lost cities of Ozymandius provides an illustration of the impact that update and maintenance have on our creations' longevity. This chapter addresses the importance of planning, guidance, and regular maintenance to retain functionality, value, and purpose in the face of the many changes and threats over a network's life cycle.

Project Management

The enterprise architect will develop a vision and extend this into a program, which will in turn span a number of projects necessary to transforming the enterprise into a cohesive and sustainable form. Success depends on proper planning, effective transfer of guidance, and strong control over change to avoid feature creep becoming a never-ending goal of Sisyphean character. The vision is enduring, programs become a part of the organizational business plan, and projects effect stepwise change from one state to the next. Together, these describe a path that the enterprise will follow, milestones and checkpoints along the way, a timeframe and criteria for completion, and metrics for measuring progress.

In addition to understanding the technologies, regulatory mandates, and line-of-business requirements of an organization, the enterprise architect should have strong knowledge of project management techniques, whether through application of a formal methodology such as PRINCE2 (Projects IN Controlled Environments) or derived from a standard such as the PMBOK (Project Management Body of Knowledge) produced by the Project Management Institute (PMI). Projects differ from programs by having a specific start and end date, defined deliverables, and a specific set of completion criteria. These factors are mandatory for effective change and provide a planned evolution to maintain sustainability. Without a clear project scope, individual projects can mutate into ever-evolving general goals that consume resources and fail to produce useful output or end-state products. Continually changing end-state goals reflect a trait termed "feature creep," which presents the greatest threat to project completion.

Tip: For each element of the enteprise, multiple projects will emerge. Programs provide a stepwise process to reach or close toward a desirable "final state" defined by the vison. Formal project and change management will ensure that each step, as a defined project, has a final goal and completion point that will then be used to develop the next step. The vision itself will likely never be attained, because the fundamental technical environment is constantly evolving.

Using the Project Management Framework (PMF) from the PMBOK, the steps become a continuous process in enterprise architectural management: initiating, planning, execution, monitoring, and closure. The Project Management Framework is a close analog to the Systems Development Life Cycle (SDLC) used in software engineering, which includes: initiation, concept development, planning, requirements analysis, design, development, integration and testing, implementation, maintenance, and disposition. The enterprise architect should be constantly addressing these steps in each element of the enterprise, with an eye toward emerging solutions and their potential usefulness for the business entity. Everything up to the end of life of a technology, service, or solution should be considered even while planning for its creation or execution.

Vision, business alignment, program, and project goals must remain living documents, reviewed regularly to address changes in business practices, regulatory mandates, technologies, and their uses. Robust entities will engage continuous improvement (CI) review with strong change management (CM) practices to ensure that business alignment remains effective while longer-term goals remain attainable. Although the process of updates is a continuous and repeated operational function, each element can be managed using well-tested project management practices, with the output of each project consumed as input for the next cycle in turn.

Hardware

Before delving into the enterprise's interconnected software and service agents, it is worth examining the hardware foundation that must support the evolving spectrum of user applications, malware defense, and sundry other elements of the enterprise. An individual computer system may serve many roles:

- **Server**—Any service that performs a task or presents data based on requests from a client
- **Client**—Any system that consumes and/or presents data provided by a system operating in a server role
- **Thin client**—Any system that serves only a presentation and input role, without its own operating environment

Note: Most systems will perform multiple roles, both hosting services and consuming data from others. An individual system may even recursively consume its own host services as a client.

The role of an individual hardware system may affect its update cycle, depending on use, criticality, and other business issues such as service-level agreement contracts. Thin client systems may be able to accept updates without disrupting the remote client operating environment, while updating a server could shut down entire operations until the process is concluded. Care and planning is critical to ensure effective, timely updates while avoiding or minimizing disruption of business.

Firmware

The most fundamental and lowest-frequency updates to hardware systems include updates to firmware. Firmware includes the internal instruction set used by a device for initiation and operation, often encoded in nonvolatile storage. A common example of this is the basic input/output system (BIOS) bootstrapping code used by a computer to start up, access its long-term storage system, and begin loading its operating system. Firmware refers to low-level operations of a device, separate from emerging FLASH-based onboard storage used for immediate boot environments.

Firmware updates often require specialized standalone applications, custom boot mechanisms, or other procedures whose function isolates the update process from the business-as-usual functions of the device being updated. In many ways, this process is as delicate as performing brain surgery on one's self, and a failed update can render a device unrecoverably nonfunctional, or "bricked." Many small- to mid-sized businesses do not plan and test firmware updates as they are released on additional test-only equipment, instead relying on ad-hoc updates to production equipment when mandated by function loss or other signifying event. Few small businesses have sufficient equipment to function as spares that can be lost in a botched firmware update test.

Firmware updates require extensive regular research, as each vendor provides one or more versions of update for its equipment. These updates may require review of batch and lot numbers on individual pieces of equipment to determine which updates are appropriate. Within a single computer, there may be many firmware elements that must be updated—the motherboard's BIOS may be complemented by specific firmware on storage controllers, video and audio controllers, internet-working systems, onboard encryption devices, and other dedicated computing elements.

Each such system may require review of type, model, lot, and batch details against an individual vendor's sites. Because of the level of effort required, even enterprises that regularly review firmware update requirements may only perform this cycle quarterly or yearly. And often, firmware updates are only appropriate if a particular condition emerges in hardware operation.

Drivers

Software device drivers couple closely with the hardware devices they facilitate. Although these should be addressed along with standard software update practices, it is important to identify and document the drivers in use within an enterprise so that changes in hardware components and updates to the drivers themselves can be addressed in the software update process. For businesses whose regulatory mandates require documentation of all software in use within the enterprise, device drivers can be difficult to properly identify. Drivers created by parties other than the hardware manufacturer, such as community-developed device drivers in many Linux distributions, can present challenges in some regulatory environments.

Components

Component-level updates are less common than they were a decade ago, a result of integrated on-board components in larger-scale integrated circuit designs. Input/output and communications components remain challenging for larger enterprises, where drivers and configuration settings may have to be adjusted when replacing a component using a similar unit from a different vendor or batch. This is particularly troublesome for governmental agencies where the procurement process is long-cycle and regularly changes vendors based on yearly bidding cycles.

Thorough testing and documentation of hardware inventories at the component level can rapidly escalate device-level total cost of ownership beyond the rip-and-replace cost. This becomes much more significant when devices are kept in operation beyond design or warranty limits, when availability of compatible components and cost per service call can generate significant additional costs in lost time and productivity.

Tech Refresh

Tech update or refresh practices form one of the most hotly debated issues in enterprise networks of all sizes. Some businesses choose to buy the best-in-class system available and press it into service for as long as possible, while others buy low-to-midrange systems and plan to replace them at the end of their warranty cycle. Other strategies exist, with a few common options:

- **Until dead**—Many businesses attempt to gain the greatest possible economic return on technology investments by maintaining equipment in service until it simply stops working and can no longer be repaired. As an example, numerous VAX/VMS clusters well over a decade old are still being used in production environments. This option provides the greatest stability in the operating environment but at times presents challenges for system integrators who may face resource constraints (remember Moore's and Kryder's laws) and compatibility with emerging technologies. Component replacement costs are also increasingly high as directly compatible equivalents become unavailable. Media and storage formats also become problematic in these environments, in which compatibility becomes a challenge for software integration efforts. Skill availability may become a major cost factor for these systems, as retirement and other business factors make experience with legacy systems more difficult to acquire and retain. This is the least agile strategy possible, with legacy elements hanging on and impeding integration of emerging options.

- **Cutting edge**—Enterprises with financial incentive and adequate resources may replace systems every year or even more often, in order to push performance to the very limits of available technology. Businesses that consume spare processing cycles for compute grids may follow this path to maximize the CPU cycles per watt enterprise-wide, while others may depend on the "latest and greatest" systems to woo and maintain their customer base. Beyond being costly, this strategy can translate into the most challenging environment for users forced to deal with constant data migration together with application reload and update issues. Shifting storage of user data to centralized servers can offset the disruption somewhat, by ensuring that data stores remain intact. Data storage remediation practices such as secure wipe and environmentally friendly equipment disposal efforts present cost-recovery issues in this strategy. This strategy provides the highest level of agility, because new systems can be acquired to meet the requirements for emerging technologies and services.

- **The plum**—Businesses may replace systems on a priority based on status, position within the organizational chart, or other internal hierarchical mechanism for individual selection. By implementing rewards of the newest technology, these enterprises have little opportunity to benefit from economies of scale and create incredible complexity for support and upgrade efforts. This strategy is exceptionally poor, due to long-term costs, support issues that will arise due to complexity generated by minor differences between systems, and ill will for those users who are not on this year's update short list. This is typically a strategy employed in immature enterprise environments, where technology purchase can be controlled by a single individual and may be used solely to produce political goodwill for that individual. This strategy should be avoided.

- **The waterfall**—As in the "plum" strategy, the waterfall employs a replacement scheme that depends on identification of the key users or functions. These systems are then replaced, with the displaced systems shifted to second-tier use, those in turn to lower tiers until the oldest systems are simply removed from service. This strategy maximizes utilization against cost but increases complexity over cyclic replacement strategies and can keep some systems in use beyond their warranty period or expected life. When used in research or engineering enterprises which demand greater processing power for specific users or functions, this can be an effective strategy. When used in politically based hierarchies in which the top dogs get the best toys, this strategy creates "have and have-not" feelings between users and develops greater complexity without adding value to the enterprise. This strategy shares the highest level of user disruption, because all systems shift one layer down with each cycle.

- **Full pulse**—Enterprises with a defined replacement cycle, typically linked to warranty or funding cycles, may elect to replace all systems each time the cycle concludes. This is the least complex enterprise possible, but almost never occurs beyond very small-scale network enterprises or those within specialized isolated environments such as extreme-environment research facilities. This strategy provides all users with equal technology and affords integrators a simple environment with a well-defined upgrade term. If the cycle exceeds the limits of Moore's and Kryder's laws, life-cycle costs increase toward the end of each replacement cycle. Shortened cycles avoid this and increase agility, but they increase costs accordingly. This strategy suffers in budgetary planning, because some years will have no replacement costs while the end-of-cycle year will require full funding for the entire enterprise. Similarly, support personnel requirements are high in replacement years and reduced during the remainder of the cycle.

- **Steady cycle**—As with the full pulse strategy, the steady cycle replaces systems on a cycle linked to fiscal or warranty constraints. Unlike full pulse, the steady cycle replaces a portion of the systems each term, allowing for easier and less variable budgeting across multiple years for mid-to-large-scale enterprise networks. User environment disruption is minimized, complexity is minimized within each term's purchase group, and all systems are replaced on a regular basis to provide a continually renewing technology base able to implement planned integration of emerging solutions.

Because of the impact of Moore's law, major software development cycles, and standard warranty periods, the most common cycle for user workstation and laptop equipment employs purchase of midrange systems on a cycle between 3 and 4 years. Server-class hardware typically enjoys higher tolerances and can be managed on a 5-year cycle, which corresponds to common manufacturing strategies such as the evolution of new blade chassis formats. A steady cycle replacement strategy provides the optimal balance between network agility and a predictable budget, while providing minimized complexity and regular replacement of all systems.

User acceptance is typically better under steady cycle replacement than under other strategies because there are no privileged users who always get the best, newest equipment. Users know when their next cycle will occur and that everyone with the same need will receive the same equipment, allowing computing equipment to be considered more as office equipment like the telephone than as a personally possessed item of greater or lesser quality and capability. This solution minimizes disruption due to replacement, as all equipment is maintained within its expected lifespan and replacement occurs only once per cycle for each device. The steady cycle strategy provides many benefits and is typically the best total-cost-of-ownership option.

- **Ad hoc**—Immature enterprise environments may employ ad-hoc purchasing to add, replace, and update systems in small numbers or individually based on equipment failure, emergent need, or other strategic determination. This is particularly common in research environments where individual researchers may enjoy independent funding or in enterprises where end-of-fiscal-year demands encourage "splurge" spending in a use-it-or-lose-it manner. This is perhaps the worst enterprise-level strategy because complexity is maximized without alignment with purchasing strategies. The result is an unplanned collection of variant technologies that can change at any time and in any way—in short, a real mess.

- **Personal**—Enterprises without coordinated purchase of systems, software, and hardware may employ instead technologies selected at individual whim or purchased as personal solutions. This is an enterprise type found in small office/home office (SOHO) environments with equipment-reimbursement stipends or within organizations constructed as community-shared resources. In higher-education environments, this type of enterprise may emerge spontaneously from collections of student personal equipment, with authentication and resource sharing added later. Personal-technology solutions do not represent a true enterprise, but more an extended workgroup, due to the variety of equipment and software that may be present in even very small environments. This is not a supportable solution for well-integrated enterprises beyond the smallest scale, although personally owned mobile devices are become increasingly common.

- **Surplus**—Volunteer organizations may at times be forced to employ only donated equipment, while unfunded organizational elements may only have access to technology resources retired from active service from funded elements. Such surplus-technology enterprises often press equipment beyond system lifespan and warranty cycles, increasing enterprise complexity and the potential for operational disruption due to equipment failure. Surplus-technology enterprises may include strategies for component-level harvesting and reconstruction of "Frankenstein" systems, requiring significant personnel for technology maintenance and support. This is an enterprise solution that is only used when no other option exists, when a temporary proof-of-concept enterprise element is needed to test an emerging business function, or when retired equipment is consumed for compute cycle farming in distributed high-performance computing environments.

Software

Although hardware selection and management present the most visible elements of the modern enterprise network, software and services define the boundaries and functions that separate an enterprise from a simple collection of devices. Minimizing variation in deployed operating systems and applications reduces support skill requirements and improves flexibility in user assignment within the extended enterprise by providing a common experience when accessing resources across multiple business elements.

Like hardware, software must be regularly updated to meet emerging functional and operational mandates as well as to resist the ever-evolving spectrum of threats to network security and resource availability. Strategies for software deployment and update must balance the need for regular, rapid update response with the need to minimize user environment disruption—all while attempting to schedule updates only during off-peak utilization periods in an environment of 24/7 resource availability and consumption.

Testing

Before new operating environments or software applications can be included in a network enterprise, it is critical to test their functionality and suitability within a protected environment in order to protect the production enterprise from unanticipated disruption or modification. A test network should be used to perform this function, created as a mirror of the settings and software solutions in use within the production environment.

While many small-to-medium-sized organizations may not enjoy adequate resources to create a duplicate network in its entirety, the use of virtualization can allow a limited-capacity equivalent to be set up with minimal hardware investment by creating an entire test network within a small number of host systems. Virtualized test networks also allow rapid rollback restoration to a known-good state in the event that software under test produces negative integration results.

Deployment

Deployment forms the first line of software update, both when a bare-metal system begins its life within the enterprise as well as in recovery following loss of function or after malware compromise. Initial deployment of operating system environments and software applications may consist of a fully configured "image," an ad-hoc installation of individually configured systems intended to meet specific user requirements, or through automated package assignment atop a standard base.

- **Ad hoc**—Ad-hoc deployment solutions are not suitable beyond very small enterprise environments, or when software licensing constraints demand per-system installation control such as when dongle-based physical keys must be installed. Ad-hoc deployment entails the greatest time expense and gains the greatest level of personalization in installation, because every package is installed manually for each system.

- **Image based**—Image-based deployment scenarios should be considered for extended enterprise network deployment and update, though hardware and software variation may create the need for multiple "images" that must be independently updated to include emerging defensive or operational requirements. Some enterprises may deploy fully configured operating systems complete with necessary software applications already installed and configured, captured as an "image" copied from a source system. Others may employ a basic image that is then modified by additional application customization.

  Deployment can be conducted by connecting systems within a protected "nursery" network in which systems can be configured and updated before being exposed to a publically accessible network with its attendant threats due to worms and other malware. Deployment may be performed over network connections to in-place systems when network bandwidth is adequate and the network is defended against malware. When network bandwidth is limited or unavailable, image deployment can also be conducted using removable media such as optical disks, USB memory sticks, or external hard drive devices.

  Virtualized environments may also employ a standard image for rapid system provisioning, allowing deployment of additional virtual systems by simply copying the source files to the new hosting location. This practice aids support functions by minimizing variation between virtual systems in the same way that purchasing strategies can minimize variation between hardware systems.

- **Base plus**—Medium to large enterprise networks should consider deployment options that depend on a standard base, often only the basic operating system and defensive applications, atop which applications are loaded based on group or location strategies reflecting organizational functions. Deployment of applications through this type of solution requires more detailed planning but can provide initial deployment as well as later update functions through the same mechanism.

  In this strategy, the base operating system and OS-integrated applications such as malware defense are captured as an image to be deployed to all systems. After identifying the proper group membership or location settings for each system within the directory service, additional packages are deployed using a management function such as the Group Policy found in Microsoft networks or by way of management utilities in heterogeneous network settings. Because the base-plus strategy can deploy a particular package to a specific system, group, or user, this system provides the greatest flexibility in application selection, at the cost of a slight delay when a new user accesses the system for the first time and triggers installation of new packages assigned to that user.

- **Virtualized**—Application and desktop virtualization solutions allow the automatic provisioning of system, service, and application suites based on system, group, user, or role-based assignment. Because no hardware preconfiguration is required, this can be the fastest setup option for highly mobile business units or during disaster recovery efforts. Once the servers and DNS namespace has been restored to direct access to a new data center, any commodity hardware systems supporting the proper remote protocols can be connected and updated functionality accessed automatically on the virtualization host. Updates applied to the desktop virtualization host or updated packages replaced in an application virtualization service will be automatically available upon the next user access without requiring update to the end-user device, though this can present a risk for data compromise if not properly secured and maintained properly.

Note: Due to the rapid growth of virtualized and cloud computing environments, software and hardware refresh cycles should be considered as related but fundamentally independent functions.

Update

Once a system is installed, configured, and deployed to its operational venue, the maintenance cycle has only just begun. Threats and exploits are continually evolving and presenting new challenges to enterprise security, while new application functionalities and system updates play a continual role in enterprise technology maintenance. A general statement to encompass this evolution comes from the extension of Moore's and Kryder's laws, and is evidenced in the major-release cycle of many commercial software vendors: "A new generation of technology is released every three years." Although this is only a rough measure and many technologies (notably security-related and mobile) change at a faster rate, it has worked well in planning for regular technology updates for more than two decades.

Patches and Service Packs

Patches and hotfixes are released regularly by software vendors to correct small groups of vulnerabilities, while rollups of these small changes are produced as service packs that allow easier update to new systems beyond the sequential application of all minor updates since the base software edition was released. New features may also be introduced in service pack updates, requiring significantly more testing before deployment into an enterprise to ensure that changes do not degrade enterprise service availability.

Zero-Day Threats

So-called "zero-day" security issues may also arise randomly, allowing an attacker the opportunity to exploit previously unknown security vulnerabilities. When these attacks arise, vendors must rush patches through that are often less well tested than scheduled updates, and these present a two-edged sword for the security and testing teams within the enterprise. Updates like these must be applied as rapidly as possible to protect the network, but testing is still necessary to ensure that rapidly produced updates do not render critical systems inoperable.

You can minimize the potential negative impact of these updates through participation in professional forums and testing groups that allow feedback to provide input from a range of enterprise configurations. Monitoring security feedback aggregation websites such as the SANS Internet Storm Center (http://isc.sans.org) can also aid in identifying emerging threats and evaluating community-developed defensive strategies.

Test Networks

Maintaining a test network that matches the same software packages and configuration settings found in the production environment is important to ensure that updates do not compromise critical application functionality. The use of virtualized computing environments makes this significantly less expensive, because a test network need not consume the same processing power as your production environment, allowing a single physical host to support multiple virtualized test servers. In some cases, a single powerful physical host might support a full test network by itself.

Automated Updates

There is no such thing as a "permanently secure" computer, due to the steady evolution of new threats and new defensive measures to meet each in turn. Physical warfare evolved from striking, piercing, and crushing weapons and animal hide defensive armor to include ever more powerful ranged weapons and metal-reinforced armor types. This in turn required the evolution of longbows and plate armor, which the emergence of crossbows made no longer viable as a form of personal defense. Mobile barriers became armored transports, while crossbows gave way to gunpowder weapons. Today's tanks and armor-piercing rounds continue this evolution, extending all the way back to the first person who developed the original "superweapon" in the form of a rock tied to a branch.

Network computing has followed the same pattern of offensive and defensive evolution, first one and then the other in a cycle of response and increasing sophistication. When new patches are released, automated tools provide attackers with rapid reverse engineering of corrected vulnerabilities, allowing directed attacks to be fashioned and released often even before operators can apply the new updates across their extended enterprise environments. Automated update services ensure that new updates can be applied automatically across large and widely distributed networks. These services are absolutely vital for all networks of more than a tiny handful of systems, and provide the greatest reduction in direct human support for workstation maintenance.

Retirement (License Recovery)

During tech refresh as well as normal system maintenance processes, machines will be reloaded or removed from service. Without a registry of software and licensing, together with a formal policy for license management, software costs may continually escalate without need. Concurrent licensing application virtualization services allow the automatic release of package-bound licensing when software sessions are terminated, but many products including antimalware defenses and service applications may require manual interaction in order to expire or release legacy software licenses when no longer in use or when storage media is securely wiped for disposal.

Malware Defense

Many forms of malware continue to evolve with the rapidity of their biological namesakes. Early self-replicating programs led to the creation of viruses, which evolved in turn to self-propagating worms and automated malware defenses necessary to defend against the growing flood of Trojan horses, keystroke loggers, browser redirects, and the many other forms of malware that can flourish in an unprotected environment.

Application of patches and hotfixes can harden the network against automated attacks, but social engineering practices can still introduce malware into the enterprise though many channels. Active defenses layered atop a hardened network can help to identify emerging threats, isolate infections from other network elements, and automatically remove many threats to the enterprise.

Note: Although many types of malware can be removed automatically, others will insert copies of their application functions into well-used files or hide within protected system restore points. Manual cleansing using protected operating modes may be required to restore function, but nothing short of a total system wipe and reload can ever ensure absolute elimination of compromise.

The use of central management software is very helpful in mid-to-large-scale networks, allowing identification of systems that have not updated recently, those that fail to update properly, and those that have been or are currently infected. Regular review of malware defense log files is critical for the identification of emerging threats and failing updates, which can provide a false sense of security to users who assume that their systems are "once secure, always secure."

Directory Entries

Software maintenance and update processes should also include regular reviews of computer accounts and service records. Directory registrations and certificates for failed and replaced systems should be removed or expired when physical devices are removed from operation, reloaded, or when securely wiped for disposal. User deprovisioning is also critical to ensure that residual data files, user profiles, and inactive accounts are similarly cleaned up on a regular basis. Like sweeping the floor, regular clean-up practices can help keep garbage from accumulating in the directory as a result of updates, replacements, and the passage of time.

Passwords

The Internet Engineering Task Force (IETF) published RFC 2196 (Site Security Handbook) back in 1997, identifying the regular expiration of passwords as a potential security threat to enterprises. Conventional wisdom has always been that regular changes to passwords should enhance security by blocking brute-force password guessing practices. Modern enterprise networks have more sophisticated authentication services capable of automatically locking out log-on attempts after multiple failed attempts within a specified window of time, alleviating this threat somewhat, but the raw processing power available to attackers now provides many other, more effective avenues for attack.

Some threats that arise from regular password changes include increased support requirements for users who have forgotten their new passwords, selection of very simple passwords and phrases, selection of passwords that change only minimally and in guessable ways (example: MyPassw0rd1, MyPassw0rd2, MyPassw0rd3…), or users creating physical notes of each new password—often stored in discoverable locations near the operating environment, such as beneath a keyboard or on a "sticky note" attached to the system monitor.

Note: Password expiration on a yearly basis has always been acceptable to my own clients in many different network environments, although I have always implemented policies for password expiration upon individual account compromise, any admin account compromise, upon change in personnel or job role, or upon personnel termination or separation.

Compromise of an admin account should trigger expiration of all account passwords, including user, administrative, and service accounts.

Summary

This chapter has focused on the need for continued management and maintenance in enterprise network operations and support. Like the bridge that is forever being painted somewhere along its length, an extended enterprise network must be perpetually updated, patched, and refreshed. Policy development, communication, and implementation are critical to ensure that users and technical implementers alike accept and support this ongoing requirement. The next chapters will examine common threats to the enterprise, defensive measures to address these threats, and strategies for disaster recovery and business continuity.

Chapter 12

Enterprise Security

In This Chapter

- Considerations for layering security measures
- An examination of common enterprise threats
- Identification of risk management strategies

A common way of describing physical security is that "a house is only as secure as its least secure door or window." This means that an unauthorized entrance requires only one open window to provide access to the entire structure. An extended enterprise network follows the same rule: An attacker need only bypass the least secure entry point to gain access to the entire structure—unless steps are taken to isolate segments of the network and to protect information assets.

This chapter addresses threats to the enterprise and some methods of mitigating these threats. Because defensive and offensive technologies continually evolve, I will not attempt to address every possible threat in specific detail, but rather to identify strategies that you can apply to your own enterprise during architecture updates. Security should form a foundation for all other architecture changes, not be layered on top of the network at some later date, and all defenses should be regularly tested and updated to meet emerging threats.

The Process of Security

Security is not a state that can be achieved once and for all time; it is an ongoing process of addressing threats to the enterprise that may arise from external attackers, internal mischief or misuse, environmental hazards, or any other vector that provides a potential undesirable change to enterprise functionality or availability. The standard view of security addresses three aspects of service and data:

- **(C)onfidentiality**—Data and services should only be available through authorized access, with unauthorized access prevented or detected and reported if controls are bypassed.
- **(I)ntegrity**—Data and services should be protected from unauthorized modification or corruption, during use and in storage.
- **(A)vailability**—Data and services should be available for use upon authorized access attempts, with outages and service interruptions monitored and reported.

Security Is like an Onion

To meet the protective goals of this C–I–A mandate, security controls should be layered to create a series of barriers against compromise, failure, or unauthorized access. Figure 12.1 illustrates this type of layering, starting with leadership and vision and drilling down to implementation settings and configuration details. Attackers and undesirable events must bypass each layer in turn in order to disrupt or modify service availability or enterprise data, providing more opportunities for denial, mitigation, and alerting.

Program Rather than Project

Although individual implementation efforts may be managed as projects (limited-term, defined end goal, and criteria), the process of security is an ongoing operation and so should be managed as a program (open-ended, regularly reviewed, with corrective actions applied during each

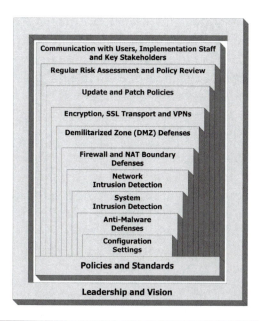

Figure 12.1 A simplified structural outline of a layered defensive strategy. Note that training and communications support all other functions, while policies and standards provide a solid basis for implementation and control. Your leadership and vision will define and align protective strategies with organization requirements and mandates.

iteration). Security planning and review should include management of a risk register, with impact, value, and responsible parties clearly identified and communicated appropriately. This registry is a living document and must be updated at each change in standards, tech refresh cycle, change in personnel, change in partnering or hosting practices, or identification of an emerging threat.

Explain Why

Implemented security measures should not be onerous or present barriers to normal operations, or users will take action to circumvent their protective action to "just get the job done." Automation of settings management, access provisioning, and event log review can all aid in smoothing out the impact of new security measures by ensuring that standards are applied uniformly and completely. Training efforts and user awareness measures such as monthly IT newsletters are an excellent way to present the "why" of a security measure prior to its "what" and "how" implementation. Users are far more likely to avoid bypassing security measures if they understand the purpose and function of each such measure.

Standardize and Simplify

Standards and policies must apply uniformly across the enterprise, to avoid an "open window" in one area that will weaken the security stance elsewhere. As with the selection of technology and software standards, care should be taken to reduce complexity in security policies, technologies, and configuration settings across the enterprise. This aids in identification of threats, application of updates, and technical support capability.

Common Enterprise Threats

Uncertainty (risk) is a constant presence in the enterprise, in that directed or automated attacks may be launched from anywhere in the world or inadvertent configuration changes may compromise data availability or access controls. Power outages, storms and earthquakes, acts of terrorism or warfare, and industrial espionage are all potential threats to the enterprise that must be addressed by security and recovery practices. We will examine disaster recovery and business continuity strategies at greater length in the next chapter.

Load Only in the Nursery

Malware is a generic term encompassing directly threatening software agents such as viruses and worms, as well as security-weakening agents such as Trojan horses, service proxy redirectors, and spyware such as keyboard loggers. A centrally managed malware-defense system is one of the most fundamental "must have" security technologies. The time between an unprotected system's connection to the Internet and its compromise by one of the more than 1 million identified types of malware is measured in minutes or less.

Care should be taken to ensure that new systems are loaded, fully updated, and provided an updated malware defense before exposure even to an internal organizational network. Like a newborn baby, an unprotected system is susceptible to illness passed from other systems without a strong immunity to resist electronic contagion. A shielded subnet used only for loading and updating systems can function as a nursery, to allow systems time for full configuration and malware protection before exposure to other systems.

Secure the Network

Network attacks may come in the form of denial-of-service attacks that overwhelm service availability through massed service requests, or may involve the unauthorized interception of data during transport between systems. Automated network profiling software can allow a would-be attacker to identify open service ports, unencrypted data transport endpoints, open-text protocols in use, and vulnerabilities in system defenses due to missing updates or outdated services still in use. Your security practices should include regular scanning of systems for vulnerabilities and network traffic for exposed data streams. Encryption between endpoints can aid in protecting data during transport, using solutions such as Secure Sockets Layer (SSL) website access, virtual private networking (VPNs) for secured access over Internet and wireless connectivity, or a public-key encryption infrastructure (PKI) implementation for point-to-point encrypted data transport, as illustrated in Figure 12.2.

Secure the Data

Encryption and access controls should also be applied to data during storage and backup archival processes, to ensure that physical access to storage media or lost backup tapes does not expose data to unauthorized review. As I discussed earlier in this book, mobile devices are at enhanced risk because of their small size and portability, and on-device encryption mandates are vital for devices used to conduct organizational business using data local to the device.

Backup media are alo at similar risk due to size, portability, information density and transport practices for offsite disaster recovery backup protection. Data should be encrypted on backup media to ensure that a lost tape does not lead to accidental release of sensitive or protected data

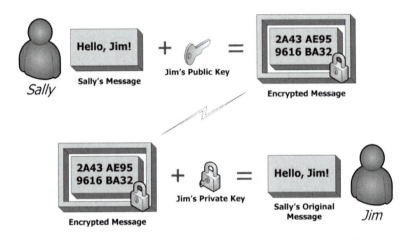

Figure 12.2 An example of a public-key encrypted message transmission between Sally (the originator, with only Jim's public key) and Jim (the receiver, using only his private key). Unauthorized interception of the message, even with the public key, provides no useful data.

assets. Data stored on file servers and in databases may also be candidates for encryption, to guard against data exposure through unauthorized access to devices and file stores.

Note: Encryption of data within a relational database can have negative consequences if it is not performed properly. Because an attribute used to create a clustered index reorganizes the order of records within a table, encryption of the clustered index attribute can cause the entire table to be re-sorted every time a single value is changed, due to the re-encryption of that attribute across all records. This can create significant processor load and record-locking issues if it is not considered during application, database, and encryption planning.

Secure the Applications

Security practices must also be put into place for application development and management strategies. As with SSL requirements for Web-based access to data, reporting tools, dashboards, and other organizational services, application design must also provide internal checks and validation to protect operational continuity and function. As I have often said, applications should be made as "idiot-resistant" as possible—"idiot-proof" is an impossible goal, because there are so many idiots who are very inventive.

Idiot resistance can be enhanced through code review and automated testing of code segments and applications, but should also include internal controls such as input validation, catching and passing failures to a secure end state, maximum allowable resource constraints, and meaningful codes for errors and unexpected termination of operations. An error page that displays information about where a failure occurred (even using cryptic numerical checkpoint values to avoid exposing details of application design) is useful when accompanied with contact information for technical support and directions for proper error reporting.

Regular review or automated monitoring of key services will allow the identification of emerging threats to the enterprise, by identifying operational characteristics outside of expected specifications. Figure 12.3 provides an example of a monitoring package being used to display real-time data on a server's operations.

Note: Detection of aberrant operational characteristics requires a baseline and established variance from the baseline against which to measure current levels of use. This baseline must be comprehensive to cover cyclic shifts in load, such as morning start-of-day log-ons compared to midnight and weekend utilization, and updated regularly to address changes in technologies and use.

Defend the Enterprise

Because the potential attack vectors (including internal "idiots" who just hit the wrong key) are without bounds but security and defensive options are limited, it is important to prioritize threats and items listed in the risk registry. Applying Dr. Joseph Juran's extrapolated Pareto's principle, defense against roughly 80% of identified risks should fall within 20% of potential protective solutions. It is important to identify the "critical few" so as to get the greatest return on mitigation efforts, knowing that some legal and regulatory mandates are absolutes and must be addressed no matter what is required.

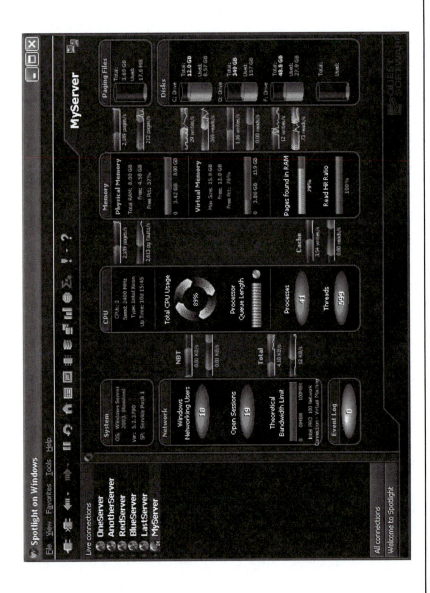

Figure 12.3 An example server monitoring dashboard displaying real-time data on process load, CPU and memory use, data throughput, and storage device levels.

Malware Defense

Malware defenses and a system-load nursery are excellent starting points for securing systems against compromise. Threat signatures and antimalware applications require regular updates on a daily (sometimes hourly) basis. Centralized automated management of malware defenses is mandatory beyond a handful of supported systems, while reporting should be reviewed daily to identify compromised systems for cleansing or wipe-and-reload service. This is not an area in which to save money at the expense of quality, because the threat is continuous and includes a high probability of significantly impacting the C–I–A mandates.

Network Protection

Encryption provides a key function in protection of data transferred through and stored within the extended enterprise. Additional services such as intrusion detection systems (IDS) can monitor network traffic (network-based) or access and application functions within a monitored host (device-based). These systems can raise an alert when nonstandard access is identified or when specific attack signatures are detected.

Network firewalls can provide defensive "walls" around protected subnets, separating network traffic and restricting access between subnets based on access rules and service port constraints. Figure 12.4 illustrates a firewall configured to segment a private network into protected internal services and systems and a public-facing, partially protected demilitarized zone (DMZ) subnet, separated from the external Internet by service port restrictions.

Firewall configuration management and log review should be regular and comprehensive, to ensure that changes to network resources, services, and use are properly managed to protect network resources from unauthorized access.

Defense Against the Unexpected

Quality and risk management disciplines attempt to address the "known known" and "known unknown" threats to an enterprise by identifying risks, prioritizing defenses to gain the greatest protection possible using available resources, and then managing identified risks in the four standard ways:

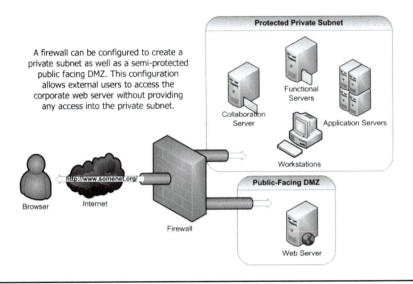

A firewall can be configured to create a private subnet as well as a semi-protected public facing DMZ. This configuration allows external users to access the corporate web server without providing any access into the private subnet.

Figure 12.4 A simplified network diagram illustrating a firewall configured for constrained access between a protected private organization network, a partially protected DMZ subnet, and the public Internet.

- **Eliminating/avoiding**—Avoiding a risk by ceasing to perform a particular activity or to use a particular technology. This is not always possible or desirable.
- **Mitigating**—Reducing the likelihood of a threat's occurrence or its potential impact by changing processes or adding defenses. This is generally the most likely mechanism for addressing identified risks.
- **Transferring**—Transferring risks may consist of outsourcing a service such as backup operations or purchasing insurance to transfer financial repercussions to an external party. This practice generally has a high cost and may not protect nontangible assets such as client loyalty or a regulatory mandate with legal but nonmonetary consequences.
- **Accepting**—Some risks must simply be accepted, either due to inability to prevent or mitigate the threat or due to cost factors that make mitigation impossible. Acceptance of risk requires careful documentation of the "why" used to make this decision, and should be communicated to senior management for written approval.

Note: Keep in mind that it is possible to outsource many security functions and operations, but it is not possible to outsource responsibility.

Emergency Response Planning

In any organization, the best possible listing of all identified risks will likely miss a few. Generally, a risk registry might identify and address up to 90% of the potential (known) threats to the enterprise. The other 10% must be identified as rapidly as possible upon occurrence, through log and service review, and addressed through mitigation practices based on a well-designed action plan that is regularly tested, reviewed, updated, and communicated to all parties. The time for disaster planning is not after the emergency exists ("Okay, the data center just disappeared into a sinkhole. . . who wants to discuss offsite backup media strategies first. . . ."). It is important to build an effective response team with clear communication channels and designated responsibility well ahead of an actual emergency in order to have any chance at response, recovery, or continuity of operations, rather than simple after-action reconstruction.

Don't Forget the Little Things

The growing use of mobile, often personally owned, devices for access to organization resources requires the creation and communication of clear security policies for all devices used for business purposes. In addition to on-device encryption mandates, additional policies might include mandates for malware defenses for remote desktops, or device update and on-idle automatic locking requirements. Because these devices continue to expand in variety and number, policies addressing mobile security requirements should be reviewed at least quarterly or upon the release of a new popular platform.

Summary

This chapter has included a review of security threats to the enterprise and examples of solutions and policies meant to mitigate the risk they present to organizational functions. Numerous regulatory and legal mandates may provide a number of "must address" constraint items in the risk registry, and should be considered first in any security prioritization efforts. Operations that depend on other functions within the organization may also play a part in determining risk priority, requiring regular review to identify changes in the organization, its functions, and technologies in use.

Communication of the "why" and "what's expected" of security measures is vital to engaging users to follow policy guidelines and avoid bypassing security measures. In the next chapter, I will examine considerations and strategies for dealing with the aftermath of a threat's occurrence.

Chapter 13

Recovering from Disaster

In This Chapter

- An examination of business continuity and disaster recovery
- Considerations for disaster recovery and response
- A review of common technologies involved in recovery operations

One question that should never be asked following a disaster or attack is "Now what?" My grandfather always commented that there was little point in locking the gate after the horses had all gotten out of the barn, and emergency management is somewhat akin to this sentiment. Disaster response, recovery, and continuity planning must be conducted well before an event occurs. Even the best plans will at times prove inadequate, and then well-established emergency communication strategies must already be in place.

Recent major events have illustrated this requirement all too clearly. Businesses in New Orleans found that there is no time to haphazardly hand out flyers detailing emergency contact information when the flood waters are already waist deep and rising. Offices in the Twin Towers could not go back and make offsite backups of critical data after the airplanes struck. Wide-scale losses of power and sudden emergencies have been headline news many times over the past decade. This chapter will address what to do before and after the next event.

Continuity of Operations Versus Disaster Recovery

When a disaster strikes, the foremost concern is preventing loss of life. Following this is retaining organizational value, which includes both tangible assets as well as intangibles such as client loyalty and trust. An alternate site or redundant data center can keep an organizational website up and taking orders even while the data center resembles a tumbled pile of rubble and EMS is still treating people in the area. Communications between clients and organizational staff may be somewhat delayed, but a virtual answering service and mobile computing systems can allow individual knowledge workers and staff members to address client requirements from a nearby coffee shop or from home until new office space is available. In some cases, a geographically distant website might serve as the initial contact point between staff members forced to evacuate ahead of a crisis.

Continuity of Operations (COO)

Organizational planning intended to address requirements for ongoing operations during and following a disaster will focus on the continuity of service and operations. These plans are immediately activated at the time of the event and continue until terminated or no longer needed. Redundant servers providing functions such as DNS and authentication services might keep workstations and SCADA controls in operation even in the event of primary data center loss. Offsite hosting of a Web portal or e-business site might allow customers to continue placing orders, even as the sales office is flooded and under water. Mobile communications and remote desktop access might allow normal business to be conducted even after a toxic spill in the headquarters lobby.

Planning for continuity of operations should identify and prioritize services that are necessary to allow continued operations, even if at a reduced level of availability or responsiveness. These plans should start with simple considerations such as redundant arrays of independent disks (RAID) for continuity in the face of a storage device failure, as well as any other "single points of failure" (also called "choke points") required for minimal operation function. Identification of the true minimum functions may require effort, due to the "everything is priority 1" mentality that pervades many organizations.

Note: Continuity planning should be a strict bare-bones listing of minimal requirements, addressing immediate-to-mid-term continuance of business function during and following an event.

Disaster Recovery (DR)

Disaster recovery planning is more comprehensive than that required for continuity of operations. Disaster recovery extends the recovery objective to include a return of all services to operational function, prioritized in terms of recovery point objectives and recovery time objective criteria as part of the business impact analysis process. Disaster recovery planning is conducted in conjunction with risk assessment practices, because each entry in the risk register should be coordinated with its appropriate recovery objectives and plans should be developed to facilitate the steps necessary for full recovery. Disaster recovery applies to full loss of function (no continuity was possible) as well as to operations shifted to continuity-of-operations status in the short term, and includes all functions of the organizational enterprise and network. The time frame for disaster recovery is flexible and may include a lag (delay) period for safety and procurement prior to initiation. Disaster recovery practices may not begin until a disaster or emergency has been declared to be at an end, and depends heavily on communication and notification strategies that have been thoroughly tested and regularly updated.

Planning for Recovery

Developing COO/DR plans should involve key stakeholders from each organizational area, to ensure that recovery time and recovery point objectives are reasonable and clearly communicated.

Business Impact Analysis (BIA)

A business impact analysis involves the identification of processes that are critical to organizational operations, as well as identification of the relative criticality and urgency for the return of each process. A bad joke I have heard many times is the suggestion that "Everything's important, so combine it all and do it at once." In both COO and DR states, prioritization of recovery activities is mandatory if chaos is to be avoided. The BIA identifies organizational processes at a high level, with greater resolution addressing requirements for recovery (services, servers, equipment, etc.) later. Many times, conducting a BIA to address technology requirements for recovery will also involve identification of many nontechnology functions and practices necessary as well, allowing the BIA to return value for time spent in many ways at once.

Like any project (limited term, specific goal), objectives developed during the BIA should be specified in terms of time. The 8/80 rule is a useful tool for breaking up recovery into work periods of between 8 and 80 hours, though recovery objectives might be expressed in work periods of one hour, one day, one week, or whatever is deemed appropriate by the planning committee and senior stakeholders. Priority for recovery actions should be based on business need, except where the order of service recovery is mandated by function (for example, the authentication service must be up before the database server can be returned to service).

For each identified business process, recovery objectives (targets and guidelines, not mandates because all plans must be flexible and able to change to meet emerging conditions) should be established for acceptable completion term and span of data loss:

- **Recovery point objective (RPO)**—This measure is used to develop backup strategies for data. It identifies how far back it is acceptable to lose data from the point of failure or loss. Weekly backups, for example, fulfill only RPOs of one week or longer.
- **Recovery time objective (RTO)**—This measure identifies how long the business process can be unavailable. Service-level agreements, contracts, and other factors both tangible and intangible will influence this determination. For high-utilization e-business sites, RTOs may be expressed in terms of minutes before unacceptable losses occur.

Following the business impact analysis, each identified business process must be decomposed into a full inventory of services and requirements for recovery, complete with contact information and contract details necessary for procurement of hardware or software if necessary.

Risk Assessment (RA)

Once a full decomposition of the BIA has been completed, each identified service and resource should be cross-checked against the risk register. Before beginning the recovery planning process, a complete risk analysis is necessary, including identification of contingencies, alternatives, and workarounds for elements that are critical to high-priority process recovery efforts. Many times, this assessment during the COO/DR planning process may reveal areas which require additional contingency reserves, alternate sites, backup equipment, and cost consequences arising from fees, fines, or other negative impacts due to service loss or failure to meet regulatory or contractually mandated service-level criteria.

Construct a Plan

After the BIA and risk assessment have been completed, you will need to create two recovery plans: one for immediate-to-short-term continuity requirements, the second for mid-to-long-term full disaster recovery. The requirements for developing a detailed plan vary widely between organization types and functions, and go well beyond the limits of this single chapter. Once the plan is completed, it is critical to test its assumptions to ensure that theoretical recovery procedures will function when applied to real-world organizational environments.

Because an actual emergency is not likely to coincide with your testing events (hopefully), develop scenarios based on identified risks and test a walk-though of the plan against each scenario. Scenarios might be a simple as a loss of power in the area, requiring a test of on-site generators and battery power backup systems, or may be as complex as a simulated pandemic in which a large portion of the workforce might be unable to leave their homes or too ill to participate in recovery actions. Testing backup personnel, alternate contact mechanisms, and strategies for procuring replacement materials by alternate personnel can aid in identifying potential points of failure and areas for additional training.

Lessons learned during simulations and tests should be used as feedback for an update to the plan. Once the plan has been finalized and approved, it should communicated to responsible parties, made available for review, tested regularly, and remain a living document to be updated to address changes in business process, organizational structure, personnel, or technology.

Technology in Recovery Planning

Because many business processes rely on technology, the CIO or IT lead will typically play a significant role in planning and implementing COO/DR planning activities. Technology is often fundamental to communication strategies, requiring special attention to recovery of authentication, e-mail and website capabilities early in the recovery process.

Alternate Data Center

Disasters may prevent normal use of the data center due to disruption of utilities (power, chilled water, and networking are all common requirements for data center operations) or outright destruction of the facility. In either case, an alternative site for data center operations may be required for COO/DR operations. Depending on the organization, the recovery site may need nontechnical elements such as food, water, and sleeping accommodations for personnel displaced over a large geographic distance due to a large-scale event such as a hurricane or earthquake.

The type of alternative data center needed depends on recovery objectives identified as a result of the BIA, and might include:

- **Hot site**—The most expensive alternative, with the fastest recovery time. Hot backup sites have redundant hardware and software found in the primary data center, and may include continuous-backup and multiple-location clustering of servers and files stores so that the total loss of a primary data center is transparent to users, whose systems simply switch to the hot failover services automatically.
- **Warm site**—Less expensive than a hot site, with a longer recovery time. Warm sites include hardware, software, and utilities necessary for data center operations recovery but require details such as system

configuration and recovery from backup media to be completed before operations resume. Warm sites often employ older equipment removed from service during the previous tech refresh cycle, reducing procurement costs but offering limited capacity in comparison to the hot site.

- **Cold site**—The least expensive alternative, with the longest recovery time requirement (except for a completely new site, which requires starting from nothing). Cold sites are locations with basic utilities such as power and water. They may not have equipment, networking, software, or other requirements for data center operational recovery. Recovery using a cold site will generally require procurement of hardware, software, or utilities before recovery becomes possible.

Alternate Equipment

Recovery following a disaster that results in loss of equipment will generally result in new types or versions of equipment supporting existing functions. Plan testing scenarios should include strategies for recovery using alternative equipment, particularly when using warm or cold backup sites that may have equipment with far less capacity than existing primary data center equipment.

As mentioned earlier in this book, server virtualization and remote desktop access can improve portability between hardware hosting alternatives, provided the hypervisor is compatible with that on the original host. Figure 13.1 illustrates some of the ways in which virtualized servers might be migrated to facilitate recovery operational requirements. Due to the hardware-independent nature of virtual machines, restoration of the virtualized server's files and appropriate network settings will return functionality with the level of resources available on the new host computer.

Alternate Communications

Following hurricanes Katrina and Rita, telephone service was lost throughout the area. Due to the extended power outage, cellular phone service became unavailable in some areas and intermittent in others. Remote personnel in many cases could not access organizational Web servers because those servers were located in data centers within the affected area. One

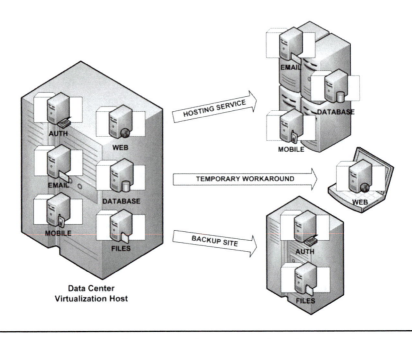

Figure 13.1   Virtualized servers can be recovered to alternative hosting solutions following a disaster.

strategy that proved highly effective in bringing team members back together was providing a simple website hosted in a remote geographic area. This website was formatted to allow viewing using many forms of mobile phone and laptop computing devices with limited connectivity (for example, no Flash components, no graphical embellishments, etc.) and served as an initial point of contact where details could be posted to provide directions for further contact and team reconstruction.

A COO/DR contact site should be named in such a way that it can be easily remembered, established in a very remote location (the other side of the country or several states away if possible), updated regularly if only with a change in date so that users can see the last update time, and communicated to all organizational members regularly. When activated, this read-only site should provide additional contact data without requiring individualized log-ons, to ensure that even new hires are able to read the contact content. Only designated individuals should be able to post data to the site, to avoid conflicting information or misleading details from being posted in the wake of a large-scale emergency.

Summary

To quote a famous tagline, "The world is an imperfect place." Because of this imperfection, it is important to safeguard valuable elements of your enterprise and plan for the "What now?" occasion so that if it arrives, everyone knows their part in recovery. This is not a quick process; it requires identifying all business processes and the technologies that support their functions. Prioritization is also critical, because it is just not possible to simply combine them all and do them at once.

Smooth recovery relies on familiarity with a well-tested and regularly updated plan, combined with effective means of communication between members who may be scattered to all quarters of the compass. In the next chapter, I will discuss some elements of computing that may play a larger role in the years ahead, but in any case, it is absolutely imperative to plan (and test, update, and retest the plan) in order to protect the technology resources of today.

Chapter 14

Future Computing

In This Chapter

- A review of multi-megapixel visualization systems
- An examination of high-performance computing technologies
- Considerations for "green IT" implementation in the enterprise

A comment often attributed to an anonymous military officer during World War II indicated that he believed "We will never need more than a slipstick [slide-rule] for calculations—anything more complicated is too likely to fail and prove worthless in a pinch." Fortunately, that prediction proved to be very far from the mark, and computing power has continued to expand at the exponential rate predicted by Moore's and Kryder's laws. Computers have progressed from building-sized constructs of tubes and wires to ultraminiaturized powerhouses capable of tremendous processing using nothing more than a battery power supply, yet able to share processing across hundreds of cores on a single chip.

Future computing can only be expected to continue this progress, enhancing processing power and distributed processing ability while reducing energy requirements and environmental impacts. This chapter will examine multiple high-performance computing models and various "green IT" strategies that can help improve the long-term "sustainable" nature of the network enterprise.

Bigger Is Better

Presentation of data is a key function of technologies in use within the enterprise. Organizations may dedicate entire rooms to multiprojector displays, while individual desktop systems may employ multiple monitors to provide users with the ability to cross-reference information or to view very large data sets, as shown in Figure 14.1.

When attempting to view very large data sets, such as all of the assets engaged in an emergency response effort or detailed geographic survey results, a single display can be used to examine the entire data set at a low resolution or zoom in for detailed examination of a single small subset of the data. Some forms of data can benefit from the ability to combine the video and graphic rendering capabilities of multiple systems to create very large displays that provide the high-resolution examination of very large data sets with changing focus and resolution.

I was recently able to visit the world's highest-resolution tiled display wall at the Texas Advanced Computing Center (TACC) at the University

Figure 14.1   A small visualization cluster sharing the combined display area of six monitors to form a single large display.

Figure 14.2   *Stallion* is the world's highest-resolution tiled display at 307 million pixels. The system features 75 high-resolution 30" displays arranged in 15 columns of five displays each. *Stallion* enables data sets to be processed on a massive scale, with more than 36 gigabytes of graphics memory, 108 gigabytes of system memory, and 100 processing cores.

For applications in life sciences, earth sciences, and fluid simulations, the extreme panoramic size helps researchers be more flexible. For example, researchers can display a single, very large data set across all the monitors, or they can display multiple views of a detailed data set at one time. They also have the ability to show a large number of time-varying sequences and do interactive 3-D modeling.

Stallion was deployed by the Texas Advanced Computing Center (TACC) at The University of Texas at Austin in 2008. The system was designed and built by members of TACC's scientific visualization and advanced computing systems groups.

(Photo and description provided courtesy of the Texas Advanced Computing Center.)

of Texas at Austin, as seen in Figure 14.2. The *Stallion* installation, deployed in 2008, allows for the direct examination of visual data up to 307 million pixels at a single time, creating a single display the size of an entire wall that is capable of simultaneously displaying multiple graphic and video streams.

Although most enterprise environments may not need a visualization studio of the magnitude of the *Stallion* installation, the combined power of multiple computers for processing, storage, visualization, and rendering data is increasingly valuable. As distribution and industrial systems grow larger and more complex, supervisory control and data acquisition (SCADA) becomes more complex as well, and financial calculations become more deeply integrated into real-time data presentation. Large-scale visualization systems become increasingly more valuable in the enterprise. Most organizations now recognize the value of dual monitors for workstations used in comparative analysis or document creation when using reference materials.

Supercomputing

True supercomputers are the top of the line in terms of raw computing power. These systems are used in government studies, atmospheric modeling, genetic and bioinformatics research, and similar uses requiring massive throughput and calculations for large data sets. These systems cost hundreds of millions of dollars and may consume enough power to light all the homes in a fair-sized city.

Because supercomputers represent the current leading edge in technology, the designation is a constantly moving target. A list of the top 500 supercomputers in the world is updated every six months, with corporations, universities, and governments competing to show the very best performance. The top system in the world today is the Cray Jaguar, which performs more than 1.75 million million (quadrillion) floating-point mathematical operations (petaflops) each second. However, current projects already in development are aimed at the 10-petaflop range of processing and beyond.

Today's desktop systems sporting high-end CPUs and powerful multicore graphics processing units (GPUs) are capable of over 9 teraflops (9 trillion floating-point mathematical operations each second) of performance individually. This power exceeds that of the #1 supercomputer in the world only 10 years ago. Many researchers feel that this power is a double-edged sword, making new forms of research and graphical representation possible while also rendering legacy forms of password and encryption protection weak in comparison to brute-force analysis.

Desk-side mini-supercomputers like the Dell/Cray CX1-iWS provide even greater processing power by combining several computer motherboards into a single case and coordinating the processing power using the Windows HPC Server operating system. These systems, along with PCs constructed using technologies such as the Intel X58 "supercomputing motherboard," place the raw processing power of a small group of computers behind an interface that functions as a normal desktop computer.

Distributed Computing

Today's supercomputers make use of specialized processing chips and supercooled information transfer electronics, but their true "speed" advantage comes from distributing pieces of a complex set of data calculations across multiple CPU or GPU cores. Calculations requiring each step to be completed and the result used for the next step do not divide into parallel processes well, while other calculations such as weather modeling and genetic comparisons can be readily split up into smaller subsets and distributed across multiple processors, with results combined upon completion.

High-end video cards include specialized multicore GPU chips that can split the rendering process into multiple smaller processes, so that each small area of the display has its own dedicated core. This power allows photo-realistic rendering of graphical imagery and advanced multilayered video content for virtual-world and gaming environment interaction. NVidia's CUDA (Compute Unified Device Architecture)-capable GPUs are also capable of sharing processing loads with the system CPU through standard C language application design.

Grid and Cluster Computing

Distributed computing can be performed outside high-end supercomputing installations by coordinating multiple independent computers toward a single task. Groups of networked computers can combine their collective processing power to provide supercomputer-like performance, although network connectivity will add latency that is not present in true supercomputers.

An example of collective computing can be found in the evolution of spam-generating botnets and denial-of-service attacks waged using coordinated groups of computers distributed around the world. Commands sent by the controlling system provide each node with instructions for its task, allowing a very large pool of computing resources to be directed toward a specified target.

Volunteer Computing

Beneficial uses of coordinated computing are also possible, such as the SETI@Home and Folding@Home projects using the Berkeley Open Infrastructure for Network Computing (BOINC) model. Users can download a small application package that operates during system idle times, performing mathematic data analysis on selected projects of interest. The total processing power of the BOINC projects currently exceeds the Cray Jaguar's power by three times the total floating-point operations available to the dedicated supercomputer, but is composed only of personal computers whose idle-time processing power has been volunteered to the BOINC projects. Private installations of the BOINC infrastructure can also be created to allow an organization to leverage its own combined desktop computing power toward dedicated high-performance computing functionality.

Grid Computing

Loosely connected groups of computers are often referred to as grid computing solutions. These systems can be dedicated to tasks such as video rendering in a "render farm" or may be composed of standard desktop systems whose processing power is only made available when the systems are idle and have "spare" computing power.

Compute grids combine processing power, while storage grids may combine part of each system's hard drive capacity into a single large virtual storage pool for use in cloud computing, comparative analysis of very large data sets, or to allow rapid capture of huge data sets exceeding individual system network throughput. The European Organisation for Nuclear Research (CERN) produces particle-smashing data in bursts that exceed the capability for capture using individual systems, and so employs a form of storage grid to capture short-term data for later transfer to long-term storage.

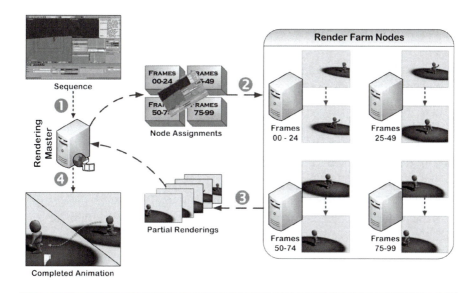

Figure 14.3   An illustration of the consumption of a render farm's nodal output to create a complete animation sequence faster than would be possible with a single rendering node.

Grid computers are also used in digital video production, splitting out groups of frames so that individual systems render only a small portion of the total video stream, as in Figure 14.3. Grids dedicated to a single task are often referred to as farms, and can use older equipment for compute and render farming past the working lifetime as production equipment.

Cluster Computing

When distributing nodes are tightly connected using dedicated high-speed networking, the result is generally termed a *cluster*. Clustered systems may provide standard operational support such as transparent load balancing across multiple public-facing systems or automatic fail-over following node failure. Many of the top 500 supercomputers are actually clustered computers, with multiple systems acting in concert while connected with high-speed dedicated networking equipment. The visualization systems illustrated earlier in this chapter are examples of visualization clusters, in which multiple computers divide rendering so that each need only handle only a small part of the overall display.

Distributed Computing and the Cloud

By combining the resources of multiple computing devices, grid and clustered computing solutions make supercomputing power available without the cost of dedicated top-500 systems. Tools used to create compute and storage grids and clusters, together with system virtualization hypervisors, have evolved into the current generation of cloud computing services, which hide the nuts-and-bolts details of "where" a service resides so that users need only request a particular scale of resources to be made available from an aggregate pool. Many technology vendors now produce specialized server hardware for high-performance and cloud computing, coordinating high-speed network attached storage with high-density blade server architectures and multicore CPU/GPU processing power.

The Sustainable Enterprise

Virtualization, distributed computing, consolidated storage solutions, remote desktops, and a myriad of other recent technology improvements offer ever greater opportunities for technology cost reductions and data center energy and cooling requirements. Policies should also be put into place to reduce the environmental impact of technology operations, including reducing water and energy requirements, reducing the environmental impact caused by production and disposal of equipment, and reduction of consumables used and discarded into public waste dumps.

These policies, collectively known as "green IT" are becoming more widely known and can provide significant benefits to the organization through reduced costs, improved public image, and tax credits. This is still a nascent field, with only one vendor-neutral professional certification covering green IT practices (the CompTIA Strata Green IT certification for data center planners). However, examples of the benefits of environmentally sustainable practices provide ready proof of their potential value to the organization.

Equipment Replacement and Disposal

Because construction of computing devices involves energy and water consumption, together with the use of hazardous chemicals and materials, extending refresh cycles provides an easy mechanism to reduce the environmental impact of technology operations. A four-year workstation replacement cycle instead of a three-year cycle, for example, reduces the number of machines that must be produced and purchased each year. Care should also be taken to ensure that equipment disposal after end-of-life addresses concerns that hazardous materials might be released into the environment.

Energy Options

Because data centers are often placed in out-of-the-way locations, they can provide excellent opportunities for early adoption of alternative-energy micropower generation systems. Energy demands of large data centers during peak hours place a strain on power generation and distribution systems that can be alleviated through partial energy sustenance provided by alternatives such as wind and solar power generation.

Selection of energy-efficient technologies certified by the Energy Star program in the United States or the TCO program in Europe can reduce energy costs while affording access to energy tax credits under a number of federal, state, and local laws and regulations. Energy tax credits may also be available for upgrading cooling systems and construction materials during data center updates.

Central management of desktop power settings can further reduce the energy impact of technology operations, by allowing computers to turn off monitors, park hard drives, and even enter reduced-power "sleep" modes when not otherwise in use. The wake-on-LAN functionality of many types of network cards can allow regular updates and other off-peak access functions to return sleeping systems to their active state long enough for maintenance.

Reducing Consumption

Paper, toner, ink, and other forms of technology consumable materials constitute a continuous cost of operations. Disposal of these materials and their packaging creates additional bulk in landfills and higher costs for waste disposal. Implementing enterprise dashboards that allow immediate access to data and electronic reporting can reduce printed output significantly. Policies mandating the use of shared high-capacity workgroup printers instead of multiple personal printers each requiring its own supplies, double-sided printing, reduced margin sizes, lighter-weight (in terms of toner or ink consumption) fonts, and white-background PowerPoint handout printouts are examples of strategies that can further reduce consumable waste and costs.

The Right Location

Selection of a data center location can affect operating costs and availability. When located in the north, summer cooling costs can be significantly reduced at the cost of potential heating requirements during winter months. Data centers placed near waterways or advantageous geological sites may be able to use geothermal or open-circulation options to dump waste heat and reduce cooling energy requirements. The use of virtual desktops and telecommuting solutions can also reduce requirements for cooled office space and transportation energy costs. Consolidating shipping of supplies and equipment can similarly reduce transportation energy requirements and may reduce procurement costs as well.

Summary

This chapter has briefly examined some ideas about the future of computing, both in terms of distributed computing as well as environmentally friendly technology management practices. Although I still have a collection of abacus and slide-rule devices to remind me of older times, I am pleased that technology has marched onward. I hope that this book has provided you with an effective starting point for architecting the future of your own enterprise network.

What the future will ultimately bring, no one can truly predict, but one aspect of technology remains ever present: *The only constant is change.*

Index

80/20 rule. *See* Pareto principle

access control, 18, 56, 91, 92, 102, 103, 108, 109, 112–115, 149, 150, 157, 159, 163, 166, 189
accessibility, 12, 13, 50, 85, 113, 142, 191, 195
account provisioning, 111
Advanced Research Projects Agency (ARPA), 172, 173
adware, 177
alternate data center, 252
AoE. *See* ATA over Ethernet
application design, 30, 83, 201, 241, 261
application development, 30, 41, 55, 63, 80, 110, 193, 209, 216, 240
application stack, 48
application virtualization, 18, 205, 229, 232
architectural framework, 16, 36
ARPA. *See* Advanced Research Projects Agency
ARPANET, 172, 173, 175, 189
asynchronous communication, 123, 131
ATA over Ethernet (AoE), 165

audit reporting, 112
authentication, 3, 5, 7, 18, 57, 63, 65, 68, 70–72, 75, 83, 85, 91, 93, 95, 97, 101–107, 110–115, 125, 149, 150, 156, 157, 159, 163, 186, 188, 189, 200, 201, 225, 233, 248, 250, 252
authentication directory, 93, 102
authentication modules (PAMs), 106
authorization, 57, 91, 92, 97, 101, 102, 105, 107, 108, 110–115, 131, 149, 163
automated updates, 231
automation, 17, 72–74, 76, 77, 114, 130, 237
availability, 20, 40, 41, 51, 63, 66, 86, 108, 109, 113, 114, 123, 124, 141, 146, 150, 153, 156, 157, 159–161, 163, 166, 168, 171, 173, 175, 183, 186, 191, 195, 197, 204–206, 210–212, 222, 223, 226, 227, 230, 236, 238, 239, 248, 266

backup, 6, 8, 54, 68, 69, 71–74, 76, 84–86, 155–163, 166, 188, 216, 239, 244, 245, 248, 250–253

bandwidth, 41, 63, 68, 94, 96, 118, 123, 140–142, 168, 183, 191, 194, 197, 212, 228
BIA. *See* business impact analysis
big iron, 8, 89
biometric, 85, 98–100, 113, 160
blended threat, 87
blog. *See* web log
boundary defense, 57
business alignment, 45, 219
business architect, 30
business continuity, 6, 28, 86, 182, 234, 238, 247
business impact analysis (BIA), 249–252
business intelligence, 6, 30, 40, 64, 83, 146, 149, 150

capacity planning, 69
Cardholder Information Security Program (CISP), 110
CAS. *See* Central Authentication Service
Central Authentication Service (CAS), 105, 113
Challenge-Handshake Authentication Protocol (CHAP), 104
change management, 20, 22, 28, 29, 63, 189, 219
CHAP. *See* Challenge-Handshake Authentication Protocol
chatroom, 139–142, 144, 147
chief architect, 22–25, 27–33, 36, 39, 40, 42, 85
chief information officer (CIO), 2, 23–25, 27, 34, 38, 60, 88, 89, 252
Children's Online Privacy Protection Act (COPPA), 84, 109
choke points, 249
C-I-A, 157

CIO. *See* chief information officer
CISP. *See* Cardholder Information Security Program
cloud computing, 19, 64, 76, 203, 209–212, 215, 216, 229, 262, 264
cluster computing, 261, 263
CobIT. *See* Control Objectives for Information Technology
cold site, 253
collaborative technology, 62, 118, 147
collective intelligence, 120, 121
commercial off-the-shelf (COTS), 12, 103
complexity, 3, 16, 31, 46–48, 54, 57, 58, 62, 65, 72, 73, 77, 86, 94, 95, 106, 114, 115, 153, 160, 207, 223–226, 238
confidentiality, 104, 157, 166, 236
consolidation, 3, 8, 65–71, 75, 76, 110, 159, 163, 164, 207
content management, 16, 148
continuity of operations (COO), 6, 22, 76, 77, 85, 86, 125, 166, 245, 248–252, 254
continuous improvement, 219
Control Objectives for Information Technology (CobIT), 35, 43, 59
COO. *See* continuity of operations
COPPA. *See* Children's Online Privacy Protection Act
COTS. *See* commercial off-the-shelf
cryptography, 42

DACs. *See* discretionary access controls
DAS. *See* direct attached storage
dashboard, 6, 64, 146, 149, 150, 195, 240, 242, 265
data center, 46, 65, 66, 68, 69, 72, 73, 75–77, 86, 88, 89, 159,

163–165, 206, 207, 211, 216, 229, 245, 248, 252, 253, 264–266

Data Center Markup Language (DCML), 65

data exposure, 8, 54, 60, 73, 85, 110, 199, 240

data mining, 42, 51, 64, 153

Data Security Standards (PCI DSS), 59, 65, 84, 110

data storage, 6, 84, 91, 151, 152, 154, 155, 157, 160, 163, 164, 168, 169, 204, 223

data structure, 40

DCML. *See* Data Center Markup Language

dedicated clouds, 210

demilitarized zone (DMZ), 57, 58, 243, 244

denial-of-service, 131, 141, 193, 239, 261

deployment, 18, 71–73, 82, 193, 195, 204, 205, 226–228, 230

device drivers, 221

DFS. *See* distributed file systems

digital signature, 100, 101, 103, 127

direct attached storage (DAS), 161–163

disaster recovery (DR), 6, 12, 28, 42, 51, 76, 77, 80, 86, 125, 129, 141, 155, 156, 160, 182, 211, 216, 229, 234, 238, 239, 241, 247–252, 254

discretionary access controls (DACs), 49, 108, 111

distributed computing, 40, 261, 264, 266

distributed file systems (DFS), 161, 163

DMZ. *See* demilitarized zone

DNS. *See* Domain Name System

document control, 148

Domain Name System (DNS), 125, 173, 184, 186–189, 229, 248

DR. *See* disaster recovery

EAP. *See* Extensible Authentication Protocol

economies of scale, 16, 67, 77, 161, 223

efficiency, 20, 27, 29, 33, 41, 62, 76, 82, 98, 143, 156, 205

electronic bulletin board, 133

electronic mail (e-mail), 3–6, 13, 19, 21, 42, 51, 62, 69, 71–72, 124–131, 134, 139, 140, 145, 153, 154, 156, 157, 166, 172, 174, 191–193, 199, 216, 252

e-mail. *See* electronic mail

emergency response, 245, 258

Energy Star, 265

enterprise architect, 16, 20–23, 26–28, 31, 35, 39, 42, 46, 47, 50–54, 57, 60, 61, 63, 74, 79, 89, 113, 150, 156, 160, 169, 201, 218, 219

enterprise information management, 46, 51

extensibility, 82

Extensible Authentication Protocol (EAP), 104

extensible markup language (XML). *See* XML

extranet, 189

facilities planning, 69

fault-tolerant, 72, 166

FEAF. *See* Federal Enterprise Architecture Framework

feature creep, 3, 62, 80, 218, 219

Federal Educational Rights Protection Act (FERPA), 84, 109

Federal Enterprise Architecture Framework (FEAF), 37
federated authentication, 105
federated data, 83
federated enterprise, 83
federated identity management, 31, 83, 93, 105, 112
FERPA. *See* Federal Educational Rights Protection Act
Fibre Channel, 165, 166
file repository, 154, 155, 158
file storage, 67, 69, 151, 153–155, 158–161, 166, 167, 189, 204
file versioning, 158
firewall, 57, 58, 127, 201, 243, 244
firmware, 188, 220, 221
forum, 29, 128, 132–134, 136, 140, 147, 230
FOSS. *See* free open-source software
free open-source software (FOSS), 10–12, 14, 56, 84, 103, 133, 146, 147

Gartner Enterprise Architecture Framework, 37
GLBA. *See* Gramm-Leach-Bliley Act
global positioning system (GPS), 101, 131, 178
Governance, 15, 16, 33–36, 38, 42, 61, 62, 90, 92, 130, 175
GPS. *See* global positioning system
Gramm-Leach-Bliley Act (GLBA), 84, 109
Green IT, 257, 258, 264
grid computing, 262
groupware, 117, 122, 124, 145, 146, 150, 158

Health Insurance Portability and Accountability Act (HIPAA), 54, 84, 85, 109, 153, 159

help desk, 69–71, 181
heterogeneous enterprise, 42
HIPAA. *See* Health Insurance Portability and Accountability Act
honeynets, 208
hotfixes, 230, 232
hot site, 252, 253
hot swap, 165
HTTP. *See* HyperText Transport Protocol
hybrid cloud, 211
HyperText Transport Protocol (HTTP), 43, 136, 173, 192, 230
hypervisor, 206, 207, 253

ICANN. *See* Internet Corporation for Assigned Names and Numbers
identification, 5, 26, 31, 34, 91, 93, 94, 96–102, 109, 110, 112–114, 119, 141, 146, 157, 171, 193, 203, 217, 223, 232, 235, 237, 238, 241, 249–251
identity management, 16, 21, 26, 31, 83, 91, 93, 105, 106, 109–115
IDS. *See* intrusion detection systems
IM. *See* instant messaging
information architecture, 51, 52
information silo, 68
Information Systems Audit and Control Association (ISACA), 35, 43
information technology infrastructure library (ITIL), 34, 35, 43, 59
inheritance, 114, 179
instant messaging (IM), 5, 6, 42, 62, 70, 139, 140, 143, 145, 153, 171, 181
integrity, 104, 157, 166, 236
interconnectivity, 65, 103, 104, 159, 162, 189

Internet Corporation for Assigned Names and Numbers (ICANN), 188

Internet SCSI (iSCSI), 165, 166

intranet, 23, 110, 135, 146, 189

intrusion detection, 243

intrusion detection systems (IDS), 243

IPSEC. *See* IP Security

IP Security (IPSEC), 104

ISACA. *See* Information Systems Audit and Control Association

iSCSI. *See* Internet SCSI

ISO/IEC 27002, 35

ITIL. *See* information technology infrastructure library

Kerberos, 97, 104, 113

kill pill, 199

Kryder, Mark, 152, 168

Kryder's law, 152, 154

LAMP, 10, 11

LAN. *See* local area network

layered defenses, 64

LDAP. *See* lightweight directory access protocol

lead architect, 2, 29, 63, 65, 68, 76, 77, 82, 84, 88, 159

legacy application, 30, 205, 207

legacy technology, 50, 89

legal mandate, 84, 88, 139, 153, 245

license recovery, 231

life cycle, 67, 88, 89, 206, 209–211, 218, 219

lightweight directory access protocol (LDAP), 102, 103, 113

listserv, 127, 172

load balancing, 63, 76, 155, 207, 263

local area network (LAN), 187, 188

location-identifying systems, 101

log files, 159, 232

low-hanging fruit, 17, 29, 52, 60, 65, 90

MACs. *See* mandatory access controls

mailing list, 127–130

maintenance cycle, 229

malware, 57, 58, 60, 73, 177, 184, 185, 220, 227, 228, 232, 238, 239, 243, 245

MAN. *See* metropolitan area network

mandatory access controls (MACs), 49, 108

maturity model, 25

Mauldin, Bill, 52

media management, 6, 73

meta-data, 40, 83

metadirectory, 83, 106

Metcalfe's Law, 118, 119

metropolitan area network (MAN), 188

mobile computing, 5, 187, 201, 248

mobile device, 163, 188, 189, 192–195, 197–199, 226, 239

mobile technologies, 41, 192, 193

Moore, Gordon, 152

Moore's law, 152, 224

MOSAIC, 174

multifactor authentication, 113

name service poisoning, 186

name squatting, 184

NAS. *See* network attached storage

NASCIO, 38, 43

NAT. *See* network address translation

network address translation (NAT), 187

network attached storage (NAS), 161–163, 264

network connectivity, 41, 68, 72, 101, 125, 162, 187, 194, 261

network management, 41
network of trust, 120

obsolescence, 88, 89
Ockham's Razor, 46
ODF. *See* Open Document Format
Office Open XML (OOXML), 13
OOXML. *See* Office Open XML
Open Document Format (ODF), 13,
   52, 53
Open Group Architecture Format
   (TOGAF), 37, 43
open-source, 10–14, 37, 38, 53, 84,
   87, 133
open standards, 1, 10, 13, 14, 177
outsourcing, 31, 53, 87, 244

PAMs. *See* authentication modules
PAP. *See* Password Authentication
   Protocol
parallel architecture, 32
parallel ATA (PATA), 164
Pareto principle (80/20 rule), 79, 80,
   89, 241
Pareto, Vilfredo, 80
Password Authentication Protocol
   (PAP), 104
password expiration, 95, 233
password management, 110, 111
password strength, 95, 111
PATA. *See* parallel ATA
patch management, 51, 73, 82, 201
Payment Card Industry (PCI), 59,
   60, 65, 84, 110
PCI. *See* Payment Card Industry
PCI DSS. *See* Data Security
   Standards
PDF. *See* Portable Document Format
permission assignment, 111
personally identifying information, 84
Peter principle, 61

PHI. *See* Protected Health
   Information
PKI. *See* public-key encryption
   infrastructure
platform architecture, 16, 17, 19, 20
PMBOK, 218, 219
PMI. *See* Project Management
   Institute
podcasting, 138
Portable Document Format (PDF),
   13, 177
portal, 5, 10, 23, 30, 63, 106, 110,
   114, 141, 146–150, 155, 158,
   172, 176, 186, 192, 195, 201,
   248
portlet, 146, 147
POSIX, 36
PRINCE2, 218
private clouds, 211
private network, 101, 187, 199, 243
program management, 27, 38, 39
project management, 2, 3, 19, 21,
   24, 28, 39, 42, 60, 63, 121, 149,
   217–219
project management framework, 217,
   219
Project Management Institute (PMI),
   21, 218
protected data, 26, 29, 54, 58, 239
Protected Health Information (PHI),
   54
PSTN. *See* public switched telephone
   network
public cloud, 210, 211
public network, 101, 188, 189
public-key encryption infrastructure
   (PKI), 104, 111, 239
public switched telephone network
   (PSTN), 140–142

quality, 26, 39, 82, 128, 225, 243

RAID. *See* redundant array of independent disks

RBAC. *See* role-based access control

really simple syndication (RSS), 136–139, 148

records retention, 6, 13

recovery point objective (RPO), 250

recovery time objective (RTO), 249, 250

redundancy, desirable, 71, 77

redundancy, undesirable, 22, 26, 47, 71

redundant array of independent disks (RAID), 72, 249

Reed, David, 118

remote access, 41, 141, 142, 148, 150, 156, 157, 195, 201

remote desktop, 144, 198, 199, 201, 205, 206, 245, 248, 253, 264

remote management, 71, 144

remote sites, 68, 71, 142, 143, 187

resource silo, 93

rich content, 152, 153

rich media, 138, 141, 160

risk acceptance, 87

risk assessment, 249, 251

risk avoidance, 87, 88

risk homeostasis, 86

risk management, 45, 79, 86, 87, 235, 243

risk mitigation, 87

risk transference, 87

role-based access control (RBAC), 49

root, 7, 8, 184–186, 188, 189

RPO. *See* recovery point objective

RSS. *See* really simple syndication

RTO. *See* recovery time objective

SAN. *See* storage area network

Sarbanes-Oxley Act, 11, 84, 109

SAS. *See* serial attached storage

SATA. *See* serial ATA

SCADA. *See* supervisory control and data acquisition

SCSI. *See* small computer system interface

SDLC. *See* Systems Development Life Cycle

search engine, 183

search poisoning, 183

Section 508, 85, 195, 196

secure erasure, 167

Secure Sockets Layer (SSL), 97, 104, 199, 201, 239, 240

self-service, 74, 111, 114, 178

sensitive data, 54, 55, 58, 68, 188

serial architecture, 32

serial ATA (SATA), 164, 165

serial attached storage (SAS), 164, 165

service-oriented architecture (SOA), 9, 41, 42, 57, 72, 103, 110, 157

service pack, 230

shared services, 67, 69

shielded subnet, 57, 58, 239

short message service (SMS), 124, 131, 132

signal boosters, 200

silo, 32, 68, 93

simple mail transfer protocol (SMTP), 4, 13, 19, 124–127, 131, 154

simple object access protocol. *See* SOAP

single points of failure, 249

single-sign-on (SSO), 103–106, 149

small computer system interface (SCSI), 164, 165

small office/home office (SOHO), 194, 225

SMS. *See* short message service

SMTP. *See* simple mail transfer protocol

SOA. *See* service-oriented
architecture
SOAP, 42
social engineering, 60, 232
social network, 118–120, 132, 140,
191
SOHO. *See* small office/home office
spam, 6, 124, 126, 130, 153, 154
SSL. *See* Secure Sockets Layer
SSO. *See* single-sign-on
stakeholder, 81, 82
standardization, 12, 16, 18, 47, 66,
72, 73, 76, 77
standard platform, 20, 50
storage area network (SAN), 161–163,
165, 166, 188, 217
storage configuration, 161, 162
storage management, 72, 130, 151,
156
storage management policies, 156
storage survey, 156
store and forward, 125
streaming media, 141, 153, 181
supercomputing, 41, 95, 173, 260,
261, 264
supervisory control and data
acquisition (SCADA), 143, 248,
260
synchronous communication, 5, 123
system modernization, 67
Systems Development Life Cycle
(SDLC), 219

TCP/IP, 13, 104, 124, 140, 165, 166,
172
technology architect, 3, 30, 47
technology modernization, 2, 3, 42,
60, 62, 63, 79
technology refresh, 67
tele-operation, 123, 143, 144
telepresence, 118, 123, 142–144

test networks, 75, 227, 230
threat, 6, 8, 18, 28, 50, 57, 58, 60,
63, 64, 76, 77, 87, 88, 92, 155,
217–219, 226, 228–238, 241,
243–246
TOGAF. *See* Open Group
Architecture Format
token, 96, 97, 102
trademark, 185
transport security, 198
Twitter, 132, 176

UDDI, 42, 83
uptime, 82, 83
user provisioning, 68, 115

value, 6, 14, 21, 22, 24, 26, 27, 29,
45, 47, 51, 52, 60, 67, 77, 79–82,
84, 85, 88–90, 92, 98, 102,
104, 110, 111, 117–120, 127,
131, 142, 149, 150, 166, 167,
172, 178, 181, 211, 218, 224,
237, 240, 241, 248, 250, 260,
264
VDI. *See* virtual desktop
infrastructure
videoconferencing, 143, 150
virtual appliance, 206
virtual desktop infrastructure (VDI),
206
virtualization, 18, 41, 64, 74–77, 88,
144, 155, 159–161, 163, 201,
203–209, 216, 227, 229, 232,
253, 264
virtualized application, 204, 205,
229
virtualized desktop, 144, 205–207
virtualized network, 208
virtualized server, 76, 159, 160, 167,
207, 253, 254
virtualized service, 204

virtual private network (VPN), 101, 187, 198, 199, 201
virtual reality, 144
virtual server, 74–76, 159
virus, 3, 6, 50, 60, 72, 73, 77, 87, 92, 154, 232, 238
visualization cluster, 263
voice communication, 140
voice-over-IP (VoIP), 42, 63, 140–142
VoIP. *See* voice-over-IP
volunteer computing, 262
VPN. *See* virtual private network

WAN. *See* wide area network
warm site, 252, 253
Web 1.0, 175–177, 179, 181, 189
Web 2.0, 176, 177, 179, 181
Web 3.0, 177, 178, 180, 181
web log (blog), 119, 132, 133
web of trust (WoT), 180
web service, 42, 58, 63, 89, 134
WEP. *See* Wired Equivalent Privacy
whiteboard, 42

wide area network (WAN), 166, 187, 188
WiFi, 41, 104, 194, 197, 199, 200
WiFi Protected Access (WPA/WPA2), 104, 199
wiki, 124, 134, 135
Wired Equivalent Privacy (WEP), 198
wireless, 63, 104, 188, 194, 197–201, 239
workflow, 111, 112, 114, 148
World Wide Web (WWW), 43, 136, 173, 175–177, 182, 186–188
worm, 73, 87, 228, 232, 238
WoT. *See* web of trust
WPA/WPA2. *See* WiFi Protected Access
WWW. *See* World Wide Web

X.500, 102, 103
XML, 13, 42, 83, 136–138, 159, 183

Zachman Framework, 37
"zero-day" threat, 230